SUNFLOWER SEEDS & SEOUL FOOD

SUNFLOWER SEEDS & SEOUL FOOD

The Best of Frederick C. Klein
"On Sports" in
The Wall Street Journal

Bonus Books, Inc., Chicago

© **1997 by Bonus Books, Inc.**

01 00 99 98 97   5 4 3 2 1

Library of Congress Cataloging-in-Publication Data

Klein, Frederick C.
    Sunflower seeds and seoul food / Frederick C. Klein "On sports" in the Wall Street journal.
        p.   cm.
    A collection of articles originally appearing from 1987 to 1996 in the author's Wall Street journal column. "On sports."
    Continues: On sports.
    Includes index.
    ISBN 1-56625-075-7 (pbk.)
    1. Sports. I. Klein, Frederick C. On sports. II. Wall Street journal.
III. Title.
GV707.K66   1997
796—dc20   96-43484

Text illustrations: Joel Davies

Bonus Books, Inc.
160 East Illinois Street
Chicago, Illinois 60611

Printed in the United States of America

To Susie

Contents

Part 4   **FUZZYBALL** / 73

Part 5   **DIMPLEDBALL** / 93

Part 6   **SPEED BALLS** / 119

Part 10 **SQUARED CIRCLES** / 199

Part 11 **TRUE-LIFE ADVENTURES** / 219

Part 12 **ODD BALLS** / 237

Preface

P
•

eople keep telling me I have the best job in the world in a way that invites an answer. Usually, I reply either by saying they may be right, or telling them I have an around-the-corner neighbor in Evanston, Illinois, who's chief photographer for *Playboy* magazine, so the title depends on one's tastes. Both responses, however, are brush-offs, and the preface to this book of my "On Sports" columns for *The Wall Street Journal* over the last 10 years seems a good place for a response that says something about both sports and writing, the two elements of the sportswriter's craft.

I think most people look at the job description as it appears, with the "sports" part coming first. Those are the fans who wish they were in our shoes because we "get" to go to such events as the baseball World Series, the professional-football Super Bowl or the Masters golf tournament, tough-ticket affairs they'd give quite a bit to attend. Often, they're the same people who ask if after, say, a Chicago Bulls game, we journalists "get" to shoot the breeze with our buddy Michael Jordan. And, say, what's Michael really like, anyway?

It's certainly true that, as Jimmy Cannon said, sports-writing allows one to be "at glad events amid friendly multitudes, gathered for the purpose of pleasure." Under such circumstances, it's hard to walk around with a sour face.

But a sportswriter goes to a game to write about it for an audience that includes many people who are knowledgeable about the subject, and some who have watched the contest at hand on television or from the arena, and that entails finding a brain-plug somewhere. The writer must take notes while the contest is in progress, and later, when the fans have gone off to their homes or parties, stare at the empty seats and try to put together sentences that will make sense in the glare of morning. It's a process that the jauntiest among us would, under torture, probably confess to finding daunting at least sometimes.

Furthermore, after one has been around sports for a while and gets to know some of the participants (although not with the intimacy that "civilians" suppose), things that the fan tends to see in black or white begin to turn gray. Partisanship—fandom—is based on drawing sharp distinctions between the home-team "good guys" and everyone else, but the closer you get to the forest, the more the trees begin to look alike, and the harder it is to prefer one woody clump above the others.

Once fanlike innocence is lost, and the rooting stops, sports become like other, less emotionally charged activities. Then the detached stance of the American journalist—generally no fiction despite what the news-media critics say—can, and usually does, reassert itself. Dave Kindred, who has written wonderfully about sports for a number of publications, puts the sportswriter's creed best when he says, "I root for my column."

When others in my business say I have the best job in the world, they mean something quite different. They look at my two-columns-a-week schedule, and compare it favorably to their own of four-or-five-a-week or more. They envy the fact that I write for two days ahead, instead of for the next day, and, thus, am not saddled with the onerous deadlines that are their banes. Also, because my newspaper is a national one, I'm not obliged to cover the teams or athletes of any particular city, meaning I can pretty much range across the sports landscape, selecting targets of opportunity. More than one colleague has told me he wants my job when I retire.

To those people, I can only shrug and say, "Sorry." If I wanted to say more, I'd point out that while it's tough enough in this day of shrinking attention spans to find something that people might want to read one day after a widely watched event, it's a mite tougher to engage their interest two days later. I also could say that landscape-ranging requires many hours in taxicabs, airports, airplanes and hotels, not all of them pleasant. I restrain myself, though, because nobody wants to hear me complain. I think that's the worst thing about my job.

When "On Sports" was started in 1977, travel was not in the picture. I'd already been a reporter for *The Wall Street Journal* for 14 years, covering a wide variety of topics ranging from business (naturally) to religion, and had introduced sports to the publication with front-page articles that began with a 1966 story about the golfer Arnold Palmer, who was, I think, the first athlete to benefit from a sustained effort (engineered by his agent, Mark McCormack) to convert his athletic celebrity to money-making, off-field endeavors. That led to other sports pieces, by me and other *Journal* writers, not all of them with business twists.

At the same time, the range of subjects that were being covered in the newspaper's editorial and op-ed pages also was expanding, and I began proposing to write sports commentary for that department, something that hadn't been done previously. It took awhile, but the idea was adopted under the provisions that it not involve travel or detract from my normal reportorial duties. The first "On Sports" column—about betting on the Super Bowl—appeared on January 7, 1977. Others followed, first at intervals of a month and then every two or three weeks.

"On Sports" went on the road, and became a full-time job for me, in September of 1983, when the *Journal* launched its daily Leisure & Arts page, a wide-ranging compendium of views and reviews. I wrote every-Friday features or essays at first, and soon added Monday or Tuesday pieces based on events I'd covered the weekend before. The latter exercises entailed gaining access to press boxes and other places that hadn't before opened themselves to my newspaper. Sometimes, that was no simple matter: I was admitted to the Baseball Writers' Association of America only after my friend, Jerome Holtzman of the *Chicago Tribune*, pointed out to the group's powers-that-be that a writer for the *Daily Worker* once had been a member. I also began hearing the lines "What does *The Wall Street Journal* want to interview me for? I don't own no stocks," from jocks with whom I wished to speak. I hear them still from time to time.

In fact, *The Wall Street Journal* has been paying increasing attention to sports, mirroring, I think, the growing national interest in the subject. In 1992, the paper put out a U.S. Open golf supplement, which I edited. We've done this annually since, along with ones for the sport's Masters Tournament, PGA Championship and Ryder Cup (the piece on Jack Nicklaus in the pages that follow is from the 1996 Masters supplement). A daily sports page was instituted for the duration of the 1992 Winter Olympics in Albertville, France, and has been resumed for every subsequent Olympics, summer or winter. A weekly, Friday sports page, with "On Sports" as a part, was inaugurated on January 6, 1995, with my early-week column still appearing on the Leisure & Arts page.

This is the second collection of "On Sports" columns to be published in book form—the first, also from Bonus Books, came out in 1987—and the column has changed since then. The main idea still is that sports are fun to watch and play, and shouldn't be taken too seriously. Indeed, their very lack of import makes them fun to write about, because as long as you get the score right you can fool around some.

But the light-hearted approach has been more difficult to maintain as the sports pie has grown, the calendar has filled past overflowing and the scramble for attention among its components has become harsher and more frantic. In the hazy past, sports may have seemed like an oasis from the struggle for gain, but few see them that way now, and the transparent grabbiness of their principals has been transmitted from owner to athlete to fan, to the improvement of none of them.

It's ironic, I think, that most-indictable element of the sports scene is the one that's supposed to be concerned with more than the doings on the field and at the box office. I refer, of course, to big-time college sports. With one hand, the main regulator of that activity—the National Collegiate Athletic Association—professes to push a "reform" agenda, but with the other it hustles to scoop up every loose dollar, and some that aren't loose.

But the same entity can't be effective as both promoter and police officer, and it's clear that the NCAA puts the financial interests of its member institutions ahead of any of those of the teenaged and young-adult athletes who entrust themselves to its care. Stadiums, "post-season" schedules and TV contracts all have grown over the last 10 years, and so have the time and psychological pressures on the so-called student-athletes who make up the college sports labor pool.

It's such a smelly situation that when I'm not bashing the NCAA, et al. (see, especially, "It's the Core That's Rotten"), I've sought out college games played by actual (non-athletic-scholarship) students ("Cantabs Edge Elis") or coaches who don't ascribe to a win-

or-die philosophy ("Honestly, Abe" and "College Football's 'Dr. No'"). Notre Dame has been playing Florida State without me lately.

Ethical questions weigh lighter on the pros because their main missions are to profit and entertain, but they, too, have been providing reasons for distress. I think that professional football is becoming a gladiatorial sport, and that the trend toward bigger, stronger and faster footballers that's so dear to National Football League marketeers isn't entirely accounted for by weightlifting and milkshakes (see "The Scales Tell the Steroids Story").

More worrisome has been the way professional teams have been holding up their home municipalities for new stadiums under the threat of moving if they don't get their way ("Supporting 'Our' Teams" and "Squeeze Play in Cincy"). The nastiest hook in that generally nasty picture—overlooked by many observers, I think—is that that main engine of the stadium-building push is the desire of team owners for more premium-priced "luxury suites" or "club seats" from which most of the taxpayers who are being asked to subsidize the facilities are barred for economic reasons. It's corporate piracy at its baldest, and it's fraying the ties that link cities to their teams.

Withal, though, sports provide a bond among men (and women, too) like few others today, one that gains importance as we become more specialized and separate in our working lives. At their highest levels, sports provide peeks into what we can be at our best that are made all the more glowing because, so often, such moments occur in games or situations in which we least expect them. When we're able to sweep aside the commercial flotsam that surrounds them, they provide thrills that are no less real for being vicarious, and at the participant level—which I write about more than most in my trade (see the section on "True-Life Adventures")—they give us a chance to test our own resources in a way everyday life usually doesn't. The older I get (I'm 59 years old at this writing) the more I like to play instead of watch, and one of these days I may give up watching altogether for playing.

In the meantime, though, there's a living to be made, and my way of doing it is about the best I can think of. And while I may or may not have the greatest job in the world, it's nice to know some people think I do.

Frederick C. Klein
February 1997

HARDBALL

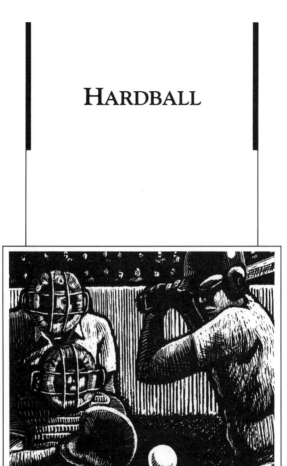

Part 1

An Unlikely
Championship Crew

OAKLAND, CALIF.

hat kind of a Los Angeles Dodgers team reigns as baseball champions of the known universe? Well, in the sixth inning Thursday night, while the Dodgers were well on their way to beating the favored Oakland Athletics in the fifth and, it turned out, final game of the World Series, the public-address announcer at Oakland Coliseum announced that the next L.A. hitter would be "third-baseman Jack Hamilton."

"Did he say that? I'm not surprised. I've been announced as 'Jim' in a bunch of places," said Jeff Hamilton after the triumph. "I started most of our games this season, and all the playoffs and World Series, but I realize my name still isn't a household word."

Even after watching the long-transplanted Brooklynites dispose of the A's in five games last week, it was tough to keep some of their identities straight, and not wonder what they were doing in such an august event. Two of their Thursday-night starters, catcher Rick Dempsey, age 38, and leftfielder Mickey Hatcher, 33, were signed by the Dodgers as free agents after being released by clubs who thought their best days were behind them. Designated hitter Mike Davis mostly occupied bench space in a campaign in which he batted .196 and hit but two home runs.

Veteran shortstop Alfredo Griffin still can man his position, but his batting has become so feeble that he was often reduced to bunting for hits. Rightfielder Mike Marshall looked like a man with a bad back, which he was.

And young Mr. Hamilton? Just so you'll know something about him when you meet him, he's 24 years old, stands 6-foot-3, hails from Flint, Mich., preferred basketball to baseball in high school, was a 29th-round (!) Dodger choice in the June 1982 draft, and plans to spend the winter lifting weights in hopes of beefing up his batting numbers, which included just six home runs and 33 runs batted in in 111 games during the regular term.

"What's outstanding about me?" he echoed. "Well, I field pretty good, and I played third baseman on a world-champion team. I'll always be able to say that last thing no matter how the rest of my career turns out."

So what does it prove? You knew one thing: Good pitching, which the Dodgers had, beats good hitting, which was the A's previous long suit. That line ought to go over the entrance at Cooperstown.

It also goes to show that baseball isn't that much of a team game—the players pretty much do their own things—and that one guy who gets something right at the right moment, like the gimpy Kirk Gibson, whose dramatic pinch-hit home run in his only appearance in the Series won game one, or the effusive Hatcher (two-run homers in games one and five), can negate the efforts of the opposing nine. That means that, in the short haul, anybody can beat anybody, except, of course, the Chicago Cubs.

The guy who had the greatest impact was Dodger pitcher Orel Hershiser, who allowed just two runs in winning games two and five for his team after similarly confounding the New York Mets in the playoffs, and the entire National League in the last month of the season.

His effort was extraordinary just because it wasn't a one-wink deal, or even a two- or three-winker. He threw shutouts in his last six scheduled starts, gave the Mets just three earned runs in 24 innings, and blanked the A's once before Thursday's 5-2 conquest. That worked out to five earned runs in 101 innings. Including the post-season, he won 26 games in 1988, and lost eight.

Much of baseball's allure, I think, stems from the fact that it uniquely combines the long haul (a regular campaign of 162 games per team) with the explosive moment. That the androgynously named Hershiser (Hers-his-er, get it? Will he be endorsing unisex towels?) was able to forestall explosions as long as he did should ensure him a place in the sport's annals.

How he was able to accomplish this was a subject of debate in the Dodgers' post-Series locker room. Pitching a baseball, it was agreed, is akin to striking a golf ball in that it is a complex act that only looks simple. A glitch in any part of the motion can doom the whole.

"The great thing about Orel is his knowledge of his own mechanics," said teammate Tim Belcher, the starter and winner of game four here. "He gets out of whack from time to time, like everyone else. But while most pitchers go through agony trying to get back on track, he has the knack of pinpointing his problem and correcting it."

Catcher Dempsey, who handled the great Baltimore Orioles' pitchers in the late 1970s and early '80s, called Hershiser's '88 effort the best single pitching season he'd witnessed, and thought it all the more remarkable because Hershiser lacks the overwhelming "stuff" of a Dwight Gooden fastball or a Jim Palmer curve.

"His best pitch is his sinker, and it's a great one. But he's got to pinpoint it to make it effective, and that's really difficult to do, inning after inning and game after game," said Dempsey. "He was able to stay in a groove longer than any pitcher I've seen. It's study, attitude and concentration, and who knows what else. All I know is that wherever I put my glove tonight [Thursday] is mostly where the ball went."

The hero himself is a man of 30 who, at 6-foot-3 and 192 pounds, looks bigger up close than on TV. He's got big ears and a Howdy Doody grin, and doesn't chew anything nasty. He's well-spoken and religious, so his expletives needn't be deleted.

"I'm proudest of the way I've learned my trade over the years," he said after the champagne had been sprayed and the locker room crowd had dispersed. "I'm not some brain-dead ball-heaver; I know the game and how to pick my spots.

"I also know that nobody can pitch a perfect game, and I sure didn't tonight. I was lucky that the A's hit most of my mistakes right at somebody. One day next season—maybe in my first start—I'm going to get shelled. I just didn't want that to happen in the post-season, with everything at stake. I've been carrying that fear around the last couple of weeks. Fear is a great motivator, you know."

• *Oct. 24, 1988*

Allen's Alley

CHICAGO

ick Allen's third and last year with the Chicago White Sox was 1974. He batted .301, hit 32 home runs and drove in 88 runs. The American League's most valuable player after a titanic 1972 season, he was the toast of a town that, lacking championship teams, lionizes its individual stars as do few others.

But Allen did not leave Chicago to the applause he could have claimed as his due. He "retired"—the sports pages called it "quit"—with two weeks to go in that season, leaving explanations to others. He would play again, but elsewhere.

Tuesday Allen was back in town, at Kroch's & Brentano's bookstore on Wabash Avenue under the Loop El, autographing copies of *Crash*, the autobiography he coauthored with the Philadelphia writer Tim Whitaker. Clearly, bygones were long gone for his fans. The store was full and people's eyes shone with the pleasure of being in his company.

"Thank you for the best three summers of my life," a middle-aged man in a camel's hair coat said, reverently, when it was his turn at the table. "There's not a week goes by that I don't think of you, swinging and hitting the ball. I wish you were still around," whispered another well-dressed business type.

Allen returned the good will, signing everything that was thrust before him, including balls, photos and jerseys, and adding inscriptions on request. When the subject came up, and sometimes when it didn't, Allen assured one and all that Chicago was his kind of town. "I only wish I'd started and ended my career here," he repeated.

Someone might have pointed out that he could have ended it here if he'd chosen, but good manners prevailed. Someone did ask him why he departed so abruptly 15 years ago. "It's a long story. It's in the book. It was about baseball," Allen replied.

It is in the book, but it's a short story and it wasn't only about baseball. A sportswriter's importunity, a dispute with a teammate, a manager he admired reminding him that he—the manager—was running things, and a baseball paradise turned into yet another purgatory for this sensitive man. The book repeats pretty much that same tale about other of the six stops Allen made in a 15-year Major League career.

Questions and contradictions followed the ballplayer on this day. The host of a morning radio call-in show on which he appeared quoted from the book that Allen, feeling "misperceived" and mislabeled, had "played angry." He asked him to elucidate. "I didn't mean angry at people, I meant angry at the ball, like a fighter takes out his anger on the heavy bag," Allen insisted.

The book has Allen musing about, but never answering, the question of how good he might have been. Asked the question directly, he was blunt. "I don't worry about 'could haves,' I was good," he declared. "I played 15 years in the Majors. I hit 351 home runs. I hit over .300 seven years. I did everything I could to help my teams win. Not many have done better."

That the biography that was supposed to define Dick Allen only puzzles, whatever its intent, should be no surprise. He always raised more questions than he answered. He was, first and foremost, the most powerful hitter of his era, not large (he stood 5-foot-11 and weighed 190 pounds) but so strong-armed and deep-chested that he could twirl a 42-ounce bat as though it were a majorette's baton. His home runs didn't simply leave ballparks, they soared out, starting low and ending high, like jet planes on takeoff. "If they got by the shortstop, they were gone," he chuckles.

He was a well-rounded player as well, adept at baseball's cherished "inside" game. He could hit and run and, when the mood struck him, bunt, as he once did to foil a Nolan Ryan no-hitter bid. A sportswriter friend of mine, who has covered the Bigs for more than 30 years, says he can recall few better baserunners.

The other hand was more like a catcher's mitt, though. Allen missed practices and games. He had a celebrated brawl with his Philadelphia Phillies' teammate, Frank Thomas. He writes that his method of securing a trade from the Phillies, the club he broke in with in 1963 and came to despise (although he returned to it after his Chicago stint), was to make "regular stops at watering holes," which is to say bars, on the way *to* the ballpark. Probably no one was photographed smoking cigarettes in a baseball uniform more often than he.

Allen is pictured smoking a cigarette in uniform on the cover of his book. He thinks, maybe, that wasn't such a good idea, because it reminds in a pointless way of his image as a baseball rebel. He says he likes less the work's title, which derives from his habit, begun in Philadelphia, where fans threw things at him, of wearing a batting helmet on the field. His Phillie teammates nicknamed him "Crash Helmet," later shortening it to "Crash."

"I didn't crash. I'm here. I'm working [in sales, for a firm that makes inflatable structures to house swimming pools, tennis courts and other sports facilities] and doing OK," the still-trim Allen said quietly. "I think a better title would have been 'Rules.'"

Rules? "Yeah. People always said there was one set of rules for me and another for the other players. Sometimes there was, but not in ways people thought.

"Take the Thomas fight," he went on. "Thomas broke the ballplayers' rule by hitting me with a bat, but the Philadelphia fans blamed me. Other players smoked and drank, but only I was abused for it. If I was a troublemaker, why was I never thrown out of a game by an umpire? And that stuff about calling me 'Richie.' No other player got hassled about his first name.

"I said baseball was racist in some ways. People used that against me, too. If baseball isn't racist, why are there no black managers? Why is Dick Allen not in the game today? Yeah, there are rules. If everybody followed them, maybe we'd be all right."

• *April 14, 1989*

All Shook Up

SAN FRANCISCO

They didn't play the third game of the World Series on Tuesday night as scheduled, and they didn't play it on Wednesday or Thursday either. But you knew that, didn't you?

They are supposed to play the game next Tuesday, in Candlestick Park here. The theory is that the stadium, damaged by Tuesday's earthquake, will be repaired by then, and that people will be able to get there. Like just about everything else, that remains to be seen. Aftershocks could intervene. But, at least, the law of averages should have swung to the favorable side.

It may seem trivial to worry about the World Series amid the destruction to the Bay Area wrought by Tuesday's quake, but the name of this column is "On Sports," so I feel obliged to do so. You might be interested to know that baseball, not survival, appeared to be the first thought of most of the crowd of 60,000-odd that had gathered at Candlestick at 5:04 p.m. Tuesday, a half-hour before game time, when the quake struck. As soon as the tremor passed, many people spontaneously arose and cheered, as though it had been a novel kind of pre-game show.

One fan, seated several rows in front of the open, upper-deck auxiliary press section where I was stationed, faced the assembled newsies and laughingly shouted, "We arranged that just for you guys!" I thought and, I'm sure, others did: "You shouldn't have bothered."

9

I'd slept through my only previous brush with natural disaster, a tornado 15 or so summers ago near Traverse City, Mich., so I was unprepared for one reaction to such things: the urge to talk about them. Perhaps primed by the daily diet of radio and TV reporters thrusting microphones into people's faces and asking how they "feel" about one calamity or another, fellow reporters and civilians who spied my press credential were eager to chat.

"It felt like I was on a station platform and a train went by," said one man, describing my own reaction. A woman said she saw the park's light standards sway. A man said he saw the upper-deck's rim undulate. I saw neither.

Dictates of good sense to the contrary not withstanding, the general inclination was to believe that the disturbance would be brief and that ball would be played. "I was near the top of the stadium, and saw a steel girder bow six feet from where I sat, but I stayed put for 10 or 15 minutes," confessed a friend. "I guess I thought, 'This is the World Series and I'm not gonna wimp out!'"

Here in the Global Village, though, folks do not stay uninformed for long. Electrical power was out in still-daylighted Candlestick Park, but battery-operated radios and television sets were plentiful. Within a few minutes, the true extent of the catastrophe was becoming clear. Its Richter Scale measurement was reported as 6.5, then 6.9, then 7.0. A section of the Bay Bridge had collapsed, as had a part of Interstate Highway 880 in Oakland. People had died.

At 5:40 p.m., scheduled game time having passed, some fans chanted "Let's Play Ball." No longer innocent, they qualified as fools. The stadium was ordered evacuated soon afterward; the announcement, made over police bullhorns, cited the power outage, but it later was revealed that there also had been stadium damage of the sort reported by my friend. Outside, I spotted two young men lugging blocks of concrete. "Pieces of Candlestick," they said.

The crowd remained good natured, even bemused. TV reporters interviewed fans in the parking lots while, a few feet away, others watched the interviews on their portable TVs. The only frenzy I saw was commercial: Booths selling World Series commemorative stamps and dated postmarks were besieged by fledgling speculators who saw future profit in the items.

The traffic jam out of the park was monumental. It took me a half-hour to move 10 feet from my parking spot in an outer lot to an aisle, and an additional hour to reach an inner roadway a half-block away. The six-mile trip to my airport hotel that had taken 20 minutes earlier in the day took more than three hours.

At my hotel, the Westin, power was out, some interior plaster had broken loose and there had been water damage, but little else. With Garpian randomness, a hotel across the street, the Amfac, had been hit harder: A large sheet of its concrete facade and several window balconies were torn away.

The Westin staff had, kindly, set out lighted candles in the ballroom, prepared a cold-cuts buffet and passed around pillows and blankets. I fell asleep on the lobby floor, next to a man wearing a Chicago Cubs jacket. I expected him to say, "I told you so," but he already was snoring.

The journalistic consensus was that the earthquake made the World Series seem unimportant. My response was that sports rarely are important, only diverting, and the quake merely highlighted that fact.

Should the rest of the Series be played at all? Sure. The quake and baseball weren't related, unlike the massacre of athletes that attended the 1972 Olympics. That heavily politicized event learned nothing from the horrifying experience, and seems doomed to repeat it.

Two ironies intrude. This has been widely dubbed the BART Series, after the local subway line, and the Bay Bridge Series. Flags fly at half-staff for the death of Bart Giamatti, the recently deceased baseball commissioner, and now the Bay Bridge lies in ruins.

A Series that was shaping up as the dullest since the one-sided Detroit-over-San Diego go of 1984 has become memorable in the least fortunate way. Still, its edge is lost. It now will be played mostly for the record, and should be wrapped up as quickly as possible, without "off" days.

And I will never again complain about a rainout.

• *Oct. 20, 1989*

One for the Books

MINNEAPOLIS

J. ohn Smoltz, the Atlanta Braves pitcher who threw seven scoreless innings in the seventh game of the World Series Sunday night, looked at his bare feet in his locker room afterward and summed up a Series in which, it seemed, the question wasn't which team would win but whether either would.

"It was like we were looking into a mirror," said the tall 24 year old. "It was like we were pantomiming each other's moves."

For nine innings the Braves and Minnesota Twins dueled scorelessly, something that never happened in a seventh game in the previous 87 years they played this thing. Then the Twins scored on a bloop double, a sacrifice bunt and a pinch hitter's one-out fly ball that plopped safely to the plastic green over an outfield that was drawn in because a run would've scored on a decent fly anyway. The 55,000 fans in the indoor Metrodome roared as one. Why, some of 'em got so excited they forgot to wave their hankies.

The final score was 1-0, and the margin of difference between the two teams seemed less, if that could be. It was, everyone agreed, a classic, and even that label seemed inadequate. How about "epic" instead?

"You had 10 scoreless innings by Jack Morris. You had double plays, line-drive outs, guys left on base. Never saw anything like it," gushed Tom Kelly, the winners' manager. But then he reverted to his usual, droller form. "After the ninth inning I wanted to take Morris out," he said. "He'd pitched nine innings with three days' rest, and who could ask for more? He insisted he was fine and I should keep him in. I said, OK, go ahead, it's just a game."

Except for a 14-5 Braves triumph in game five that gave them a 3-2 Series lead, the entire Series was in that mold, and it added up to the kind of baseball fans pray for. Of the seven games, five were decided by a single run and three went into extra innings. All were won by the home team, which meant the crowds always went home happy. There were heroes large and small, and some of the largest were small (or, at least, short) guys, like the Braves' unheralded Mark Lemke, the Series' leading batsman, and the Twins' Kirby Puckett, the sixth game's star.

The subject of the Series' place in history was raised as early as Saturday night, after a 4-3 Twins win on Puckett's 11th-inning home run made a seventh game necessary. As usual, Kelly got the last word. It came as his post-game press conference was breaking up and a TV reporter asked a question as many were leaving. "Stick around. This may be the one that turns up all the good stuff," the manager said.

"Tom, has this Series been a classic?" the TV guy asked.

"You can keep walking, folks," laughed Kelly, adding, "All I can say is people tell me it's very good."

That certainly could be said about game six, which will be worth a history-book page of its own one day. Atlanta lost, but not for lack of trying; its batsmen hit Twins starter Scott Erickson so hard that his teammates would have been justified asking for shields as well as gloves. But most of the drives were either snagged by Twins or went just foul.

Still, the Braves scored three times, and that would have been enough for the win—and the title—if not for Puckett. The stumpy veteran, who'd had just three hits in 18 previous at-bats, drove in a run with a triple and later scored in the first inning, saved at least a run with a leaping catch of a Ron Gant drive in inning three, and led off the 12th by hitting a waist-high change-up from reliever Charlie Leibrandt over the left-field wall.

Puckett said he went to the plate in the fateful inning with the thought of waiting for a pitch that was "up" in the strike zone. "They'd been getting me with low stuff, and I didn't want that to happen again," he said.

His feelings on a Series that included a four-hour, 12-inning marathon in Atlanta the previous Tuesday? "I feel drained, like I've gone 15 rounds with Evander Holyfield."

But everybody got off the canvas for Sunday, and the effort exceeded that of the night before. While there were no runs through regulation play, there were many missed opportunities. The Braves had runners in scoring position in the second, third, fourth and fifth innings, and in the eighth had them on second and third with none out, but to no avail. The Twins started slower off the talented Smoltz, but loaded the bases in the eighth after he was gone and had runners on first and second with none out in the ninth, only to have both threats killed by double plays.

It couldn't go on that way forever, though, and Dan Gladden led off the Twins' tenth with a broken-bat double. He moved to third on Chuck Knoblauch's bunt, and, after a couple of intentional walks loaded the bases, came in on the Gene Larkin fly that was scored as a single.

"Somebody had to score; I'm just glad it was us," said Larkin, a sore-kneed reserve. He added: "I was relaxed when I went up to the plate, but my stomach was in knots when I was on the bench watching."

The outcomes of these events usually prove nothing beyond which team played best in the contests at hand, but this Series underscored a couple of more general points. One is that, while many bemoan the passage of quirky old ballparks like the Polo Grounds, a successor exists in the tent-roofed, bouncy-turfed Metrodome. Something, after all, has to account for the Twins' 11-1 post-season record in the placid-appearing place, including its 1987 championship run.

The second has to do with competition and player free agency. That both (or either) the Twins and Braves went from last place to first in a season was unprecedented, but it shouldn't have been all that surprising in the light of recent trends. Back in 1976, when free agency took effect, it was widely predicted that the best players would congregate in sunny California or New York, the media capital, leaving other teams bereft. The actual result has been the opposite: an era of playing-field parity unmatched in modern professional sports. Over the past 16 seasons, 12 different teams have claimed titles and none has won more than two.

The Twins and Braves both plumbed the free-agent market in the last off-season, to good effect. Minnesota signed Morris, the workhorse pitcher; designated hitter Chili Davis and third-baseman

Mike Pagliarulo. The Braves corralled three-fourths of their starting infield in first-baseman Sid Bream, shortstop Rafael Belliard and third-baseman Terry Pendleton.

And while money played a role in all those moves (it always does), other factors did, too. The 36-year-old Morris, a longtime Detroit Tigers ace, is a St. Paul native who said he wanted to end his career in his home town. Davis, ex of the California Angels, knew some Twins players and envied the fun they were finding in the game. The religious Bream said "the Lord" led him to Atlanta from Pittsburgh by "opening some windows and closing some doors" during the negotiating process.

As it turned out, the biggest prize was Morris, who was named the Series' most valuable player for winning games one and seven. Combative to the ends of his walrus mustache, he's also a wary man who seems uncomfortable outside the insularity of locker-room society. Yet after Sunday's game he wept in describing his joy in victory.

"Doing it where I grew up was special," he said. "Everyone can understand that."

● *Oct. 29, 1991*

Mustard and Memories

CLEVELAND

T· his is the last year the Cleveland Indians will be playing in 62-year-old Cleveland Stadium, and that fact is being marked in a number of ways. Indian players are wearing a commemorative logo on their uniform sleeves; at various times during the season the team will give away cups, pennants, sports bags, balls, pins and prints honoring the place; and a local newspaper is running a daily box recalling notable baseball feats that took place there.

Really, though, few will mourn when the Tribe moves to the new ballpark now being built on the other side of their city's downtown. Cavernous old Cleveland Stadium, with its seating capacity of 74,000, ain't Wrigley Field, Fenway Park or, even, Tiger Stadium. In the view of most, it's too big, too gloomy, too chilly on nights when the breeze is off Lake Erie, and houses too many memories of a team that's been baseball's Bad Luck Bears.

A few years back, when he was an Indian first baseman, Mike Hargrove said there was nothing wrong with Cleveland Stadium that a case of dynamite couldn't cure. He's the team's manager now, and if he's changed his mind on the subject, he's kept it to himself. The wonder is that no one took up his suggestion.

But there's at least one Clevelander who says he'll be sorry to see the Indians move, and one can only believe him. He's 51-year-old David Dwoskin, and he's unusual as both a fan and a man. The pivotal event of his life was when, as a 10-year-old, his father took him to his first Indians' game, and he ate his first ballpark hot dog.

It wasn't so much the dog that got him, but the mustard. "It was brown, spicy and delicious, and like nothing I'd had before," recalls the baldish, bearded, bouncy Dwoskin, eyes sparkling. "I still remember it."

Aiding his memory is that, beginning some years later, he made that mustard his livelihood. In 1969, having closed the kosher butcher shop his father had run before him, he decided to follow his heart. He sought out the family that owned the recipe for the condiment he loved and volunteered to go on the road selling it. A few years later, he bought the recipe and took over its manufacture himself.

The mustard had no name when he signed on—it was produced only for institutional customers—so he gave it one: The Authentic Stadium Mustard. It's a bulky tag, but it provided the desired tie between the taste of the product and the crack of the bat and the roar of the crowd. "I thought other people would associate mustard with baseball, like I do," he explains. The stadium referred to, of course, was Cleveland Stadium.

The excellence of Stadium Mustard has been attested in past years by *Fortune* magazine, in an article about Cleveland, and by this newspaper—that is, by me—in an article about the Indians. The actor Karl Malden has testified, without solicitation, that he loves the stuff. So have many other, less famous people.

And while Dwoskin did not concoct the product's original recipe, based on a Canadian-grown mustard seed, he is its stern protector. "I started in the business knowing next to nothing, but today I'm an expert," he avers. "I can smell any mustard blindfolded and tell you the brand. I can *look* at any batch of mine and know immediately whether or not it's perfect. If it's not perfect—if it's not the exact same mustard I ate as a kid—it doesn't get shipped."

As food companies go, the one that makes Stadium Mustard is small, and likely to stay that way. Dwoskin's Davis Food Co., which he operates out of his home in the Cleveland suburb of Mayfield Heights, doesn't advertise because it wouldn't pay to take on the big ad budgets of such conglomerate-owned competing brands as French's, Gulden's and Grey Poupon. Some of his distributors are native Clevelanders who moved away, couldn't get the product in their new home areas, and offered to sell it there.

Nonetheless, Stadium Mustard is available in retail stores in 30 states, and in some 150 stadiums, including the Metrodome in Minneapolis and the Silverdome in Pontiac, Mich. "When I started out, I'd put 50 cases in the trunk of my car and not come home until they were sold," notes Dwoskin. "Now, we ship by the truckload."

It's a matter of pride to the entrepreneur that Cleveland Stadium remains his biggest single outlet; for example, 400 gallons of his mustard were consumed there when 73,290 people, he among them, came out for the Indians' season opener on April 5.

It's also satisfying to him that his product is linked to Indian baseball, however tangentially. "I grew up like some kids, playing whatever sport was in season, but baseball always was special," he said as we watched the Tribe play the California Angels before a more typical crowd of 10,057 on a recent Monday night that was about 15 degrees chillier in the ballpark than elsewhere in town. "Green never seemed greener than in the grass on the field here, white never whiter than on the Indians' uniforms.

"Some people say it's tough to be an Indians' fan because they've lost for so long [the team won its last pennant in 1954 and has finished higher than fourth place just four times since], but I've never thought so. I took winning and losing seriously when I was a kid and we had great players like Early Wynn and Al Rosen and Larry Doby and Jim Hegan, but I still like the game even though I don't care so much about that anymore. What's important is that it's Major League baseball, and it's always good, and we have it all summer in Cleveland, whenever we want it.

"I think it's great that they're building a new stadium, but I'm going to miss this place," he went on. "Yeah, Cleveland Stadium's big, but you can show up 10 minutes before a game and buy a good ticket, and after this season you probably won't be able to do that.

"And the memories—the nostalgia—won't be there. I mean, my dad took me here, and then I took my kids. When I think of baseball, I think of this place. Probably always will."

• *May 14, 1993*

Note: The Indians have thrived in their new Jacobs Field home, but David Dwoskin didn't get the mustard concession in the place.

Ray Miller's Three Commandments

BRADENTON, FLA.

R ay Miller might be excused if he feels more like a camp counselor than a baseball pitching coach these days. He was introduced to his Pittsburgh Pirates "replacement" staff three weeks ago, and has about three weeks more to get them ready for opening day, should things come to that.

"Can't do much in that time, just make sure they know how to cover first base on ground balls and get them into a game or two so we can look at 'em," he says with a shrug. "They'll have to use the pitches God gave 'em."

Chances are, though, Miller might slip in a mention of his rules of pitching that he has toted around the big leagues since he surfaced as the Baltimore Orioles' pitching coach 17 years ago. In fact, his new and, one hopes, temporary students won't have to ask about them, because they're printed on the front of the T-shirt he wears under his Pirate doubleknits. "Work Fast. Throw Strikes. Change Speeds," it reads. If he thought it'd do any good, he'd have them tatooed on his chest.

That Miller is a man with a plan sets him apart from the majority of his colleagues. Like other sports, baseball is taught mostly by pragmatists, whose motto, if they had one, would be "Whatever Works." They fiddle with a pitcher's delivery or a hitter's swing until the guy gets off a few good ones, then hope he remembers whatever it was he did right.

Some of Miller's charges have had quite-substantial reminders of their successes. The Orioles' Mike Flanagan won the American League Cy Young Award in 1979 and his teammate, Steve Stone, won it the next year. The Pirates' Doug Drabek got the National League piece of that august prize in 1990, the coach's fourth season in the erstwhile Steel City. Jim Palmer, Scott MacGregor, Mike Boddiker and John Smiley are among others who have mentioned the coach thankfully while collecting individual laurels, in addition to sharing their teams' World Series, league-championship or divisional titles.

The large and husky Miller, who is 49 years old, bows to those worthies in return. "The one thing you can't teach is talent, and the good ones have a lot of it," he says. He does not run on about this subject apropos the game's current situation, but no elaboration is necessary.

As a younger man, Miller had some pitching talent, and believes that, with better coaching, it might have taken him to The Show. Alas, about all he got was the standard bullpen exhortation to "drop and drive, push off hard." He did that, and averaged a strikeout an inning over his 10 years as a pro. But too many walks, and too little craft, kept him a minor leaguer.

Wisdom arrived late—too late for Ray Miller the player. He says some of it came from Joe Altobelli, who managed the Rochester, N.Y., team for which he played his last two years, and who gave him a start as an instructor in the Orioles' chain. "Joe preached the mental side of the game, and the need for a teacher to be patient because things always take longer than you'd think," Miller notes. "I kind of took it from there."

But although it ended short of his goal, the coach doesn't believe his playing career was wasted. "You'll notice that 'throw hard' isn't one of my rules," he remarks. "I'm my own bad example."

The first of Miller's dicta—"Work Fast"—is the most common-sensical, and (probably thus) the least widely observed. It has nothing to do with how or what a pitcher throws. "Working fast keeps the fielders on their toes, and fielders are a pitcher's best friends," he says. "It also makes the umpires love you. Get 'em to dinner on time, and maybe they'll give you the benefit of the doubt."

The necessity to throw strikes—especially on first pitches—likewise seems apparent, but not entirely in the way some might think. "Knowing that a pitcher will be over the plate affects a batter's psychology," Miller avers. "It makes him go up knowing that if he doesn't swing, he's out. That gives a pitcher a big edge, I think."

The business about changing speeds is the most pitcherly of the Miller rules, and the heart of his philosophy. Even so, it has as much to do with batting as pitching.

"It's about understanding the big-league hitter, and respecting the difference between him and the guys a pitcher faced at other levels of the game," says the coach. "A pitcher gets to the majors by throwing the ball past hitters, but he stays there by getting them to hit him with less than their best swings. He might be able to throw a ball 95 miles an hour, but if that's all he can do he'll be watching it come back faster by the second or third time they see him. He *will* get hit. The only question is, how hard?

"A pitcher who can vary his speeds keeps a hitter off balance," Miller continues. "If he's got a 70-mile-an-hour changeup, it's going to make his 85-mile-an-hour fastball look faster. The more speed a pitcher has, the better off he is, but mostly because that gives him a greater possible range of speeds by letting him dial up as well as down. A pitcher shouldn't throw all out more than three or four times a game, but it's nice if he has something left when he does."

And if all he has left is a slower delivery, well, that's not always bad either. "A hitter fears two things," says Miller. "One is getting hit by a pitch, the other is looking bad by getting caught swinging way out in front on a slow one. Let him know you can change speeds, and, all of a sudden, your marginal fastball isn't so marginal any more. I wish I'd known that 25 years ago."

● *March 10, 1995*

Tony Gwynn
Takes His Cuts

PEORIA, ARIZ.

T. he purpose of the drill during the first week of the San Diego Padres' spring exercises was to give pitchers a taste of throwing hard to real hitters. Most of the Padre batsmen enlisted for the task treated it perfunctorily, posing with their bats while cracking wise to one another about the efforts of the pitcher, reliever Trevor Hoffman.

Tony Gwynn would save his jokes for later. *Before* taking his turn, he stood to the side of the batting cage and took a half-dozen full-dress practice cuts, silently rehearsing his batter's box mantra of "bat back, left elbow up, front foot soft." To Gwynn, every swing matters, and none is to be wasted.

The 35-year-old Tony Gwynn has wasted few swings in a Major League career that's entering its 14th campaign. At least partly in consequence, he's posted the sort of batting numbers usually associated with baseball's earlier eras, when games were played in the daytime, pitchers were expected to go nine innings and hitters didn't strain their eyes watching television or reading the stock tables.

Gwynn won the National League batting championship last year—his sixth such title—with an average of .368, 22 points higher than that of his runnerup. When the players' strike ended the 1994 season in mid-August, he was averaging .394 and bidding to become the majors' first .400 hitter in 53 years.

The left-hander has spent 13 full seasons in the bigs, and has hit better than .300 in each. His lifetime batting average of .336 is the highest of any active player. That's the kind of number one associates with Ted Williams, Lou Gehrig and George Sisler. They don't make 'em like that any more, we're told. Not often, anyway.

"Tony's the best hitter in the game today, without a doubt," says Rod Carew, the California Angels' batting coach and the man with whom Gwynn is most often compared. Carew's lifetime average, over 19 seasons ending in 1985, was .328.

"Tony uses the whole field, same as I did," Carew says. "There's no single way to get him out, also same as me. He's got such good hands that he can wait on a pitch longer than most hitters and still get a good piece of it. And I know he works at his hitting, just like I did. Nobody gets the kind of numbers he does just doing what comes naturally."

Work, however, is what you make it, and Gwynn wonders aloud if its definition encompasses doing things one likes to do. Whatever, he's never far from a bat, in season or out.

"I take two weeks off a year—from about Oct. 1 to about the 15th—and the rest of the time I hit almost every day," he says. "I don't have a fixed schedule in the off-season; I may feel like swinging at 10 in the morning, or four in the afternoon, or nine at night. If I'm not at a batting cage, I'm in my backyard hitting wiffle balls off a tee, and I keep a bedspread hung in my garage to hit balls against in case I get the urge to take some swings at night. It's the repetition that counts, feeling the rhythm, feeling the stroke.

"I spend a lot of time watching video tapes of myself hitting," he goes on. "I've got one tape of myself getting base hits, and another of me hitting balls hard whether they went for hits or not. I'll play them between drills in the off-season, to keep the pictures in my mind. During the season, I tape every game, and play back my at-bats afterwards, along with one or both of the tapes of me hitting the ball well. That way, if I get off the track mechanically, I can catch it right away.

"I'm always watching the good hitters on the other teams, trying to pick up pointers. When we play the [San Francisco] Giants, I'll always watch Barry Bonds, especially for how he handles the inside pitch, because that's my weakness. I also keep a book on the pitchers —what they like to throw and when. It's a mental book, because I'm not much for writing things down, but I manage to remember it pretty well.

"I track the pitchers so I know their tendencies, but I usually don't go up to the plate guessing on pitches. I've talked to Ted Williams about hitting, and he said he guessed a lot and thought I should, too, but that's not my style.

"Still, sometimes I feel I know what a pitcher's going to throw, and go with it. A couple years ago, in the All-Star Game, I came up against David Cone with runners on first and second and one out, and got ahead in the count, 2-0. Cone's got a great fastball, and I'm sure everybody in the park was thinking he'd use it then, but I remembered he'd gotten me out on forkballs a couple of times, and I decided to look for one. He threw it, and I hit it down the line for a double. But I'd hate to try to make a living playing guessing games.

"My style is to react to the pitch—to see the ball and hit it someplace hard. I read that Williams in his prime could count the stitches on the ball as it came in. I don't see that well—I've been wearing glasses off the field the last few years—but I can pick up the spin on the ball out of the pitcher's hand, and that's enough. I guess the knowledge about pitchers that I store comes out kind of by osmosis. The periods I'm hitting the best are the ones when I'm thinking the least when I'm up there."

Gwynn has done some thinking about his career, and has set several goals for its remainder. One, of course, is to get back to the World Series (the Padres were there once during his tenure, in 1984), but others must cooperate for him to do that. His other goals are personal—to play five more years and pass the 3,000-hit mark.

Chances are that if he does one, he'll also do the other with room to spare; he'll enter this season with 2,401 hits, and since he seldom strikes out or walks (he's a singles hitter, so pitchers feel they may as well give him his whacks) he should have more than enough opportunities. And anyone who swings a bat as often as he does is sure to connect lots of times.

• *March 8, 1996*

Seeds of Change

S
•
ome day, many years from now, archaeologists will un-earth small but intense accumulations of sunflower-seed shells in various urban parts of what we now call the United States. They probably will conclude that strange tribes dwelled there, with dietary habits quite different from those of other residents of the land.

But—ha!—the joke will be on them. What they re-ally will have stumbled upon will be the bullpens of Ma-jor League Baseball parks, the inhabitants of which, through years of munching and spitting, are creating de-posits of seed hulls that could survive long after other traces of the game have vanished. This is not to say that only pitchers are into sunflower seeds; other players are, too, but, because of their positions afield, their shell-spitting is more widely scattered.

Those in the know say the movement of baseballers of many stripes toward seeds, and away from chewing to-bacco, has been pronounced of late. It might be likened to the one toward bagels and away from muffins as the breakfast-food choice of the broader society.

Baseball's Establishment, beset on other fronts, sees the seed-eating trend as a welcome ray of sunshine. A few years back, on grounds of health and public image, the game's overseers began a campaign to purge tobacco in all its forms from their sport. In 1991, they banned tobacco use from the dugouts and clubhouses of their

25

rookie leagues. The next year they extended the fiat to Class A leagues, and the year after that to the rest of the minors.

The major leagues remain exempt from the prohibition because that would require an agreement with the players' union that hasn't been forthcoming, among other things. Anyone who's seen Pittsburgh Pirate manager Jim Leyland sneak a cigarette in a dugout runway between innings, or come within 10 feet of the Philadelphia Phillies' Lenny Dykstra while he's at work on his chaw, knows that tobacco use remains alive in the National Pastime.

But big-leaguers who've made the switch to seeds from chewing tobacco say they're glad they've done so on a number of counts. "My wife likes me a lot better now when I come home from the ballpark," offers Steve Sparks, a pitcher for the Milwaukee Brewers, who are in training at Chandler, Ariz., near here.

If they wanted to, the seed eaters also could take satisfaction in the fact they're aiding a domestic industry. Commercial sunflower cultivation occupies some 3.5 million acres in the U.S., mostly in the Dakotas, Minnesota, Kansas and Nebraska. Most sunflower seeds are sold as birdfeed or crushed to make oil, leaving only about one-seventh of the crop to be roasted and salted for direct human consumption. But one sunflower head produces about 1,000 seeds, and about 18,000 of the plants can be grown on an acre of land. That would seem to leave plenty of seeds to go around for others besides ballplayers.

The sunflower seed has other things to recommend it. It's a nutritious morsel, high in vitamin E and the "good" kind of fat (polyunsaturated), it contains no cholesterol, and it isn't sugary like most chewing gum. It's more hygienic than tobacco juice, whose nasty stains must be scrubbed from artificial playing surfaces.

Moreover, "it's not just the taste or food value of the seed people like, but the process of shelling and eating it," says Richard Bell, president of David & Sons, the Fresno, Calif., company that's the largest U.S. packager of the product. "It's something satisfying you can do while you're doing something else."

To that list of pluses, the big-leaguers can add a couple more. One is that they get their seeds free because David & Sons gives them away to teams in the name of promotion. The other is that—unlike chewing tobacco or gum—there are competitive aspects to seed munching that appeal particularly to athletes. That's because extracting the kernel from the shell "takes tooth-tongue coordination," notes Shawn Boskie, a California Angels pitcher. "No player'd be caught dead opening a seed with his fingers."

There are, indeed, legends of the seed-eating art. Among them is Reggie Jackson, the former Oakland A's and New York Yankees outfielder. "He could eat 'em and spit the shells like a machine gun," says Bell with awe.

Jackson's nearest contemporary counterpart may be Glenallen Hill, a San Francisco Giants outfielder. He'll pack 30 or 40 seeds into his cheek before he takes the field for an inning, and consume them all before the third out is made. "I never lose a kernel or swallow a shell," he asserts. He stands 6 foot 2 inches and weighs 220 pounds, so one does not lightly challenge his claim.

If there's a problem with seeds, it's that their shells aren't aerodynamically suited for impressive spitting. That means they're usually simply expectorated, falling where they may. Ever equal to such challenges, however, players have found that holding a shell-half between the thumb and index finger of one hand and flicking it with the third finger of the other produces a satisfactory flight. Contests for distance are a bullpen staple, as are those for accuracy from dugouts, the usual target being the other team's nearest baseline coach.

Finally, sunflower seeds lend themselves to the kind of rituals baseball players cherish. One is practiced by Mark Dewey, a Giants reliever.

"I don't like salt on my seeds, so I'll take my bag out to the bullpen at the start of a game and roll it around in my hands to get the salt loose. That may take two or three innings," he says. "Then I'll make a small hole in one end and pat the bag to get rid of the salt.

"The neat thing about doing it that way is that the salt gets real powdery, like talc, and makes a cloud coming out. It drives the other guys crazy. I get as much kick out of that as I do from the chewing and spitting."

• *March 22, 1996*

OVALBALL

Part 2

Let's Take the Foot
Out of Football

I. have learned from experience that if you want to talk to football fans about anything substantive regarding their game, you'd better do it between seasons. Once the ol' pigskin is teed up for real, the only things those folks are interested in discussing are the hit Billy Joe put on Jimmy Clyde last Saturday or Sunday, how many Bloody Marys they downed at their tailgate picnics, or how the point spreads for the coming weekend's games will affect their eagerness to take a flyer.

Thus, I wish to take advantage of this last pre-football-season day by advancing what the late Dr. Swift, of literary fame, would call a modest proposal. I would like to see what's left of the foot taken out of football. I mean everything: no more kickoffs, punts, field goals or points after touchdowns. Send the kickers to the so-called soccer fields where they belong, and leave the gridirons to the true combatants.

Now, you probably think that's radical, but viewed through the kaleidoscope of history, it isn't. I have this from no less an authority than David Nelson, the foremost expert on football history and rules. Nelson used to be football coach and athletics director at the University of Delaware; now he's dean of that institution's school of physical education. He has been a member of the NCAA's football rules committee since 1958, and its secretary since 1961. His book on football's evolution, titled

"Anatomy of a Game," will be published by the NCAA sometime early next year.

Nelson says that, for most intents and purposes, American football gave the boot to the foot a long time ago. He points out that the contest from which football traces its origin, between Rutgers and Princeton in 1869, really was mostly soccer, and that its score, 6-4, counted the number of times each team kicked the ball between the goalposts and *under* the crossbar. Fifteen years later, football rules still emphasized kicking: A field goal counted five points, the kick-after-touchdown four, the touchdown two and the safety one.

The kick ceased being a method of advancing the ball offensively in 1923, when punts were declared no longer to be "free" kicks that either team could recover. Statutes covering kicking have hardened since, but not calcified; goal posts have been widened and narrowed and moved forward and back, kicking tees have been approved and disallowed, points of kickoff origin have been changed.

"Football people act like they're 30 degrees to the right of Genghis Khan, but they've been flexible on occasion," Nelson notes. I asked him if he liked my idea. He laughed heartily and remarked that he's had similar notions from time to time. "I've kept them to myself because they'd call out the boys in the white jackets for anyone in my position who proposed them," he confesses. "But maybe after I retire . . ."

The boys in white jackets don't bother with calls about newspaper columnists, so I have no hesitancy about proceeding. In fact, I'm confident the rationale for my position would win over even the boobyhatch reps, should they drop by to discuss it with me.

The reason to abolish the field goal is, I think, clear: It's wholly uncharacteristic of the game as it's now played. Eleven sweaty guys heave and haul the ball into scoring range, but when they're stymied out trots a fella wearing a clean uniform to perform an altogether different sort of act, and sometimes with an altogether different accent. "I go keek a touchdown," says sport's ultimate specialist, in Alex Karras's memorable words. One needn't be a xenophobe to see the situation's ridiculous side.

The same goes for the point after touchdown. This vestige of football's past is not only uncharacteristic of the game, it's also dully predictable. Extra-point kicks succeeded 95.6% of the time last year in both (!) the National Football League and NCAA Division I games. 'Nuf said. I suppose the "t" in touchdown needs to be crossed to prevent wholesale ties, so I suggest a play from scrimmage from far enough out to make it a good deal less than a sure thing; say, eight or 10 yards.

Getting rid of kickoffs would be no big deal; they're a way to get the ball into play at the start of halves and after scores, and simply giving the offensive team the ball at its own 30 or 35 yard line would accomplish the same purpose without kicking up a fuss, so to speak.

My objection to the punt is a bit more complex. Modern football's character—and, I think, main appeal—lies in its analogy to territorial combat; whoever called it the "100-Yard War" was on target. There's no equivalent of the punt in war, so eliminate the thing and let 'em fight it out. A team that fails to score a touchdown or get a first down would surrender the ball where it stands. If a team's defense pushes a foe's offense into its own end zone, call it a "touchback" and award six points, just like for a touchdown. Fair is fair.

Taking the foot out of football would permit a name change that would better describe the sport. "Battleball" is my candidate, but I'm open to suggestion. We could then join the rest of the world and get rid of the silly term "soccer" for the game where the foot really is supreme. It also would junk those big slingshots at the ends of the fields, giving people sitting in the end zones an unobstructed view of the proceedings.

Why should we do all this? For a better, more entertaining game, of course. Denied the outlet of the punt, teams would have no choice but to go all out offensively and, probably, employ a more "open" style as well. The most exciting part of present-day football, the fourth-down play, would occur again and again. Eliminating the field goal and kicked extra-point, and granting defenses the opportunity for scoreboard parity, would put the glory where it belongs—where the sweat is.

If you like my idea, write and say so. Don't write to me; I want to stay on good terms with my postman. Write to Pete Rozelle at the NFL, 410 Park Avenue, New York, N.Y. 10022, or Dick Schultz at the NCAA in Mission, Kan., 66222 (no street address necessary). For ease of handling, mark your envelope "NO KICKS."

• *Sept. 8, 1989*

Note: Neither Mr. Rozelle nor Mr. Schultz reported being inundated with mail.

Covering the
Spuds Bowl

MIAMI

Y.
ou know you are at a first-class sporting event when, just off the lobby of the Hyatt Regency Hotel, news-media headquarters for the Super Bowl, an elevator door opens to reveal Spuds MacKenzie, in the arms of an attendant.

"Going up?" asks a hotel guest.

"Going down," answers the attendant. And down the thing goes.

America's favorite English bull terrier is encountered again later that afternoon at a reception hosted by Spuds's employer, the Budweiser beer people, to promote the commercials they will run during Sunday's Super Bowl telecast. That's right, a reception to hype TV commercials.

Later, I will say more about Spuds and those commercials, but allow me to digress for a paragraph or four about my intermittent quest to discover the essence of Super Bowl week. It's about football, to be sure, but there are only three or so hours of that on Sunday, so other things must be arranged to fill the time of the news folks and others who get here early because, well, everyone else gets here early. There are rounds of interviews with the coaches and players, at which those gentlemen say how difficult it is to concentrate on the game with all the interviews they must do. Then there are parties, mostly with a commercial twist, designed to sell things.

This week, as you have no doubt heard, there also were riots in the predominantly black Overtown neighborhood, sparked by a policeman whose method of stopping a speeding motorcyclist was to shoot and kill him. The outbreaks provided some unscheduled employment for reporters, and pained Miamians eager to present a shiny civic face to the nation in this week of all weeks. The riots have, however, not seriously damped the air of commercial festivity. "Super Partygoers Upbeat but Concerned," headlined a *Miami Herald* story on Wednesday.

That got us close to the week's core. Closer yet was another *Miami Herald* piece, which detailed the preparations for all the sponsored entertainments taking place here. Among other things, the story revealed that partygoers will eat 65,000 shrimp and 16,000 stone crabs, utilize almost five miles of stretch limousines—as many as 1,000 cars—and soil more than 10 miles of tablecloths.

It continued, "To decorate the 26 corporate-village tents and NBC's reception tent at the stadium on game day, designer Neil Goldberg is using 1,500 pounds of glitter; 70,000 pounds of helium (enough to lift more than five African bush elephants); 1,728 hot-glue sticks and ribbons equal to 150 times the length of the football field." That answered all my questions except two: How many elephants are "more than five," and what if they don't want to be lifted?

Levitating Spuds MacKenzie would take a good deal less than 70,000 pounds of helium, one possible reason Budweiser picked him to plug its products. Also, the dog could be counted upon not to object. He was a most cooperative co-host at the event that unveiled the six, 30-second spots that will run during the San Francisco 49ers-Cincinnati Bengals contest. Together, they will make up Bud Bowl I, a football game between animated bottles of Bud Light and the company's regular beer, which henceforth will be called Bud Heavy here.

I arrived at the gathering eager to be enlightened, but was diverted by a bar dispensing the host's two brews. "Gimme a light," I grinned at the bartender, hoping to be beamed into a spaceship or, at least, have searchlights flash from my eyes and ears in the manner of the product's commercials. All I got was a beer.

The next diversion was the chance to be photographed with ol' Spuds and two of the three comely Spudettes, the girls with whom he usually appears. Watching those who preceded me, I was struck by Spuds's docile conduct. Indeed, dressed in an undoggylike miniature tuxedo, complete with trousers, red bow tie and cumberbund, he seemed almost comatose as the camera clicked.

My interest was piqued, and when my turn came I tried to pump the Spudettes on this and other matters. "Hi," I said. "What are your names?"

"Sandy and Leslie," said the brunette, not indicating which was which.

"Where's your blond partner?" I asked.

"At home," said Sandy/Leslie. "On vacation," said Leslie/Sandy.

"Is Spuds sedated?" I asked.

"He's mellow," said one. "Laid back," said the other.

Much the same information policy was followed by a besuited male Bud representative I spoke to next. "Is Spuds male or female?" I asked.

"Spuds is beyond gender," he replied.

"I heard he was a girl," I persisted.

"You hear all sorts of rumors, like that he died in a hot tub accident," the fellow frowned, ending the conversation.

The business part of the session was an out-of-focus movie in which beer bottles, sans arms and legs, somehow propelled a football and themselves around a field while an audience of Bud cans cheered. First the Lights scored, then the Heavies. Who wins? Whaddaya think? You'll have to watch to find out.

"It'll be a better game than the Super Bowl," predicted sportscaster Bob Costas, there to introduce the thing. "It'll keep you watching when one of the real teams is ahead, 52-3."

It occured to me that Costas was not only probably right, but also prophetic. Some day the Super Bowl will fulfill its destiny, as a come-on for the Bud Bowl.

Mellow/sedated Spuds, however, was not impressed. Seated in the front row in the lap of a Spudette, he fell asleep/passed out.

● *Jan. 20, 1989*

The Scales Tell the Steroids Story

hen I visited the training camp of the National Football League Indianapolis Colts two weeks ago, I was given a roster listing the players by height, weight and position. The numbers in the weight column seemed extraordinarily large, even for pro footballers. A tally revealed that of the 89 men listed, 21 weighed 280 pounds or more and 11 of those were at or over 300 pounds.

Curious, I later dug up the roster I'd received when I was at the Colts' camp in 1984. It listed 100 players, of whom only one had weighed in at more than 280 pounds. That gentleman—an offensive lineman listed at 289— still is with the team. His weight today is 308 pounds.

Assuming that the Colts are an average NFL team —and their record of 24 wins and 24 losses over the past three seasons indicates just that—something is up in the league besides the numbers on the scales. The NFL's powers-that-be, as well as those of the football colleges that feed it, say it's weight training, large meals and a form of natural selection that's funneling more very big men into their sport. Others believe that anabolic steroids also are involved, despite recent (and, many say, belated) efforts to ban them. The evidence of the senses favors the latter view.

In case you're coming in late, a few words of explanation are in order. Steroids are substances that, combined with exercise, promote gains in stamina, muscle and weight. That's helpful for football linemen and linebackers, the sport's heavy-duty positions. Their use also has been linked to such less-happy effects as mood swings, sterility and ailments of the heart, liver and kidneys. It's particularly an issue in sports because steroids give users an artificial—and thus unfair—advantage.

The debate over the extent of steroid use in football has been going on for some time, but with the advent of year-around drug testing in the NFL and NCAA in 1990, it has boiled down lately to three things: what the tests show, what the athletes say, and the true state of affairs. It helps to think of these as steps, although goodness knows where they lead.

The bottom step is what the tests show, which is miniscule steroid use in big-time football. The NFL began drug testing in earnest (i.e., with penalties) in the training camps before the 1989 season. Of some 2,000 players tested, 13, or 0.6%, were suspended for coming up positive. Last year, the league instituted random testing in-season and out, and conducted some 6,000 tests. The number of positives dipped to three.

The story is much the same at the collegiate level. Last year, for the first time, the NCAA began a program of random steroid testing in Division I football; of the 4,383 players involved, 17 tested positive, one tested positive for a diuretic that can be used as a steroid mask, and there were six no-shows. Even adding them all as positives yields a fraction of 1%.

Officials of both organizations admit that their tests aren't sensitive to all steroid or steroid-like products. Still, they believe they have the situation well in hand. "Even if our tests aren't perfect they function as a deterrent, and we think actual use is very low," declares Frank Uryasz, the NCAA's director of sports sciences. "I think of drug use as a room full of windows," offers John Lombardo, professor of family medicine at Ohio State University and an NFL adviser on steroids. "I believe we've closed almost all of them."

Self-reported drug use by players in surveys that guarantee anonymity tell a somewhat different story. In one, reported in the magazine *Physician and Sportsmedicine* in February, 10% of a sample of 895 NCAA varsity football players said in 1989 that they'd used steroids within the previous 12 months.

The NFL Players Association and Bruce Courson, a former Pittsburgh Steeler and Tampa Bay Buccaneer lineman, last fall mailed a similar questionnaire to 1,600 active or recent NFL players.

The response was too small to generalize from; only 120 players answered. But that's still a sizable number, and 28%—and 67% of the responding offensive linemen—said they'd used steroids sometime in their careers. Three percent said they used them during the previous season.

The poor response to the survey underlines the veil of secrecy that surrounds the subject of steroid use in sports. "It's against the rules, and against the way athletes want to be perceived," says Courson, who admits using the drugs during his playing days and says they caused irreparable damage to his heart. "It isn't attractive to be regarded as a pumped-up freak who cheated to win. That's why so few players speak out about steroids even after their careers are done."

To get around that barrier, one group of researchers tackled the subject indirectly, asking college footballers about their opponents' use of the drugs. The idea was to get them to project their feelings, and, perhaps, practices. The findings, published last year in the journal *Clinical Sports Medicine*, reported that more than 97% of 351 players questioned said they thought at least some of their foes have used steroids, with the mean response at 29%. More than 80% said they thought steroid use was "a problem" for their sport.

Charles Yesalis, professor of health and human development at Pennsylvania State University, was the principal author of the projection study. He's a longtime student of steroids and athletics. "I think that in college football, actual use falls somewhere between the 10% self-reporting figure and the 29% the players projected," he says. "It's nowhere near that less-than-1% figure the NCAA puts out."

Prof. Yesalis says he doesn't know for sure what proportion of NFL players use the drugs, but says he's taken close note of the testimony of admitted users, the latest of whom was Lyle Alzado, the former Oakland Raider: "You keep hearing that 50% to 75% of the linemen use them, and lesser proportions of other positions. You have to be impressed by the unanimity.

"The fact is there are steroid-type drugs that aren't on the NFL's controlled list, and others that the tests can't detect. Testing may have reduced usage some, but only while players find new ways to beat it. The size of the athletes certainly isn't going down. The only reasonable conclusion is that just the dumb ones are getting caught."

Courson says the NFL Players Association study indicated that a large majority of steroid users would stop if they were convinced their competitors would, but they felt that such assurances weren't forthcoming. Sixty percent of all who answered, and 76% of the users, said their coaches either approved of or didn't care about the practice. And 78% said they believed the league instituted steroid testing because of concern about its image rather than issues involving health or fair play.

"I know older guys in the league who still use steroids," says Courson, whose book on his struggles with the drugs, *False Glory*, is due out this fall. "They tell me that the players coming out of college are much more sophisticated about it than they were. I suspect that, overall, not much has changed."

He adds: "It think you'll see real change only when the incentives to cheat disappear. And the way the money in the league is climbing, things are headed in the exact opposite direction."

• *Aug. 28, 1991*

The Border War

DALLAS

O il brings wealth, but it does not foster amity between bordering states that have it. Witness Iran and Iraq, and Iraq and Kuwait. Also Texas and Oklahoma.

Among those examples, it's hard to say whose relations are worse. "When you hear a Texan or an Oklahoman call each other neighbor, it just means they share ownership in an oil well," Gary Cartwright, a writer from Texas, has written. "They are like tribes connected by a common hatred, two people who look upon one another with the special loathing usually reserved for cannibalism."

Fortunately for them, and for the world at large, Texas and Oklahoma (or, as the Sooners put it, Oklahoma and Texas) battle mainly on the football field, but the rivalry is no less intense for that. The universities bearing the names of the two states had it out for the 86th time here Saturday, with the underdog Longhorns prevailing, 10-7, under the sort of unusual circumstances that have come to be usual in the series. The fray was staged at the usual place—the Cotton Bowl here, which is roughly equidistant between the UT campus at Austin and OU's Norman home—and before the usual full house, described to me by one Texas native as "75,000 people, all obnoxious."

I thought the tenor of the contest was best summed up by a scalper out front. She was offering a $30 ticket for $100, but with a caveat. "If you're a Texas fan you don't want to buy this," she said. "It's in the Oklahoma section."

41

The winning play was not a pass or run, a field goal or, even, an extra point. It was a fumble recovery followed by a 30-yard return, into the Oklahoma end zone, early in the fourth quarter. Its perpetrator was a defensive back named Bubba (no kidding) Jacques (pronounced Jacks, of course). He's a home-state boy, from Conroe.

Many of the Oklahoma players were from Texas, too—44 of the Sooners' current 93-man roster, to be exact—and that's one reason Texans don't like Oklahoma. They also don't like it that Oklahoma rubs this in. "Texas: A Great Supporter of OU Football," headlines a story in the current Sooner media guide, which points out that 40 of the 92 Sooners who have earned All-American honors hailed from the Lone Star State.

Texas produces enough football players to fill many rosters, but it has been guilty of some piracy in return. Darrell Royal, adjudged UT's best coach ever during his 1958-76 tenure, not only was an Oklahoma native, but quarterbacked the Sooners against the school he later would serve. Oklahomans weren't noticeably perturbed about that, though. They dislike Texas because it is bigger, richer, more populous and, in total volume, louder. "If we win this game, it shuts 'em up for awhile," declared William Ossler, a red-clad OU booster, before Saturday's festivities.

The accent on noise is fitting, because OU-UT isn't just football, it's a multi-faceted event that includes many opportunities for boisterousness. The first takes place in downtown Dallas on the game's eve. In the past, this very large gathering was a kind of civilian version of football without helmets, in which ordinary folks got a chance to exchange whacks. But novel police tactics, like imposing one-way walking restrictions on downtown streets, has helped put a damper on the rough stuff, and last Friday's edition was described as good natured.

The fest continues Saturday morning at the Texas State Fair, which occupies the area immediately around the Cotton Bowl and of which the game is an annual part. Partisans of both teams roam the Midway, chomping corn dogs, swilling Lone Star beer and Dr Pepper, and gesturing at one another in various fashions, usually being too pooped from the night before to holler much.

Inside the old stadium, whose seating is split 50-50 between the schools, the fans revive, pitting patriotic hymns such as "Boomer Sooner" against "The Eyes of Texas," in considerable volume. The uproar continues back on the Midway after the game, but by that time partisans of the loser tend to become dispirited and slink off in search of quieter locales.

That this fate befell the Oklahomans on Saturday was unexpected, mainly because the Sooners came here with a 4-0 won-lost mark, to Texas's soggy 1-2, and a No. 6 national ranking. Finally off a two-year NCAA probation, and with third-year coach Gary Gibbs ordering his charges to throw the ball with a frequency that has no doubt dismayed his predecessor, Barry Switzer, the Sooners were bidding to recapture the glory that fled, along with Switzer, when the team was penalized for behaving more like a motorcycle gang than a band of collegians.

The Sooners lived up to their name early on, spending the best part of the first half in Longhorn territory. They took a 7-0 lead in the first quarter on a 24-yard touchdown pass from quarterback Cale Gundy to flanker Ted Long, and offered their field goal kicker, Scott Blanton, opportunities from 32, 37 and 47 yards. Alas for OU, Blanton missed them all.

Texas, meantime, mustered only one good first-half charge, in quarter two, but Jason Post made the field goal, from 30 yards. That was to be about that for offense on both sides, as the Texas defense in particular stiffened. It did even better in the last period, when tackle James Patton forced Sooner fullback Mike McKinley to fumble and Jacques, coming in from his safety position, scooped up the bouncing spheroid and carried it into the end zone. Subsequent Sooner thrusts died amid quarterback sacks and incomplete passes.

The win was welcomed by Texas's fifth-season coach David McWilliams, who, while not making Horns boosters forget Royal, at least has beaten OU these last three years, all on late scores. Smiling, he later ascribed the win to three things: "Defense, defense and defense."

Hero Jacques grinned, too, in describing his winning play. "The ball bounced once and I missed it, but it came back to me, like it was on a string," he said. His feeling when he saw that his path to the end zone was clear, he added, was "Woo!"

And as Sooner backers will attest, "Woo!" spelled backwards is "Oow!"

• *Oct. 14, 1991*

College Football's 'Dr. No'

COLLEGEVILLE, MINN.

J. ohn Gagliardi, who is in his 40th year as head football coach at St. John's University, a Catholic institution in this central Minnesota lake country, says he learned most of what he knows about his profession from his old high-school coach in Trinidad, Colo.

"Whatever he did, I've done pretty much the opposite," says the 65-year-old. "There's more than one way to teach something, you know."

And there's more than one way to coach football, although you'd hardly know it from observing the vast majority of men who oversee our leading autumn sport. Unlike those worthies, Gagliardi does not lead his charges through scrimmages or lengthy calisthenics. His players aren't required to run wind sprints or laps. They do not spend long hours in dark rooms watching their mistakes repeated endlessly on film or videotape.

They do not spend long hours on anything connected with football; St. John's holds no practices on Sundays or Mondays, and their sessions on other days rarely last longer than 90 minutes. College students have plenty to do as it is, the coach believes.

Gagliardi, in brief, is football's "Dr. No," and he's gone to the trouble of writing down things most coaches do that he doesn't. The list numbers 63, and could be longer. "I go to clinics and hear about the stuff other coaches are doing with computers," he notes. "I don't do any of it, but I figure that one 'no'—no computers—covers it."

One thing Gagliardi-coached teams *have* done is win. His won-lost-tied record in 44 collegiate seasons is 288-94-9, and that victory total places him fifth among all U.S. college coaches, ever. He's had but two losing years in that span.

At St. John's, an all-male institution with an enrollment of about 1,800, he's won 18 Minnesota Intercollegiate Athletic Conference titles and three national crowns, in 1963, 1965 and 1976, in NCAA Division III, members of which award no athletic scholarships.

His Johnnies have gone to the national playoffs 10 times, including last year, where their only loss in a 12-game season was to University of Dayton, the eventual runnerup. That St. John's unit led its division in passing, no small feat for a school in its frosty clime. This year's team is 2-0 going into tomorrow's game with St. Olaf College.

This is Gagliardi's 50th season as a head coach all told, and, no, that's not a misprint. The first team he directed, at age 16, was the Trinidad Catholic High squad, for which he also was the starting tailback. In 1943, his senior year, the school's regular coach was drafted into the military soon after the season began. His teammates picked him to lead them the remainder of the campaign. With some trepidation, the school's principal acquiesced.

"I got rid of the things I hated as a player—the running, the hard calisthenics, the tackle scrimmaging," Gagliardi recalls. "As far as I could see, they served mainly to keep us banged up and sore. I wanted to find out what it was like to be healthy for a game."

His team found that out, plus what it was like to be champs— their 7-1 mark led their conference. The school was so pleased it kept him on as coach the following year, while he stayed home waiting to be drafted (he wasn't), and for two years after that, while he was a student at Colorado College.

He got another high-school head coaching job during his junior and senior years at college, meaning that, when he received his degree at age 22, he'd already put six seasons of experience on his resume. His first job after graduation also was as a head coach, at Carroll College in Helena, Mont., where he was the athletic trainer as well.

"I never played college football because I was busy coaching, and never was an assistant football coach anywhere," Gagliardi points out. "I can't say I've felt a lack because of either."

Lured by a salary increase to $4,200 a year from $2,400, and by a respite from taping ankles, Gagliardi came to St. John's in 1953. He's stayed despite offers to coach elsewhere, including a bid from Bud Grant to join his Minnesota Vikings staff. Grant's two sons played for Gagliardi at St. John's.

Gagliardi and his wife, Peggy, have raised four children in their on-campus home while he's honed his philosophy of coaching minimalism. His 63 nos take in drills (no blocking sleds or other practice apparatus, no outdoor workouts in bad weather, no compulsory weight lifting), rhetoric (no slogans, no using words such as "hit" or "kill," no hazing of freshmen) and coaching behavior (no whistles, no clipboards, no special uniforms).

And though it's not a rule, he prefers that his players call him John. "Every time a kid calls me 'Coach,' I feel like calling him 'Player,'" says he.

There are, to be sure, plenty of things that Gagliardi's teams do. They run their plays in practice, repeatedly and at full speed, and woe be unto him who gets an assignment wrong. They watch some game film on Mondays, but only of their successful plays of the Saturday before; their coach believes that positive examples are the best teaching aids. Even though they don't practice it, on grounds it leads to injuries, they're expected to tackle spiritedly in games. That they do so is attested by the less-than-10 points a game they permitted last season, and their total of eight points surrendered so far in this one.

And while neither sprints, laps nor weightlifting are prescribed, players are expected to do what it takes to be football-fit if normal practice exertions don't suffice. "You're supposed to learn self-sufficiency in college," Gagliardi says. "Mama's not here to tell you to study, and a coach shouldn't be there telling you to keep in shape."

What a half-century of coaching has taught him, he summarizes, is the importance of the mental side of his sport. "If you sent me an all-pro offensive lineman on a game day, and he didn't know our plays, I'm not sure I could use him," he says. "Now, if you sent me an all-pro quarterback or wide receiver . . ."

• *Sept. 25, 1992*

Dirtiest Word in Football: 'Loser'

ATLANTA

T.

he jocks-and-coaches union that cuts across sports lines —no less real for being unofficial—has decreed that losing is akin to death, and more than a bit shameful. Enter a losers' locker room after the least-important game and you're likely to find the players striking dejected poses, barely able to speak for humiliation and chagrin. Any other sort of behavior would put them at risk of being considered insufficiently serious.

The fact is, however, that losing is the common lot of those who engage in sports. Except for Rocky Marciano and the occasional racehorse, everybody loses sometime, and depending on how you define it, most lose most of the time. If the late football coach George Allen was correct when he said "Every time you win, you're reborn; when you lose, you die a little," few athletes would reach their majority.

The subject of winning and losing, unadorned, is especially apt this week in this Southern metropolis, site of the professional football championship Super Bowl between the Dallas Cowboys and Buffalo Bills. The contest won't be played out until Sunday, but one team—the defending-champion Cowboys—already has been cast in the role of winner, and its foe assigned the less-desirable part. Indeed, because they lost this game the past three times it was played, the Bills have been treated as if they have a lot of nerve being here at all.

47

This perception persists although all and sundry know that the Bills are, at worst, a very good club, winners of 58 of 76 games over the past four seasons. One of their victories in the current campaign was over the Cowboys.

Yet Jimmy Johnson, the Dallas coach, has been permitted to turn every interview session into a sermon on success (the distillation of his wisdom is that winning is something that's accomplished by "winners," as in "we have winners everywhere in our organization"), while Marv Levy, his Buffalo counterpart, is asked to second-guess his past practices. "The past is history," Levy insists. He's surely right about this— he's a Harvard man, after all—but we treat his words with skepticism.

It's been asserted that Levy's sin—the failure to win the "big one"—is uniquely grievous in football; we don't heap similar scorn upon, say, baseball pennant winners who don't win the World Series, or unsuccessful finalists in the NCAA basketball tourney. "Maybe next year we'll try the World Series," Levy said Wednesday in response to one question along those lines.

There may be a point there; it has been football, the game closest to war, that's produced our most memorable (and absolute) quotes about winning and losing. "Winning isn't everything. It's the only thing," usually is attributed to Vince Lombardi, but the reference books say Henry "Red" Sanders, another old football coach, really said it. "Good losers get into the habit of losing," said Knute Rockne. "Without winners, there wouldn't be any goddamned civilization," said Woody Hayes.

But all those guys were coaches, and a couple days of quote-shagging here this week suggests that their troops—er, players—may have somewhat different ideas. Football is a team game, which means that credit or blame usually is collective rather than individual. That this is an idea many football players find comforting is seen in their willingness to absolve from blame those of their number who may have been more responsible than most for memorable defeats.

Yes, Buffalo kicker Scott Norwood—no longer with the team— did miss the last-play field goal that would have won the Bills' first Super Bowl appearance, in 1991, but he was a fine fellow who helped win other games and one shouldn't overlook other players' miscues that day, his teammates still chorus.

And, yes, Leon Lett, the Dallas defensive lineman, did cost his team a Thanksgiving Day victory over Miami when his ill-advised swipe at the ball after a missed field goal turned into a Cowboy fumble, but that, too, was forgivable. "We gave Leon a ball with a piece of string tied to it later, but that was a team thing. He knew we were kidding," averred Russell Maryland, Lett's linemate.

Insight into how a large dose of defeat can be less than lethal is provided by the Bills' Steve Tasker. He's an unusual player in a couple of respects. At 5-foot-9 and 180 pounds, he's an ordinary-size man in a giants' game. He was a part-time player in college who has made a 10-year professional career in that role, as a member of the so-called "special teams" that cover and return kicks.

Tasker comes from Leoti, Kan., a town that, he says, has one, blinking traffic signal and a single one-way street, which runs in front of the elementary school. He mainly ran track in high school and, unrecruited, attended a community college for a year. From there he went to Northwestern University, an estimable institution but a perennial football nonpower. The teams he played on there, mostly as a kick returner, won but seven of 33 games.

Signed by the Houston Oilers as a special-teamer for his speed, Tasker was waived in 1986 after suffering two serious knee injuries in as many seasons. Buffalo picked him up for the same chores. He's made the Pro Bowl five times since in that capacity and was named the most valuable player of last year's game. "Most guys who come to the pros were stars in college, and consider special teams a step down. Not me," he says of his prowess.

Tasker thinks his Northwestern years were worthwhile despite the dearth of victories. "We accomplished some things there that were good for the football program, and I loved just playing," he says. He's liked being a pro more, "because I've showed I can do what I do at the very highest level."

He goes on: "If we lose again, I'm sure some people will continue to define us by our losses, but I won't. I'll recall being a member of some very good teams."

Vince Lombardi said what he *did* say was: "Winning isn't everything, but making the effort to win is." He also said, "If you can't accept losing, you can't win."

Maybe he really was a saint. Maybe Steve Tasker is, too. And maybe the Bills will win the Vince Lombardi Trophy on Sunday.

• *Jan. 28, 1994*

Note: The Bills lost that Sunday, but Northwestern, Steve Tasker's alma mater, went to the Rose Bowl two years later.

Cantabs Edge Elis

NEW HAVEN, CONN.

It seemed the right thing to do, so before Saturday's Yale-Harvard football game here I walked through the parking lots around the Yale Bowl looking for people wearing raccoon coats. I found two—Mr. and Mrs. F. Steele Blackall III, of Providence, R.I. Blackall, a 1947 graduate of Yale, was happy to tell me about the garments.

"As far as we know, they're both pre-1910; mine was my father's, and Patty's came down from her own family," he beamed. "We wear them once a year, for the Yale-Harvard game. This will be the 59th we've attended. We have zero interest in other college or professional football, but we love the Ivy League games. They're a throwback to the time when you could be sure the players had to pass their courses."

He continued: "We're throwbacks, too, no question. We have this wonderful newspaper picture of us wearing our coats, taken 20 or 30 years ago, with a caption saying how we looked like a caricature of a bygone era. If that was true then, what must we look like now?"

I told him I thought they looked fine, and that, on a chilly day like Saturday, I wished I had a coat like his. And besides, what's wrong with being a throwback?

As it turned out, nothing much was wrong with the game, either. In about as good a contest as you'll see, underdog Harvard, facing its first winless Ivy League campaign since the conference was formally constituted in

1956, gave up a touchdown to fall behind with a minute and a half left, then roared back and scored one of their own to win, 22-21. The victory ended their season with a two-win, eight-loss record, but capturing The Game makes up for much adversity.

"Our team banquet next week is going to be a whole lot more fun because of this," smiled Eion Hu, Harvard's junior tailback from Ringwood, N.J. He set a school record for the series by rushing for 175 yards, the last two of which, with 29 seconds left, were for the deciding score.

There are, of course, many who question the claim that Harvard-versus-Yale is The Game. Cal-Stanford in the West, Alabama-Auburn in the South and Ohio State-Michigan in the middle are among the annual outings that their proponents say have usurped that title, and each occasionally bears on the question of who's currently best among the roiling collegiate pack.

The answer is that, with 118 meetings dating from 1875, Harvard-Yale was The Game before those others were *a* game, and the two institutions did more than any others to make big-time college football what it is. For proof one need only read the recently published account of Harvard's 1905 season from the diary of William T. Reid, the school's football coach in that time when the Ivies ruled the sport.

In the earnest manner of his day, Reid despaired of some of his players' lack of academic industry and bemoaned having to intervene with profs to keep them eligible and use his clout with Boston sportswriters to keep their extracurricular brawls out of the newspapers. Many a present-day coach might find instruction in the way he handled those problems.

Some years ago, Yale, Harvard and the other Ivies turned their backs on such headaches by eliminating athletic scholarships, thereby seeing to it that their student-athletes were, really, students. This has helped their administrators and coaches sleep at night, but it lowered the schools' gridiron status considerably.

The balance between virtue and ambition is ever-shifting, though, and as crowds at Ivy games, and those of other low-profile leagues, have dwindled, some reemphasis has occurred. In 1983, the conference adopted a complex bit of business called the Academic Index that eases admissions standards for some jocks and, assertedly, gives some league members a recruiting edge over others. Freshmen were made eligible for varsity football in 1993, and, last year, spring practice was allowed. Now, there's agitation to permit the Ivy winner to enter the NCAA Division 1-AA football playoff, ending a long-time ban against post-season play.

More off-putting is the admission by some in the Ancient Eight that more than academic brilliance and financial need go into filling their football rosters. "If the dean of admissions and the financial-aid people aren't in your corner, you're in trouble," Al Bagnoli, coach of the 1993 and '94 Ivy champ Penn, has said.

But the Ivies remain a long way from the campus-or-carwash philosophy, and this is reflected in ways both small and large. For example, Saturday's pre-game scene outside the old bowl included a free-lunch tent for Yale undergrads (hey, they're paying $28,000 a year to attend), a demonstration-site display by a Mercedes-Benz dealer (future customers, you know) and a group of young women wearing Yale caps sweetly singing "Moonlight Serenade" and other oldies before some appreciative grownups. I never did learn what that was about.

Inside, before a crowd of 35,000, the tone was set by Tim Murphy, Harvard's second-year head coach. Despite rain and temperatures in the 30s, he stalked his sideline wearing a short-sleeved shirt, a la Woody Hayes. His tough-guy counterparts were running-back Hu and his quarterbacks, senior Vin Ferrara and sophomore Jay Snowden. Murphy began alternating the latter pair when Yale, whose three wins this year included one over league-titlist Princeton, went up 15-10 in the third quarter and appeared to be pulling clear.

Snowden, primarily a runner, led the drive that gave the Crimson a 16-15 edge midway through the fourth quarter. Then he threw an interception that allowed the Bulldogs to reclaim the lead. Getting the ball back with 1:39 left, Murphy returned passer Ferrara to the game, and he completed three throws that moved his team from its own 38 to the Yale four. Back in went Snowden. His and Hu's running got the final four, and their fellow students swarmed the field at the gun, as in raccoon-coat days.

Said Snowden: "Getting that [initial fourth-quarter] TD was my greatest feeling ever. Throwing that interception was my worst feeling ever. Getting that last TD was the greatest again." Said Murphy, who claimed he never noticed the cold: "There's really something about this game."

● *Nov. 20, 1995*

ROUNDBALL

Part 3

Honestly, Abe

Peering through tinted glasses and past the Nikes propped on his desk, Abe Lemons discusses his current Oklahoma City University basketball team.

"We've got nine guys on the squad, three of 'em freshmen," he says between puffs of a cigar. "Our leading scorer's a 5-foot-10 guard. We list our tallest boy at 6-foot-6, but I'm 6-3 and can look him in the eye without lifting my head.

"One of our kids is from Colombia. He doesn't speak much English. I know a little Spanish, so we communicate some. We'll get along better as soon as I learn how to say 'don't shoot' in Spanish."

On the court, however, this motley crew manages to perform creditably; its record stands at six wins and four losses. Things promise to improve when a raft of rangy scholars who have transferred in from other schools become eligible to play in the second semester. Last year's OCU team went 34-1, the sole loss coming in the National Association of Intercollegiate Athletics (NAIA) tourney.

Wins are par for the course for Abe Lemons's teams. Going into this, his 32nd season as a college head coach, they had produced 550 of them, against 304 losses. So, too, are the laughs.

"I'm part Indian," Abe says. "Every time I dance, it starts to rain."

Here's Abe on pre-game pep-talks: "One night I told my boys that if they won, I'd give 'em jewels, cars, girls, anything they wanted. They won and wanted to know where their stuff was. I told them I'd checked up on it and had learned it was against NCAA rules."

Here's Abe on the coach's role: "All I do is coach and put my players on the floor. If they win, fine. If they lose, it's their fault."

And here's Abe on coachly humor, which is about as common in his profession as losers with large offices: "Why not have some fun? We're not exactly doing brain surgery. Besides, you gotta keep the sportswriters from gettin' bored."

At age 64, Lemons is a rarer bird yet because he's a winner with a small office. His record, the seventh best among active coaches, is all the more remarkable because it has been achieved at schools in Oklahoma and Texas. In those states, he notes, "men love their families and football, not necessarily in that order."

This is his second stint at OCU, a Methodist Church-connected institution with an enrollment of 3,000 students that a few seasons back quit the NCAA's Division I Midwest City Conference to play a local schedule in the small-school NAIA. Among his other stops was the University of Texas. He was fired there in 1982 despite the fact his teams won 64% of their games over six seasons, and a National Invitational Tourney title in 1978.

The ouster still grates. "I don't know why I was fired at Texas; they never told me," he shrugs. "People didn't like some of the things I said, I guess. I said once that I'd recruit a communist or a Democrat if he could sink a free throw, and it came back to me that I'd called Democrats communists. Another time I was talking about a new arena they were building. I said it had 16,000 seats and six parking places. I really did say that.

"I'm making less money than I did at Texas, but otherwise I'm not sorry to be back at OCU. I have kinfolk around here," says Lemons, who grew up in Walters, Okla., south of Oklahoma City. "And the pace is easier. Here we just play basketball and go home. There's no Dick Vitale on TV telling people all the things I did wrong."

In keeping with their coach's observation that the team with the most points always wins, Lemons's teams try to score a lot, and often do. He eschews any grander strategic plans. "I speak at coaches' clinics sometimes, but mostly I tell stories. They put me on between the juggler and seal acts," he says. "I never went in much for X's and O's. It depends too much who your X or O is. If my X is Michael Jordan,

your whole team of O's won't stop him. I mostly try to get good players and not get in their way."

He avers that he takes a similar approach toward his charges'
academic performance. "I laugh when I hear a coach say *he* graduates
this many players. I never graduated any of mine—they graduated
themselves. I tell 'em the facilities are here, and it's up to them to use
'em. I also tell them a few facts of life, like that it can get cold awful
fast when you're on the street without a diploma."

The coach is being too modest in the latter respect, says Eddie
Jackson, who played on his OCU teams in the mid-1960s and is now
an officer at an Oklahoma City bank. "He'd joke around, but he'd
also come down hard on you if you weren't working up to your potential," Jackson says. "That went for off the court as well as on."

And, indeed, the jokes end at the court's edge. Last week Abe's
boys hosted Northwestern Oklahoma State at cozy Frederickson
Field House, which has 3,000 seats and about seven parking spaces.
State is a smaller school (1,800 students) with taller players. Still,
OCU raced to a 77-59 lead midway through the second half. Then
the team's attention waned and the visitors crept to within six points
with two minutes left.

Abe was not pleased. "This is serious damned business! Wake
up!" he shouted at his players during a time-out. They did, and held
on to win, 89-84.

Later, Lemons and his squad trooped to the nearby Student
Union for a "Talk-Back," at which they answer questions about the
game posed by fans. The coach enjoys the give and take and thinks
it's good for his players to learn to think on their feet.

With Abe as master of ceremonies, they'd better. "I see the stat-
istician gave you just two rebounds. How 'bout explaining that?" he
said to Greg Miles, a 6-5 starting forward.

"Two rebounds? No way that's right, coach! I coulda got two rebounds just standing there," said the young man in mock surprise.

"I think that's the way you got 'em," said Abe.

• *Dec. 4, 1987*

Goofing Off
Like Always

OMAHA, NEB.

"Sweet Lou" Dunbar, the gleaming-eyed, knock-kneed top banana of the Harlem Globetrotters, hunched at the free-throw line here Tuesday night, as his teammates and their full-time foes, the Washington Generals, lined the lane in anticipation. Up went the shot, and the players lurched into position for a rebound. Back came the shot—the basketball was attached to Dunbar's hand with a rubber band—and the players sprawled comically.

Just about everyone in the Omaha Civic Auditorium crowd of 7,000 knew what was coming, but they laughed anyway. And why shouldn't they? It's a funny bit. People laughed at it the night before in Wichita, Kan. They would laugh at it the next night in Lincoln, Neb. Their fathers laughed at it. So did *their* fathers.

On the court, Sterling Forbes, a pleasant-faced Globetrotter forward, smiled, too, as his father had smiled when he wore the team's star-spangled jersey and striped shorts. "Dad and I compare notes about the things we do," says Forbes. "There's not much I'm doing that he didn't."

Even if you don't see them for a while, its nice to know the Globies are still out there, and up to their old tricks. It's been 64 years since Abe Saperstein loaded a bunch of black basketball players into his flivver in Chicago and drove them 50 miles west to little Hinckley, Ill., to perform for 300 people in a cold gym. They've since strutted their stuff before more than 100 million people in 110 lands, and done everything there is to do with a basketball but eat one.

"We started out playing ball, but we've transcended that," says Charles "Tex" Harrison, who began with the team as a player in 1954 and remains as its coach and player-development head. "I think what we're doing now is more important."

There was a time when the Trotters played ball truly, and well. Team lore has it that they didn't begin clowning until a 1939 game in which they were leading 112-5, and got bored. Noting the crowd's reaction, Saperstein told his charges it was all right to fool around more.

Playing it straight, the Globetrotters won a 1940 tournament billed as the world's professional championship. Later that decade and early the next, they played eight games against the Minneapolis Lakers, the best club in the then-fledgling National Basketball Association, winning three. In 11 of the years from 1950 through 1962, they staged national tours with a group of honest-to-goodness college all-stars, and won two-thirds of the contests.

The opening of all levels of basketball to blacks dulled the Globetrotter's competitive edge; they haven't played anyone but their Washington General partners-in-travel for some time. Suffice it to say they've been unbeaten since 1971.

The show, however, has retained its luster. For the past few years there have been two Globetrotter teams, known as the "National" and "International" units, although both play world-wide schedules and each is busy about 275 days a year.

The units perform abroad from September through December, barnstorm North America from January until mid-April, then return overseas until mid-July, leaving just six summer weeks for concentrated R&R. "The only way we could book more dates is if the year went beyond 365 days," says Joe Anzivino. He's the team's longtime general manager, since 1986 in the employ of Minneapolis-based International Broadcasting Corp. The company has various interests, but none in broadcasting.

Trotting with the Trotters is taxing, to say the least. Between Jan. 2 and April 14, the International unit that played here Tuesday has but three days off, and the vast majority of its stands are one-nighters. Laundry gets lost, meals are skipped, large bodies must be pried into small airline seats.

"You know how travelers say they sometimes don't know what city they're in? Happens to me all the time," smiles Tyrone Brown, the unit's dribbling whiz. "Worst thing is, when I ask one of the other guys, he'll say he doesn't know, either."

Globetrotter management won't say what players earn for all that. "It's a nice living, but nowhere near NBA standards," allows Anzivino. "Some get into six figures, but not most."

Regardless, those who drop out can be replaced quickly. The team receives so many job applications that it limits tryouts to invitees, and these far exceed the three to five newcomers it adds annually. "We don't look for guys who can do tricks. We look for good players who can handle the ball well and learn *our* tricks," notes Harrison.

Character references also are sought, because the Trotters are, after all, family entertainment. "If we can't get somebody we know to vouch for a player, we'll likely give him a pass," says the coach. "The only place we want to see our guys' names is in the sports pages."

In fact, the Trotters rarely appear in the sports pages these days, their act being far more show biz than sport. But if all people wanted was basketball, they'd be home flicking their TV dials. On this night in Omaha, as on all other nights, the Globies rolled out their full repertoire.

In the pre-game warmup, as much a part of the show as the game proper, Matthew "Show Biz" Jackson bumped in a basket off his head and made another on a behind-his-back shot from half court (OK, it was on about his 20th try). To the tune of "Sweet Georgia Brown," the Trotters wove their familiar, but still wondrous, ball-handling routines.

They pulled the old confetti-in-the-water-bucket gag, and the one where the 6-foot-10 Dunbar grabs a woman spectator's purse, pretends to forget whose it is, then evilly displays its contents to the crowd in search of "identification." ("See here? She carries Tylenol. Must be married," he leered.) They hid basketballs under their own shirts and under those of the hapless Generals, and made general sport of the short, portly ref. All drew laughs.

"When I first joined the team, I used to wonder if it'd last out the season," says the 58-year-old Harrison. "Now, I'm sure it'll outlast me."

• *Feb. 15, 1991*

What Michael Did Last Night

CHICAGO

A friend of mine who's a Chicago Bulls fan believes that, after every Bulls game, the sports pages of the Chicago newspapers should run a box headlined "Here Are the Unbelievable Things Michael Jordan Did Last Night." That way, he says, he wouldn't have to read long game accounts to ferret them out.

My response was that his idea probably would founder on the problem of definition. After watching Jordan play professional basketball for nine seasons now, people's notions about what's believable and what's not have changed.

The opponents of His Highness Michael have gone through just that sort of transformation. After Jordan scored 55 points Wednesday night in Chicago Stadium in leading his team to a 111-105 victory that gave it a commanding three-games-to-one lead in the best-of-seven NBA championship series with the Phoenix Suns, Kevin Johnson, the Suns point guard, was asked if he could take in what had just happened.

"I can't say it was unbelievable. It was definitely believable," said KJ. "We've all seen Michael do things like that before."

Jordan did not pop eyes with individual moves that heretofore had been associated only with institutions like the Cirque du Soleil. He did not score after shifting hands with the basketball in midair, as he did during the

1991 finals against the Los Angeles Lakers. He did not approach the hoop face forward and do a 180-degree twirl before flipping in the spheroid over his head, as he did during a midseason contest last season. He did not score 69 points, as he did against a good Cleveland Cavaliers team on a March evening in 1990, or 63, as he did in a 1986 playoff game against a better Boston Celtics crew that was title-bound.

But all things considered, it's doubtful that the gifted Jordan has played a better 46 (of 48) minutes than he did on Wednesday. There were his points, of course, on 21 baskets and 13 free throws, and there was the occasion, a game that, if it had been lost (and it nearly was), would have been a profound setback to the Bulls' hopes for a third-straight league title.

There also was his defensive play, which best can be summarized by a look at the stats of Dan Majerle, the Phoenician whom he most often guarded. Majerle is his team's, and the league's, most prolific three-point shooter, and his six treys paced the Suns' 129-121 win here Sunday night. Yet on Wednesday, he got off but five three-point shots, and two of the three he made (accounting for six of his 14 points) came during a one-minute, 15-second span late in the second quarter when Phil Jackson, the Chicago coach, tried to give his star some rest. Needless to say, that experiment was quickly aborted.

And there was, finally, the last three of Jordan's 55 tallies, which will live long in highlight-film history. They came with 13 seconds left and the Bulls holding a precarious, 106-104 lead. Jordan got the ball near midcourt and, dribbling left-handed, headed past Majerle for the basket. Charles Barkley, the burly Suns star, moved to bar his path, but as he and Jordan collided, Jordan neatly switched the ball to his right hand and threw up a shot from his hip. It hit the back-board and spun in, and he later made the free throw that the collision occasioned. The official's call on the play was a close one—charging against Jordan seemed a possibility. But Barkley later opined that it was proper. "I didn't get over in time to draw a charge," he confessed.

The 6-foot-6 Jordan's points came on jump shots of up to 20 feet, mostly when he was guarded by the 6-foot-1 Johnson, and on drives to the hoop, mostly when he was guarded by the taller but slower Majerle or Richard Dumas. It was a measure of Jordan's ability to get past Majerle that that worthy, who has some reputation as a defender and is the Suns' main Jordan cop, picked up only one foul all evening. Michael was past him before he could get in a hack.

Paul Westphal, the Phoenix coach, absolved his minions of blame. "We can't stop [Jordan]. Nobody can," he said. He added: "The difference tonight was that they had Michael and we didn't."

That was an excellent synopsis of an excellent game, easily the best of this playoff series. Except for game one in Phoenix, in which the Suns suffered from stage fright, the series has been close but not always well played, as exemplified by the you-take-it-no-you-take-it triple-over-time contest on Sunday.

Wednesday's game made up for that. It was an edgy sort of contest, not at all the blowout that the success-gorged Chicago Stadium faithful had come to see. In each quarter the Bulls pulled to comfortable-seeming leads, only to have the Suns grind back behind the indefatigable Barkley, who had 32 points, and Johnson, who had 19. Their last surge brought them from eight behind, with 3½ minutes left, to 104-106 at the 1:26 mark, and they would have tied if the Bulls' Scottie Pippen hadn't stripped the ball from poor Majerle on a subsequent two-on-one fast break. But, then, Michael barred the door.

A couple of other things seem worth saying. One is that Jordan has performed in these playoffs under the self-created clouds of a late-night trip to an Atlantic City casino during the semifinal series in New York and of the claim by a former golfing partner that Jordan failed to fully repay $1.2 million in golfing losses. While the facts of those matters are in doubt, one must conclude it takes a pretty stolid character to slough them off the way he has.

Further, there's the curious matter that Jordan is often called upon to apologize for large scoring outputs on grounds that it detracts from his teammates' effectiveness. He would have little of this after Wednesday's fray, saying, "I saw my opportunities and I took 'em."

There'll be another game here tonight, and a couple of "if necessaries" in Phoenix Sunday and Wednesday, but they probably won't be necessary because no team has come back from a 3-1 deficit to win an NBA final. That's all the more reason for you to get a tape of Wednesday night's game. You'll want to tell your grandkids you saw Jordan at his best, and they may ask for proof.

• *June 18, 1993*

Basketball Is Beautiful

WOODSTOCK, NY

Charley Rosen says it's not true that he's a lunatic. Well, not all the time, anyway.

"I'm a purist, an honest man, and I hate to see a beautiful thing defiled," he says. "There have been times when my sense of injustice has gotten the better of me."

The beautiful thing of which Rosen speaks is basketball. He has coached it for a good many years, and while his present post is a modest one—he directs the women's team at the State University of New York at New Paltz—his perspective remains unique. For nine years he was an assistant or head coach in the Continental Basketball Association, the sport's professional minor-league netherworld. And with seven books on basketball to his credit, six of them novels, he's the game's foremost literary chronicler.

At his ease, the 6-foot-8 52-year-old is a pleasant and reflective person, a self-described overage hippie whose identification with the 1970s counterculture led him to establish his home in this upstate New York community that is its spiritual capital. Once ball meets floor, however, that tranquility has ofttimes proved fragile.

Rosen once spent a dismal hour in a Cedar Rapids, Iowa, jail for taking a swing at an opposing coach after a game in that city, but most of the disturbers of his peace have been referees. He racked up $1,700 in fines for technical fouls during one CBA season; at $25 a clip, that comes out to quite a few.

He disputes published reports that, fuming over a call he considered unjust, he attempted to throw his 50th-birthday cake at a referee during a halftime ceremony honoring him in Oklahoma City when he coached there. "I was holding a balloon in one hand and this very big cake in the other, and the cake slipped," he claims. But he adds: "As I was losing control of it, I did think of trying to flip it in his [the ref's] direction."

As Rosen sees it, the problem with many—yea, most—referees is simple: They don't understand the game he describes as "ballet with defense." Basketball at its best, he says, is not five players against five others; instead, all 10 play the same game. This condition does not obtain automatically—it must be developed by skilled athletes following the sport's principles and their own instincts. But once it does, "there's a flow to it that has a life of its own. The players don't know if they're winning or losing, or very much care. It transcends that sort of concern."

But just when the action is getting groovy, some dumb ref'll blow his whistle and bring everyone back to earth. "Just about all referees think they have to grab the game and bend it," he says. "Most have never really played basketball, so they have no feel for it—they're like blind men talking about art. But there they are, in total control. Can you blame me for freaking out? The real wonder is why anyone with sense keeps coming back for more."

But come back Rosen has, again and again. Big and strong as a youth, and anything but balletic, he played college ball at Hunter College in his native New York, hardly the game's big time. Reason told him his future lay elsewhere, but he still continued to deliver hook shots and elbows in Gotham's playgrounds.

He taught English in high school and college. His first published novel, *Have Jump Shot, Will Travel*, was nominated for a National Book Award. He got *this* far from receiving a Ph.D. in medieval studies from St. John's University, but balked when asked to revise his dissertation, titled *Pseudo-Dionysius and the Allegory in the General Prologue to the Canterbury Tales*, and soon after fled academe for his first love. He explains: "Writing that BS the first time convinced me I didn't want to spend a lifetime teaching it."

He coached for a couple seasons at Bard College in New York, and did some NBA scouting. Then friend Phil Jackson, a former New York Knick, asked him to be his assistant coach with the CBA's Albany Patroons. For Jackson, the post led to NBA titles with the

Chicago Bulls. For Rosen, it led to more CBA jobs, as head coach in Savannah, Ga., Rockford, Ill., Oklahoma City, and finally, in 1991-1992, Albany.

His CBA stay was highlighted by a championship-finals berth at Rockford in 1989; the dozen or so of his players who graduated to the bigs; and his 1992 novel, *The Cockroach Basketball League*, which he says was aimed at capturing the "basic absurdity" of the circuit. "The main thing about the CBA was that everybody—coaches, players, refs—wanted to be somewhere else, and thought he was there only because somebody screwed him," he avers.

Unfortunately, that included him. "The plan was for me to join Jackson as an assistant in Chicago, but I guess I didn't fit the Bulls' corporate image," he allows. "I'm the spirit of Woodstock past, and all the trouble I got into didn't help."

As a character in *Cockroach* puts it, though, "Coaching beats working. It also beats not working." So after a year devoted to penning his next novel, *The House of Moses All-Stars* (it's about a bearded touring basketball team in the 1930s), Rosen is back on the bench with the New Paltz women.

Even the CBA it ain't: Six of his 10 charges are freshmen, one of the others is a 31-year-old mother of two, and his tallest player, who stands 6-foot-0, "has small hands and feet and wants to play the game with her fingertips." He's had to clean up his language and cease threatening to trade his players to Yakima if they botch a pattern, and his technical-foul total through eight games stands at what the TV pitchmen might call a "low, low three."

He's loving it. "The girls are bright and hardworking, and want nothing more from the game than to play it. It doesn't get any purer than that," he says.

Now if the refs would just get lost . . .

● *Jan. 7, 1994*

Bigger Basketballers

I know it sounds odd, but I think that if you look at something long enough, you can stop seeing it. The example I have in mind is the makeup of the National Basketball Association, whose 50th season commenced last week.

Flick an NBA game onto your television screen, or take in one from a balcony seat in an arena, and all those players standing 6 foot 7 inches, 6 foot 8 or 6 foot 9 performing alongside one another quickly come to look ordinary. Encounter one of them strolling in your local shopping mall, though, and you're startled to see someone so tall.

Thus it is that the trend to taller basketball players at the professional level—and at lesser ones as well—goes largely unremarked. The game's terminology reinforces this lack of recognition: What else can one conclude when a near-7-footer can be dubbed a "small forward"?

Unremarked doesn't mean unremarkable, however, and basketball's continuing elevation reflects significant developments in both nature and nurture. "I was 6 foot 2 as a teenager, and was both the tallest kid in my school and the worst player on its basketball team," recalls 59-year-old Dr. David Comings, director of medical genetics at the City of Hope Medical Center in Duarte, Calif. "If I'd been born 40 years later, it's possible I'd be a couple of inches taller, and I'm absolutely sure that somebody'd have seen to it that I played basketball better."

The tall have always been with us, of course, and have played the hoops game since Dr. James Naismith first hung his peach baskets 104 years ago, but not always in great numbers, and not always well. The big men of the sport's formative years weren't especially big by today's standards. The first widely celebrated 7-footer, Bob Kurland of Oklahoma A & M and 1948 U.S. Olympic fame, later confessed that he really stood 6 feet 10½ inches. That also was the height of George Mikan, the dominant player of the NBA's early years. Hank Luisetti, whose feats at Stanford University led to his being considered the best player of the pre-World War II years, stood but 6 feet 2½ inches.

The NBA's precursor league had two 7-footers during its inaugural campaign of 1946-47—Elmore Morgenthaler of the Providence Steamrollers and Ralph Siewert of the St. Louis Bombers and Toronto Huskies—but both averaged only about a point a game and their careers ended shortly thereafter. Don Otten performed well for several league teams in the early 1950s, but historians say his height was listed as 6 foot 11 as often as it was 7 foot. The next honest-to-gosh NBA 7-footer was Walter Dukes, who debuted with the 1955-56 New York Knickerbockers. The first giant star was the 7-foot-2-inch Wilt Chamberlain, who came along in 1959.

By contrast, 46 men listed on current NBA rosters are 7 feet tall or taller, and two teams have no player as "short" as the 6-foot-2½-inch average height of the Philadelphia Warriors team that was champion of the league's first season. In 1969-70, the first season the league-wide statistic was kept, the average NBA player stood 6 feet 5¾ inches tall. The average of the players on this year's opening rosters was 6 feet 7¼ inches.

The role in all that of nurture—training and coaching—is clear. In times past, most youngsters 6 foot 6 or taller were classifiable as stiffs, able to accomplish only the simplest court tasks, but basketball's rising popularity, and the money that can be earned by today's stars, have lately brought such lads the kind of early personal attention that leads to later competence.

That's been reinforced by the basketball telecasts that have come to saturate the airwaves from November through June. "With slow-motion TV replays and coaches as commentators, every pro and major-college game today is like a clinic. It's no accident that big players now can do things that only the best smaller men used to do," says Ray Meyer, who coached the sport at DePaul University from the 1940's Mikan days into the '80s.

Nature's contribution to the game's evolution in this land is murkier, because statistics on the height of the population are both intermittent and sketchy, but there's evidence that it also has played a part. Population growth alone means there are more tall people than there used to be, and their numbers may be increasing proportionally as well.

The National Center for Health Statistics says that, in a survey taken between 1976 and 1980, the average American male between 25 and 34 years old was about 5 foot 9½ inches tall, up from 5 feet 9 inches in a 1960-62 test. NCHS also reports that the proportion of those 6 foot 3 inches or taller—the tallest category—increased from about 1.6% of the male population in a 1971-74 study to 1.7% in the 1976-80 one. That wasn't much of a percentage boost, but it added some 300,000 men to the 6-foot-3-inch-plus group.

Some researchers believe the numbers point to larger gains among the very tall. "When you see a general statistic like average male height rise in a population as big as the U.S.'s, chances are good that the numbers in the extreme categories have increased more dramatically," says the above-mentioned Dr. Comings.

Dr. Allan J. Ryan agrees, and then some. He's the founding editor of the Minneapolis-based publication *Physician and Sportsmedicine*, and a frequent writer on the size of athletes. "All signs point to there being quite a few more very tall people than there once were, more than the figures show," says he.

He elucidates: "The phenomenon of hybrid vigor is well known in biology, and it certainly applies to a population as racially and ethnically diverse as the U.S.'s. We know that growth is stimulated by the kind of better childhood nutrition we've seen in recent decades, and it's becoming clear that more physical exercise early in life has the same effect. Add to that the evidence of our senses—I see a lot more tall people around than I used to, and I'm sure you do, too—and the conclusion is inescapable."

In other words, it's a slam dunk.

• *Nov. 10, 1995*

A Coach Who Cares

S·ince the NCAA began to require their publication a few years ago, athlete-graduation-rate statistics have come to rival in prominence those for field-goal percentages of yards per carry in the public-relations output of many of our big-time sports colleges. This is considered progress in some quarters, but I'm not sure it should be.

My view, based on observation tinged with skepticism over the claims to virtue of a financially aggressive enterprise based upon the labor of people in or barely out of their teens, is that colleges that will recruit anyone also can graduate anyone, and that some schools that boast high jock-graduation rates ought to look into the influence their athletic establishments exert over their academic departments.

It's thus to his credit, I think, that the story of which Rick Majerus, the head basketball coach at the University of Utah here, claims to be proudest involves a youth who never got a college diploma.

"When I came here in 1989, a 6-foot-6 kid named Walter Watts was already on our team," Majerus says. "He could barely read, and at about 320 pounds he wasn't much good on the basketball court, either. We got him a tutor and with a lot of effort—mainly his—his reading level went way up. We cracked down on him about his eating habits, and his weight went way down. He played three good years for us, then left to try a couple of pro sports. When he didn't make it, he went back home to California and opened a barber shop.

"He's got eight or 10 chairs now, and doing well. We've called him, and tried to talk him into coming back for his degree. He says thanks but no thanks. He says he got more out of college than he ever thought he would, or could. I take that as a real compliment."

Majerus could brag about his players' graduation stats if he chose; they've been good here and at Ball State and Marquette, his previous college head-coaching stops. His won-lost record—the usual measure of coachly success—likewise stands out: Before the current season, his seventh at Utah, his teams had an overall 223-96 mark, and after wins over Hawaii and San Diego State last week, this year's bunch is 21-4 and leads the Western Athletic Conference. His 1990-91 team made the round of 16 in the NCAA tournament. This one was ranked seventh nationally in last week's Associated Press poll, and could go farther.

That's especially impressive at a school like Utah. The state is sparsely populated, and the African-Americans who form the backbone of most major-college hoops squads are in a very small minority (two of the 14 Ute players are black, and both are from around Los Angeles). Moreover, until a couple of recruiting coups this year, most of the best in-state players who are members of the locally dominant Mormon church have opted to attend church-connected Brigham Young U. rather than the state school.

Based on appearances, the 47-year-old Majerus is an unlikely figure to have thrived in such a setting. He's urban (raised in Milwaukee, the son of a trade-union official), overweight and rumpled, and a divorced man whose hotel-room, single-guy existence clashes with the area's conspicuous embrace of "family values."

He does it partly because he's funny ("Fifty percent of the people who live out here are in the Federal witness-protection program," he cracks), but mostly because his sincerity shines through the one-liners in a way that makes his players believe him and a traveling sportswriter want to. "Other coaches may talk about being there for their players, but Rick means it," testifies Brandon Jessie, a Utah senior guard. "He's got no kids of his own, so we're his kids."

What Majerus is sincere about is that his players take away more from college than a paper diploma and the ability to set a pick. That's a conviction that's grown with his years in the college game that began when he talked his way first into a spot on the basketball bench as a Marquette undergrad, and, later, into a job there on the staff of coach Al McGuire.

"I have to admit, I was basically into X's and O's as a young guy, and what I really wanted was to coach in the NBA. But after I got my wish [as an assistant to Don Nelson with the Milwaukee Bucks in 1986-87] I missed the contact with the kids, and got back to it as soon as I could," he says.

He goes on: "You get to know your college players in ways you can't know your players in the pros, and with that goes the ability to make a difference in their lives at a crucial period. I try to use it to open their eyes to what I think education ought to be about.

"The first thing I tell them is that, unless they're the equivalent of a genius, their chances of making a living as a basketball player are nil. I've had only one kid at Utah who I thought had a real shot to make the NBA—he's Keith Van Horn [a 6-foot-9 junior forward] on our present team—and I have no idea how he'll do there. The second is that going to college while being an athlete is a big job, but if they handle it well they'll be in good shape for what's to come in their lives.

"But mostly I want them to use their college years to try new things. That's tough for athletes, because they tend to get put in boxes labeled 'jock' and are expected to be in the gym or weight room every minute they're not in class. We try to break that by taking advantage of what's here.

"Every year I take the kids to see a stage play in town; most of them have never been to one before they come to school. We go hiking in the mountains, and horseback riding. We go to movies together and talk about them later. When we travel for games, we visit the historical sites, like Pearl Harbor in Hawaii.

"I encourage them to get out on campus and make friends outside the team, to join clubs and go to the dances and stay up all night in the dorm playing cards. But I also tell 'em that if they're playing cards the night before a game, they'd better quit in time to be in bed by 11."

• *Feb. 20, 1996*

FUZZYBALL

Part 4

Jack Kramer at—and on—Wimbledon

LONDON

J

ack Kramer approached Entrance 4 at the All-England Lawn Tennis and Croquet Club on Monday morning and attached his member's button to his jacket lapel. The uniformed guard at the gate nodded and passed him into the grounds of The Championships. Things haven't always gone so smoothly here for the man who probably has done more in—and, maybe, for—professional tennis than any other.

"They made me a member when I won the singles title here in 1947, but they took it back about six months later when I turned pro," Kramer noted. "Then in 1968, when they finally permitted the pros to compete, they let all us 'defrocked' old champs back in. It was," he laughed, "sort of a retroactive amnesty."

But that wasn't the end of Kramer's travail with tennis's most self-conscious shrine. "I'd done Wimbledon commentary for BBC television for 14 years to 1973, when the pros got into an argument with the powers-that-be over Davis Cup play," he said. "I was executive director of the Association of Tennis Professionals, and I represented the group's point of view. Neither side budged and a boycott of Wimbledon took place that year. The club chose to take it personally and said it didn't want me broadcasting from here after my contract expired the next year. I haven't been sore at them *all* that time, but that and other things have kept me away since."

Still, Kramer went on, it was nice to be back, even for a day. "There's something special about this place, and if I stayed mad at everyone I disagreed with in tennis, I wouldn't have talked to anyone for years," he smiled. "Disagreement is the one thing that's been constant in the game as long as I've been in it."

Indeed, at age 66, and 40 years after his triumph here, Kramer remains in the fray, if not in its thick. He runs a tournament in Los Angeles for Volvo, is chairman of the Southern California Tennis Association, and is active in junior-development programs for the U.S. Tennis Association.

Perhaps most notably, Wilson Sporting Goods Co., with whom he has been associated since he turned pro, just came out with a new line of mid-sized graphite rackets that bear his name. Wilson's wood Jack Kramer signature model sold some 10 million copies before it was discontinued in 1981, by far the most of any racket. Look in your basement and you'll probably find one. The company picked Kramer over the current pros to sign its new line because of the "trust factor" that attaches to his name, a spokesman said. "Today's sports stars go to the highest bidder when it comes to endorsements," the Wilson man added, needlessly.

Kramer finds both pleasure and chagrin in that comment. The chagrin comes because, as a longtime tennis promoter and official, he's more than familiar with the inconsistency of the breed. "The trouble with tennis is that it's ungoverned, and maybe ungovernable," he says. "As soon as someone gets to be a star today, he wants to go his own way, and no one has the authority to say he can't. Your top half-dozen players schedule exhibitions that conflict with tournament dates. John McEnroe can walk off a court in the middle of a match for no apparent reason and get away with it. I'm all for free enterprise, but there ought to be a limit."

It wasn't like that in the old days, Kramer goes on. "When I turned pro, there was no circuit. No. 1 played No. 2, best of 100 matches, anywhere we could get a booking. You played hard because whoever lost was out of work." Under that format, he was world's pro champ in 1948, '49, '51 and '53, defeating Bobby Riggs, Pancho Gonzales, Pancho Segura and Frank Sedgman, respectively.

Kramer was an early exponent of the serve-and-volley "big game," and he believes that the eclipse of that style among young players is a main reason for the decline of U.S. male players on the international scene. "The emphasis among American coaches today is to teach kids to win when they're young," he says. "That means they learn to hit topspin forehands from the baseline with the semi-western grip, and the two-handed backhand. The trouble is, those two strokes will kill your volley from both sides, and you've got to come to the net to win at Wimbledon and Flushing Meadows. Our top kids have to learn a whole new style when they turn 18, and most of them can't.

"Another reason is that our instructional programs haven't penetrated the inner cities, where a lot of our best athletes are. Goodness knows we've tried, but the money to do it isn't there. Can you imagine Magic Johnson playing tennis? It'll have to stay a dream for now."

First prize for men's singles here this year is $248,000. When Kramer won the title, he got a cup. He lived on a $75-a-week travel stipend from the USTA, then the USLTA (the "L" standing for "lawn"), plus a couple hundred dollars a month under the table from a sporting-goods concern. "I brought my own meat because it was short in England after the war, and in those days we thought we weren't training if we didn't eat steak for breakfast," he says. Kramer defeated Tom Brown in a final whose 45-minute length still holds the record for brevity.

Except for the corporate-hospitality tents on the grounds, and the repair of a bomb-caused hole in the roof of the players' quarters, Wimbledon looks much the same as 40 years ago, Kramer allows. The All-England club's hesitancy to adopt new things hasn't changed much, either, he adds. "I remember in 1972, I tried to negotiate some things on behalf of the players," he recalls. "We wanted two tickets a day for every contestant, the use of yellow balls because they were easier to see, and the removal of a referee no one liked. They gave us 60 pairs of tickets we could raffle off among the 128 men in the singles draw. The ref stayed.

"The yellow balls came in 1986. Fourteen years isn't so bad."

• *July 1, 1987*

Lendl's Quest

I think I should begin this piece by saying that I like Ivan Lendl, the tennis player. He is punctual and polite, and able to make small jokes in a language not his own (English), no small feat. I interviewed him once, and he invited me to his home, showed me around and offered me a Diet Coke. That may be no more than expected in most circles, but in jockdom it passes for high hospitality.

He is conscious of the history of his sport and concerned about his place in it, other attributes that many top athletes do not share. Further, he does not pretend to disdain what he has not been able to obtain, another minority position among the accomplished.

As anyone who can follow the bouncing ball knows, what Lendl hasn't been able to obtain is a Wimbledon singles title, which would round out a rare career "Grand Slam" of the major singles championships. How much he wants one has been a main topic of discussion at these proceedings, which enter the men's semifinal round today with him still in it.

The bony-faced Ivan and the assembled press have spent the fortnight fencing about the meaning of the word "obsessed." The former Czech lad, now a 30-year-old Connecticut squire, won't accept that psychologically loaded label, but has said he would trade all of his previous Grand Slam crowns, numbering eight (three French, three U.S. and two Australian Opens), for the

All-England bauble. That might not amount to obsession, but the price Faust paid wasn't much higher.

Lendl has gone about his quest in his characteristic way, which is to work very hard at it; this is a guy who, if he's not playing tennis, is running, bicycling, pumping iron or engaging in some other athletically useful activity. He and his coach, Tony Roche, have noticed that Wimbledon is played on grass, and have shaped their spring schedules around spending as much time as possible on the surface. This entailed skipping the claybound French Open, where Ivan is very much at home, and at which he would have been the favorite.

It's here appropriate to note that finding a grass tennis court is no easy matter. The things are difficult and expensive to maintain, yield bad bounces in the best of times and wear down easily; by the time this tournament is over, Wimbledon's famed and pampered Centre Court will be as much brown as green, and have well-worn ruts along its back and center lines.

I have played tennis for 25-odd (really odd) years, and have never set foot on a grass court. Neither, I'd guess, have you. There are some here in England, of course, and a scattering in Australia and the U.S., mostly at clubs that also have "cricket" or "croquet" in their names. The surface is, in a word, archaic, which is why it's silly to call Wimbledon the world's tennis championship, as some do. But that's another subject.

If any of the above indicates that Lendl has been a failure in this tournament over the years, it's unintentional. He's reached the finals twice—in 1986 and 1987—and last year led Boris Becker, the eventual champion, two sets to one in a semifinal before bowing. He thus reasoned that a little improvement would go a long way, and that greater grass-court familiarity would provide it.

Asked the other day what he's worked on, he mentioned his footwork and return of serve, and, naturally, his volleying, the last of which dispenses with erratic grass-court bounces. But he added: "Mostly it's just spending the time on grass; not having to pack all my preparation into a few days. This year, if it rained, we could do something else and not worry that we were losing time we couldn't make up."

It could be that Ivan is right, but it also could be that he's wrong, and that longer lawn time won't help him. My view is that the ability to play successful grass-court tennis is a knack, like juggling or being able to memorize whole pages of a telephone book at a glance. Players of all styles and nationalities have won here, some with little or no background on the stuff.

Sweden, for example, has about as many grass courts as it has Club Meds, but its Bjorn Borg won Wimbledon five times, and he was a bred-in-the-bone base liner to boot. Germany has a similar lack, but in 1985 a 17-year-old Becker showed up in the men's draw for the first time, said the German equivalent of "aw, shucks," and whupped everybody country-style. He's done it twice more since, without special preparations, and is back in the semis again today.

It could be that Lendl secretly shares my view, because he has shown little pleasure in his labors here to date. He dropped a set in his first-round match with Cristian Miniussi (ranked 116th), another in round three to Bryan Shelton (No. 125), another in the fourth round to Alex Antonitsch (48), and yet another in Wednesday's quarterfinal with Brad Pearce (120), a chunky Utahan whose main previous distinction was that he'd made the doubles final in a tournament in Schenectady.

Poor Ivan has grouched around more than usual, and continually taps his shoes with his racket between points. That latter gesture perhaps expresses a wish to be back home on clay, where shoe-tapping serves a purpose (to knock out the dirt).

After his match with Shelton, a pleasant but limited young player from Huntsville, Ala., Lendl explained how the wham-bam of grass-court tennis offended his methodical nature. He noted that while Shelton's forehand was lacking, "you can't expose his weakness on grass. His serve is big, and every now and then you get a funny hop on the serve, and then he comes in and hits some decent volleys." So instead of something like 6-3, 6-2, 6-1, the scores were 7-6, 6-7, 6-4, 6-4, and "whew."

It's true that Lendl has been aggressive here, looking, for a change, a bit more comfortable at the net than a hooked salmon. It's also true that after beating the Austrian Antonitsch on Tuesday he declared, "I'll never stay back again," meaning that he wouldn't revert to his base-lining ways.

But he quickly smiled and said he was kidding, which sounded truest of all. If he does win here, Wimbledon just might never see him again.

• *July 6, 1990*

Note: Lendl retired without winning at Wimbledon.

Who Needs the Davis Cup?

ST. PETERSBURG, FLA.

D
•

wight Filley Davis was Secretary of War in the cabinet of President Calvin Coolidge, who made no wars, proving that Davis knew a cushy job when he saw one. As a sprig of 21, just out of Harvard, Davis conceived and donated the trophy for a tennis competition designed to promote amity between nations, proving that youthful ideas aren't always the best.

The 1990 edition of the Davis Cup, which is as old as this century, was concluded over the weekend, and it was peculiar even for an event that is known for quirks. Its final round was contested here in sunny Florida, but indoors, in a dome designed for baseball and, its builders insist, hockey. It was played on clay, a surface as American as *foie gras*. And one of its heroes wore lime and black, not red, white and blue.

The U.S. won, as it has on 28 other occasions, defeating Australia, but before imparting details of the triumph allow me to question, quickly, whether the whole Davis Cup trip is necessary. While it may be true that the year-around, multi-nation event provides a window to big-time tennis for some countries, it hardly seems required at a time when the top eight players in a recent men's professional rankings list represented seven different lands.

The Davis Cup turns an individual sport into a team one, and compounds the felony with a best-of-five match format that allows one fella to win the thing virtually alone by taking two singles matches and teaming with another player to capture the doubles. That's happened often, most lately when West Germany's Boris Becker *schmeissed* the Swedes with minimal help in last year's final.

As for the amity part, forget it. Tennis might have been a genteel activity at Dwight's first fest, when only England and the U.S. competed, but it has livened up since. The enduring image of the tourney is of a bunch of matches in converted bullrings, with the spectators ringing bells, waving flags and screeching unpleasant-sounding things at visiting players.

Of the many crimes against civility committed under Davis Cup auspices, the 1980 final between Czechoslovakia and Italy, in Prague, stands out. Some Italian spectators took to protesting the umpire's calls so vociferously that they were roughed up and arrested by Czech police, whereupon the Italian player, Adriano Panatta, refused to continue until they were released. Eventually, they were, and Panatta lost in four sets. On his way off the court, he spit in the ump's face.

The Aussies speak our language, more or less, so intimidating them with unintelligible verbiage might have been difficult. Thus, the host U.S. Tennis Association played the traditional "get the guests" game with the court's surface. Possessing two skilled clay-courts players in Andre Agassi and Michael Chang, and knowing that the Australians like the ball-gripping stuff about as much as would Dick Allen's horse, the USTA exercised its home-team prerogative and dictated a dirt floor for the final. It even made arrangements to import the clay from Germany before the Aussies pointed out that the rules call for Davis Cup courts to at least be made of native substances.

The decision to play on clay was questionable on a number of grounds. One was that there are about 2,000 clay courts in the U.S., and, maybe, 200,000 hardcourts. Another is that, while fine in its proper place, which is the French Open, clay-court tennis can be as entertaining as watching bricklayers build a wall.

A third and, to my mind, crucial objection is that, at a time when tennis's lure in the nation at large is lowish, the USTA chose to forgo sending its Boomers—old-lion John McEnroe and new U.S. Open champ Pete Sampras—against the Aussie's ex-Wimbledon winner Pat Cash, et al., in a strength-against-strength test on a fast surface in this showcase event. I mean, which pairings would you rather have seen?

The 18,000 people who showed up for Friday night's two singles matches at least saw a lot of tennis—almost seven hours of it, ending just before midnight. Many of them did what any other sensible people would do under the circumstances, which is to come late and leave early. The clay takes its toll all around.

Most of the weekend's drama was contained in Friday's opener. It pitted the 20-year-old Agassi, he of the lime-and-black duds and two-toned hair, against the day-older Richard Fromberg, a gangly, heretofore unnoticed Aussie from Tasmania. Fromberg, ranked 25th among the men pros, outserved his fourth-ranked foe, took advantage of his fits of carelessness, and, generally, gave the folks their money's worth before succumbing, 4-6, 6-2, 4-6, 6-2, 6-4.

Agassi later revealed he'd been ill with flu before the match, said he hadn't eaten the previous Sunday, Monday or Tuesday (!), and opined he'd have won easier if he'd been healthier. "Maybe I'm so strong that I'm strong even when I'm weak," he marveled. Neale Fraser, Australia's Davis Cup captain, provided an alternate assessment for the match's closeness. "I think we've found a top-10 player in Fromy," said he.

Whatever the background of the Agassi win, it took some pressure off the 18-year-old Chang, the 1989 French Open titlist. Perfectly matched against the hard-hitting but erratic Darren Cahill, this terrier of the baseline was able to accomplish what every tennis player seeks, which is to give his opponent a good workout. After his 6-2, 7-6, 6-0 win, nice-kid Chang left the court arm-in-arm with his mom. By contrast, Agassi travels with a hulking bodyguard.

The crowd reconvened for the doubles on Saturday, and was rewarded when the American team of Rick Leach and Jim Pugh, the defending Wimbledon champs, beat the Australian pair of John Fitzgerald and Cash, 6-4, 6-2, 3-6 and 7-6. That gave the U.S. a decisive, 3-0 lead, and rendered academic the results of Sunday's two singles matches.

And that's another thing about the Davis Cup: Sometimes it's over before it's over. Obviously, Yogi never played much tennis.

• *Dec. 3, 1990*

This Dodo Isn't Extinct

M
•

onica Seles, claiming heinous but unspecified injuries, ditched Wimbledon last summer, spoiling her chance for a grand slam of the major international women's tennis singles championships, but what's the big deal? On Saturday, another tennis-playing lady completed either a double or quadruple grand slam, depending on how you're counting.

Dorothy "Dodo" Cheney, a cheerful 75 year old from Santa Monica, Calif., won the U.S. Tennis Association's national women's 75-and-over grass court singles championship here, after teaming with Melanie McAleer of Ocala, Fla., to win the doubles the day before. That brought to 16 the number of national titles Cheney had won this year: the singles and doubles crowns on all four surfaces—hard court, clay, indoor and grass—contested in both the USTA's 70-and-over and 75-and-over divisions.

"What would I call what I've done?" she echoed. "A double grand slam, I suppose, but that wouldn't include the doubles, would it? I've never done it before, and I haven't heard of anyone else doing it, either. I guess I'll just leave the naming to others."

But of one thing there was no doubt, and it was as true before Saturday as after. It's that Dodo Cheney is a most remarkable athlete. As a girl and young woman named Dorothy Bundy she was a nationally ranked tennis player, swapping strokes with the likes of Alice Marble, Pauline Betz, Margaret Osborne and Doris Hart. They won their titles and moved on to other things, but Dodo kept right on swinging in the age-group divisions that, in five-year increments, make up the vast bulk of the USTA's tournament activities.

She was first among the 40s and 50s, then the scourge of the 60s and 70s. "We keep hoping she'll slow down, but we're the ones getting slower while she keeps right on going," said Billie Burr, Cheney's singles victim Saturday. In all, Cheney has won 217 of the marble-sized gold tennis balls the USTA awards to its age-group singles and doubles winners. No one has won more, and it's unlikely anyone else ever will.

Cheney said she likes the prizes, all right, but it's the tennis she really enjoys. She noted that she comes from a tennis-playing family—her mother, May Sutton, was a Wimbledon and U.S. Open titlist—and "tennis was something all of us did together." She continued that practice in her own family: son Brian has won national age-group crowns, daughter Christy is a top-ranked 35-year-old in Southern California, and "all of my [eight] grandchildren play." Two of the latter, she asserted, are "budding stars." She said she knows this "because they can beat grandma."

She continued: "People ask me why I don't quit. I ask them why in the world I should. The women who play in these things are very nice—the hard losers dropped out long ago—and I can usually get a bridge game going after the day's play. In my era, you know, tournament tennis wasn't the terribly, terribly serious business it is today. I remember in one tournament, on Long Island in New York, I was scheduled for an afternoon match but up and went fishing with a couple of boys instead. They defaulted me, but nobody was very upset."

Cheney and 14 of her fellow senior citizens gathered for last week's doings in the 75-and-over and 80-and-over divisions at the Palm Coast Players Club in this resort-retirement community north of Daytona Beach, and while none took time off to fish, their pleasure in being here was obvious. A main topic of conversation was the grass-court playing surface, which they, like most players, rarely see. But there were many other topics.

"Such an interesting group of women!" exclaimed Edna Shalala, a finalist in the 80s singles. "I'd have been willing to come here for the talk alone."

And, indeed, the word remarkable applied fully to many of the contestants. Shalala, for instance, is a practicing lawyer in Rocky

River, Ohio, and her daughter, Donna, is chancellor of the University of Wisconsin at Madison. As Billie Worth, Burr was Mary Martin's understudy in "South Pacific" and "Peter Pan" on Broadway, and starred in the national road company of "Annie Get Your Gun," among other roles. Jacqueline Piatigorsky, an 80s entrant, is a sculptor, writer and widow of Gregor Piatigorsky, the cellist. Liu Shangku Tao, who won titles in the 80s singles and doubles, is a member of the national legislature in her native Taiwan.

But when tennis time came around, Cheney clearly took the spotlight. Dressed in her trademark wide-billed bonnet and lacy tennis togs set off by a strand of pearls, she bounced through her three singles matches with the loss of only four games. This was despite the fact that grass is her least favorite surface.

In her singles final against Burr, Cheney displayed a wicked sliced forehand and a volley that was effective even though it usually came from outside the service line. When Burr hit a winner, Cheney emitted a congratulatory "Yes!" and when she muffed a shot of her own she exclaimed, "Oh, my!" But she didn't do either often in a 6-1, 6-1 triumph.

"Billie was nervous; she's played better before," Cheney said of her foe. Burr had played two lengthy, three-set matches to reach the finals, but eschewed claiming fatigue. This was the third time she'd been runner-up to Cheney in a USTA event, and despaired that she'd never get a first "unless Dodo misses a plane." But she took solace in the fact that she regularly beats younger women—and men—at her home club in West Palm Beach, Fla.

In the 80s, the dark-haired Tao (everybody called her "Madame") played a quite different game, hitting hard, flat ground strokes past Shalala for a 6-2, 6-0 decision. The winner, an age-group tourney veteran who jogs daily, said she enjoys playing on grass because it feels good underfoot and accentuates her quickness. Shalala, a U.S. Amateur contestant in the 1930s who'd reverted to recreational tennis until recently, laid her loss to her foe's greater experience. "I never thought I'd say that again at my age," she smiled.

• Nov. 19, 1991

Jimmy vs. Martina

LAS VEGAS

They scheduled an unusual double-header at Caesars Palace here last weekend: professional wrestling and boxing.

Actually, it was tennis and boxing. The tennis part was Friday night's Jimmy Connors-Martina Navratilova match. It was intergender, but to hear some describe it beforehand you'd have thought it was interspecies. Arthur Ashe called the match "professional wrestling," which is longhand for hokum. For the tennis Establishment, that was a mild view.

The boxing part, on Saturday night, was to have pitted Terry Norris against Simon Brown, and nobody was scoffing. Norris, a superwelterweight champ, was a strong claimant to the hypothetical but weightier title of best-fighter-around, pound-for-pound, and in the rugged Brown, a recent welter ex-king, he had a credible opponent. That match shaped up as sport, raw and pure.

The Caesars folks are old hands at sizing up attractions, and knew what to do with both "bouts." They put Jimmy-Martina in their main room, an outdoor stadium seating 14,000 people, and Norris-Brown in their Sports Pavilion, a shed with a capacity of about 4,200. And sure enough, the tennisers packed 'em in, while the box fighters sold only about 3,200 tickets and would have performed before many empty benches had not Brown canceled out at the last moment due to an attack of dizziness officially diagnosed as vertigo.

But leave us not be too harsh on either promoters or public; 10 years from now, or even a week from Wednesday, which do you think would be more discussed, Connors's 7-5, 6-2 victory, or any conceivable outcome of Norris-Brown? If you picked the latter, you'll never get on Family Feud.

This is not to say that Jimmy-Martina was scintillating tennis, because it wasn't. The two had logged a combined 40-odd years of top-level competition, and 26 Grand Slam singles titles, but that didn't inoculate them against stage fright in their sport's first highly hyped battle of the sexes since an in-her-prime Billie Jean King beat old-guy Bobby Riggs in the Houston Astrodome 19 years ago.

You could make a case that for all its undeniable hokiness (Billie Jean was carried into the arena on a sedan chair, Bobby wore a jacket advertising a confection called Sugar Daddy), King-Riggs was the most influential tennis match ever played. Millions of people who didn't know which end of a racket to hold tuned in, and a goodly number of them decided to take up the game. It launched a five-year tennis boom that resulted, among other things, in fistfights over court time in parks across the nation.

The primary engine of that event was Riggs, a hustler in word and deed; at a time when gender issues were just getting hot, his MCP rhetoric hit the box-office spot. The lead-in to Friday night's encounter was considerably tamer; both contestants spoke well of each other before and after the affair and, presumably, during it, too.

But the money at stake here—$500,000 for the winner on top of guarantees for each player variously reported as $250,000 or $500,000 (does it matter which?)—was enough to fluster the most court-hardened. The 35-year-old Navratilova owned up to her jitters, saying she came in more nervous than in any match she'd played. Our Jimbo, usually not much given to introspection, still confessed to playing "conservatively" at first, and said he was daunted a bit by match rules that gave his foe half of each doubles alley, or 4½ feet of extra side space, into which to hit. He also was limited to one serve.

Whatever, the pair hacked through the first set like two weekend players. Connors hit a couple of shots into the bottom of the net in the first game en route to having his service broken. He broke back in game six when Martina double faulted at game point, and won the set's 12th and last game in the same manner. His returns didn't blister as they did in days of yore, meaning a month ago at the U.S. Open, and serve-and-volleyer Martina didn't get to the net with her usual frequency or authority.

Jimmy played better in set two. Martina didn't, and the 6-2 game score resulted. Martina said afterward that Jimmy didn't so much win as she lost, and that seemed accurate enough. She did tip her visor in his direction, but not for what you might expect. "The pace of his shots wasn't overwhelming—Chris Evert and Monica Seles hit the ball about as hard—but he got such depth it was difficult for me to come in," she said.

Connors assessment was similarly keyed: "I kept the ball in play, and served pretty well," he allowed. Indeed, he spun in 93% of his first and only serves, and lost fewer points on faults (five) than Navratilova did on double faults (eight).

That a 40-year-old male nine years from his last major-championship triumph, the 1983 U.S. Open, could beat one of the world's half-dozen best females, albeit one on the downslope, surprised few; Connors was a 7-1 choice in Caesars's sports-betting den. Make no mistake, though; it was a legitimate match with reasonable rules that brought attention to a sport that could use some. They oughta do this more often than every 19 years.

The Norris-Brown bout was called off at 5:45 p.m. Saturday, 45 minutes after the preliminary card was to have started. It was a fight-fan's fight, as opposed to one that has broad public appeal, but a win would have helped boost the muscular, 25-year-old Norris, already a victor over Sugar Ray Leonard, Donald Curry and Meldrick Taylor, to that coveted higher rung. Brown, 29, held one welterweight belt or another from 1988 through last year. His physician said tests showed no serious ailment, but that it would be at least a week before any rescheduling could be discussed.

The cancellation sent ticket holders into the Las Vegas evening in search of entertainment. The way out was through the hotel's casino, and some stayed. But that's why they hold these things here in the first place, isn't it?

• *Sept. 28, 1992*

A Chat With 'Little Pancho'

NEW YORK

T. ennis used to have two notable Panchos. Now, it just has one.

The better-known of the two—Pancho Gonzales—died in July at age 67 in a Las Vegas hospital, of stomach cancer, while the Wimbledon tournament was in progress. He was a two-time champion of the amateur predecessor of the U.S. Open, whose 1995 edition began its annual two-week run yesterday at Flushing Meadows in this city's borough of Queens. He was the dominant figure in the professional game's road-show era, between 1950 and the middle '60s, and a presence for longer than that.

The other is Pancho Segura. He's still very much around at age 74. If he's not already at this year's Open, he'll be here soon, renewing acquaintances, seeing and being seen, and looking to latch on as a coach/adviser to a top male player. The last fellow he served in that capacity was Jimmy Connors, who did pretty well.

"I won't work again unless it's with one of the top guys—I'm too old to be fooling around with some plumber," Segura said the other day from his home near Carlsbad, Calif. "I don't want to be teaching somebody how to hit the ball; I want to tell him how to get the most out of the shots he already has. I can name a half-dozen players who'd be better than they are if they could do that. Much better."

Segura, however, does not foresee turning any of the present crop of pros into another Pancho Gonzales. He thinks that a couple of them—Andre Agassi and Pete Sampras—play at Gonzales's best level in many respects, but they've already got coaches. As for the rest, he can only shrug. "Not many guys ever played as well as Gonzales; he had the big serve, the speed, the body flexibility, the discipline," he says. "Not many ever will."

Segura knows from whence he speaks, because he knew Gonzales as well as anyone did. The two met across the net for the first time in a 1944 clay-court tourney match in Kansas City, which Segura won. They played each other hundreds of times after that, first as amateurs and then as pros trekking around the world for the one-night stands that comprised most of the play-for-pay action then. Often, they'd share a car during their travels.

"We played four or five nights a week, in front of anywhere from 100 people to 15,000," Segura recalls of the barnstorming days. "We played on everything—carpets, rubber mats, wood floors in gyms. Once we played on ice. That was in Cortina, Italy. A man who called himself a baron was the promoter. We showed up at the arena, and it was an ice rink. They spread some canvas on top of the ice for a court, but our feet still got cold."

Gonzales headlined those shows, along with Jack Kramer or the Australian Frank Sedgman, while Segura usually was a second banana. Still, they sometimes wound up facing one another. "Guys would get hurt or sick, so everybody played everybody," Segura notes. Gonzales won most of their matches, but Segura avers that he didn't always deserve to. "He was the star, so he always got the line calls," Segura says with a cackling laugh.

Lean, dark and 6-foot-2, Gonzales looked as well as acted like a leading man. He won the U.S. Nationals in 1948 and '49 and led the U.S. to a Davis Cup triumph in the latter year. He won the U.S. Pro title—then the world's most important for nonamateurs—eight times between 1953 and 1961. His temper sometimes got the better of him on court, but never seemed to affect his game much.

Segura was a quite-different type. Unfailingly pleasant, he stood but 5-foot-6 and was skinny and bandy-legged as a result of a childhood case of rickets. One of nine children of a tennis-club caretaker in Guayaquil, Ecuador, his small size forced him to heft a racket with both hands when he first took up the sport.

He continued to hit a two-handed forehand as an adult. His backhand looked two-handed, too, although he says he released his top hand just before contact with the ball from that side. Despite his unorthodox strokes, he had a brilliant array of passing shots and lobs and won a roomful of trophies, including three U.S. Intercollegiate titles at the University of Miami and U.S. Pro crowns in 1950, '51 and '52.

But the pair had things in common. First, of course, was the nickname they shared despite the fact that Gonzales's real first name was Ricardo and Segura's was Francisco. "In those days, Americans thought all Hispanics were Mexicans, and everybody knew about Pancho Villa, the Mexican bandit. So that's what they called us, even though I'm from Ecuador and he was born in Los Angeles," says Segura.

He adds: "We never minded the name; we used it among ourselves. He called himself 'Big Pancho,' and called me 'Little Pancho.' I still think of us that way."

Court longevity was another common characteristic; both men played top-flight tennis into their 40s. Gonzales was a quarterfinalist at the first U.S. Open at age 40, in 1968, and won an open professional tourney at 44. In 1962, a 41-year-old Segura took a 28-year-old Ken Rosewall to five sets in a tournament match before losing, and in 1968, at 47, he helped win a 62-game doubles set in Wimbledon's main draw. "Both of us said we wouldn't quit competing, that they'd have to drag us away, and they almost did," Segura says.

Both continued in tennis after their tournament days were done, appearing at celebrity outings and the like. In addition to his individual coaching, Segura had a long stint as head pro at the La Costa Resort in Carlsbad, near San Diego. He still closely follows the men's tour and its members, noting who can and can't do what.

And at every opportunity, he tells people he'd like to see the tiebreaker abandoned for the fifth set of all men's matches in Grand Slam events, and for the third set of women's matches.

"I'm a best-of-five guy—play till you drop," he says with an audible smile. "Big Pancho was, too."

• *Aug. 29, 1995*

DIMPLEDBALL

•

Part 5

Acing the Course

Arnold Palmer plays quite a bit of golf, some of it pretty good, so it probably will come as no shock to learn that he has recorded 13 holes-in-one in his 50 or so years as a swinger. That total, however, is but a fraction of the 60 aces posted by one Mancil Davis, a 33-year-old former club pro who lives in Dallas.

Davis began marking ones on his scorecards in 1967, as a lad of 12 in Odessa, Texas, and he has posted at least one every year since. One year he had eight of them, three coming within five days. He has holed 'em off trees, rocks and sprinkler heads. One came on a hole that measured 379 yards, though he modestly notes that it was a dogleg and that his shot probably traveled no farther than 280 yards.

He further points out that a dozen of his holes-in-one came in exhibitions or other nonregulation events, and that his "official" count is 48. Still, that's a professional record. A self-described "OK player" who says he's always glad to break 75, he professes amazement at his knack. "I don't want to know how I'm doing it," he says. "I figure that if I ever find out, I'm in trouble."

It is appropriate that Davis, an "average-guy" pro, holds the holes-in-one mark for his ilk, because the hole-in-one is the ultimate average-guy sporting achievement. The best most of us can do is dream of making an 80-yard run on a football field (in a game, that is) or taking

Fernando Valenzuela downtown. But any mope with a golf club in his hand has a chance at an ace every time he takes to the links.

Just what that chance is is a matter of some dispute. *Golf Digest* magazine, which has been keeping track of witnessed holes-in-one since 1952 and has recorded some 700,000 of them, calculates that, based on the several hundred million rounds of golf a year played world-wide, a player has about a 33,000-to-1 shot at an ace when he tees up on a par-three hole.

A six-year-old Dallas-based outfit called the National Hole-In-One Association, which writes insurance for hole-in-one prize contests, puts the figure at about 15,000-to-1. That's based on the 281 claims it has paid in 20,000 such events in which an estimated 4.3 million shots were fired.

The company, which employs the prolific Davis as a spokesman, charges a premium of between 2% and 5% of the value of the prize being offered, based on the length of the hole and the number and quality of the contestants. Its payouts have ranged from a $100,000 check to a Midwest City, Okla., man last month, to a $5,000 casket put up by an association of funeral directors. It also sends catalogs to hole-in-one shooters offering to sell them trophies commemorating their achievement. Isn't that nice?

Even at 15,000-to-1, of course, the hole-in-one is a statistically stupendous feat. A person who plays golf 25 times a year on full-sized courses will take 100 tee shots on par-three holes. At that rate, he'll sink one ace every 150 years.

Thus, what is truly amazing about holes-in-one is the way they sometimes occur in bunches. In September 1986, in a pro-am event before a PGA Seniors tourney in Potomac, Md., the aforementioned Palmer aced the 187-yard third hole two days in a row. *Golf Digest* found that not only had seven other players in the U.S.—all amateurs—dropped tee shots on the same hole on consecutive days that year, but one, Terry Carpenter, a 28-handicap woman, aced the same hole twice *in the same day* on a nine-hole layout in Beeville, Texas.

Wanna hear a better one? On Aug. 7 at the Crown Colony Country Club in Lufkin, Texas, Waymond Daniels stepped to the 14th tee one down to Steve Roper in a club match-play championship round, and aced the 155-yard hole. "I guess I shouldn't bother to shoot," Roper said to his foe. But he did, and his ball plopped into the cup on top of Daniels's ball.

The magazine's record for lifetime aces is 58, held by Norman Manley, a low-handicap amateur from Long Beach, Calif. He's a motion-picture film projectionist who plays golf almost every day. In 1964, Manley reported acing consecutive par-four holes, measuring 330 yards and 290 yards, respectively. That's a record, too, according to *Golf Digest*.

The longest hole-in-one on record was a 447-yarder in 1965 by Robert Mitera of Omaha, Neb., at the aptly named Miracle Hills Golf Club in that city, and the hole was no dogleg. Mitera's drive, aided by a strong following wind, hit hard ground on the downslope of a hill some 290 yards from the tee and rolled the remaining distance into the cup. Mitera didn't see the ball drop, but a foursome on the green did. "About 40 guys have since sworn they were in that group," notes club director Jerry Wilke.

The oldest person to rack up a witnessed ace was 99-year-old Otto Bucher of Geneva, Switzerland. The youngest was six-year-old Tommy Moore of Hagerstown, Md., on a 145-yard hole, in 1968. Tommy got another before he turned seven—on the same hole.

On June 8, Randall Eddlemon of Wilmont, Ark., aced the 160-yard fourth hole at the Alpine Country Club in Pineville, La., with a seven iron. Eddlemon has one arm as a result of a childhood accident. On July 26, Anthony O'Connor of Derby Line, Vt., aced a 151-yard hole at nearby Newport Country Club. Mr. O'Connor has one arm, and uses two artificial legs as a result of a childhood accident.

Here's a funny one. A man from Lexington, Ohio, got a hole-in-one with a mouth full of Novocain just after a trip to his dentist. Six months later he visited the dentist again, and got another ace that afternoon.

I suppose all this has you wondering why you haven't hit your ace, so here are some tips from pro Davis: "Don't use tees on par-three iron shots because you don't ordinarily use tees with irons. Aim for the hole, not just the green. Relax. And pray."

• *Aug. 28, 1987*

The Open Returns to The Club

BROOKLINE, MASS.

T•

he sign outside the rambling, yellow-and-white golf clubhouse in this estate-dotted suburb of Boston reads "The
Country Club—A.D. 1882."

A.D.? Well, it is *The* Country Club, so it's possible
someone might think it was founded in 1882 B.C. Best
not to take chances.

The basic message, though, is clear: This spread is
old, at least by American standards. Equally apparent is its
New England brand of understatement. Why go through
the trouble of giving a place a more elaborate name when
everyone who needs to know about it already does?

The U.S. Golf Association, overseer of the annual
U.S. Open tournament, has been serving up golf history
with some of its recent offerings (remember the 1986
number at bucolic old Shinnecock Hills on Long Island?), and we will get a large dollop with this year's
event, which begins here on Thursday. The Country
Club was the place, 75 years ago, where Francis Ouimet,
a skinny, necktie-wearing 20-year-old, upset the British
aces Harry Vardon and Ted Ray to win the 1913 Open
and establish The Humbling Game as Ours, not Theirs.

Whether Ouimet did us any favors remains debat-
able in some quarters, but not here. Inside TCC's clubhouse are grainy photographs of the chill, rainy
September playoff in which Ouimet triumphed, as well
as a much-later portrait of the hero himself, dressed in

formal garb. After his victory, former caddy Ouimet, who grew up just across the road, was granted "the privilege of the golf course without dues for a year." The waiver was renewed annually until the golfer reached a more serious age, at which time he was elevated to membership by the club's assembled Cabots, Peabodys and Saltonstalls.

Also in the clubhouse is a possible clue to Ouimet's win. A bronze statue of Vardon, standing atop a trophy case, shows the Britisher's left arm to be badly bent in his backswing. Surely, Francis's form was superior.

Golf at TCC predates the Open, or any other national tourney. They've been at it here since 1893, when a six-hole course was built, at a cost of $50, near the horse-racing and shooting grounds at which original members sought diversion. In an exhibition held to introduce the fledgling sport, one Arthur Hunnewell, playing in the first threesome, scored a hole-in-one. It's recorded that audience reaction to the feat was muted. Wasn't putting the ball in the hole what golf was supposed to be about?

Despite this auspicious start, TCC never has been obsessed with golf, and only about 400 of its 1,200 current members play regularly. "It's a family place, where people come to do a variety of things," notes member Thomas Frost, an investment-research-firm executive. Besides three nine-hole courses, TCC has a swimming pool, indoor and outdoor tennis courts, a curling rink and ponds for winter ice skating.

Besides Ouimet, who died in 1967, TCC's most notable athletic achievers have been women: Olympic figure-skating champion Tenley Albright; Hazel Wightman, donor of tennis's Wightman Cup; and the golfing Curtis sisters, Margaret and Harriot, for whom the sport's Curtis Cup is named. That's a bit ironic, because the club admits women only as "associate" (non-equity-holding) members. Mr. Frost, however, hastens to assert that the designation is a "technicality." Says he, "We'll never sell our property, so there'll never be any equity to distribute."

There is more to recommend TCC as an Open host than its antiquity or the bloodlines of its members. As I'm sure the cries and whimpers of the assembled players next week will attest, this is one heckuva tough course. The last time they played the Open here, in 1963, Julius Boros, Arnold Palmer and Jackie Cupit battled high winds and higher rough to tie for the lead after the 72 holes with scores of 293. That's been the highest count in the event since 1935.

Boros's one-under-par 70 in the 18-hole playoff (to Cupit's 73 and Palmer's 76) was only the sixth sub-par round of that tourney.

About 200 yards have been added to the course since '63, but at 7,010 yards its length still will frighten few in this long-hitting era. The main difficulty of the layout lies in its undulating fairways and tiny, rough-fringed and very fast greens. Some ESP also may be required to negotiate the course successfully: On a dozen holes, greens can't be fully glimpsed from drive-landing areas or fairways can't be seen from tees.

It's agreed that the toughest part of the course is holes 10, 11, 12 and 13, all long par-fours. Ten is a 439-yard dogleg right to a small and severely banked green. The 453-yard 11th requires a blind tee shot followed by a longish iron to a green guarded in front by water and in back by trees. Palmer took three triple-bogeys there in 1963, including one in the playoff.

On the 450-yard 12th, you can see only the top of the flagstick from the fairway, and the green is no more than 30 feet across. On the 13th, measuring 433 yards, you must steer your drive, because the fairway slopes steeply into a pond.

Players with a historical bent will be leery of the 17th. It's an innocuous-looking, 381-yard par four, but Vardon's 1913 hopes died there when his drive caught a fairway bunker in the playoff with Ouimet, and Cupit drove into another in the fourth round 50 years later and the resulting six cost him his lead. It's interesting to note that the "Vardon bunker" is about 215 yards from the tee, and the "Cupit bunker" is about 235 yards out. Greg Norman's drives are still rising at those distances.

In an article in *Golf Digest* magazine, Jack Nicklaus opined that the key to scoring well at TCC is to find level landing areas for one's drives. Don Callahan, the club's lean, baldish home pro, thinks the more-humble chip shot will tell the tale.

"Everybody will miss greens, maybe as many as six or seven a round, and the guys who do best will be the ones who can get down in two from the high-grass fringes," Callahan says. "That's what Boros did here in '63: Dropped those soft little wedge shots of his next to the pins. Old Julius knew you couldn't bully this course, you have to baby it."

● *June 10, 1988*

Worst, and Loving It

I get around pretty well with my job, but there still have been sporting events I wish I'd covered. I wish I'd seen Buster Douglas knock out Mike Tyson in Tokyo in 1990, and Mike Powell break Bob Beamon's long-jump record last year. I'd like to have been at the 1982 California-Stanford football game, when California runners lateraled a half-dozen times and knocked over a couple of parading Stanford bandsmen in returning a last-play kickoff for the winning touchdown.

And I wish I'd been at the Tournament Players Club in Ponte Vedra, Fla., on that June day in 1985 when Angelo Spagnolo earned the right to be called America's worst avid golfer.

I mean, you can't say you've seen it all unless you were there. *Golf Digest* magazine, which staged the as-yet-unrepeated event, scoured the nation for worthy contenders for an honor that thousands could claim. That it chose wisely was attested by the fact that the four men tapped to play for the title logged a combined 836 strokes for their 18-hole, 7½-hour round.

Winner Spagnolo—actually, he lost—was a chubby 31-year-old supermarket manager from this southern suburb of Pittsburgh, and like a true champion, he prevailed convincingly. His score of 257 was 49 strokes worse than the runner-up's, and included a 66 on the course's 17th hole, a 132-yard par three to an island green. The

101

history-minded were quick to note that Spagnolo's 18-hole score equaled Mike Souchak's 72-hole low-scoring record for the PGA Tour, set at the 1955 Texas Open.

Seven years now have passed, and the week the gods of golf are going at it in the U.S. Open at Pebble Beach seems a good time to recall Spagnolo's feat. That's because most golfers have more in common with the Angelo Spagnolos of this world than with the Freddy Coupleses.

The grocer himself, a man of apparently limitless good humor, was more than happy to harken back, if only because he still reaps various and, perhaps, surprising rewards from that day. "It was a wonderful event," smiles the 38-year-old father of two boys. "It totally changed my life."

Before going further, it's probably necessary to record Spagnolo's assertion, voiced previously by others, that the worst golfer tourney was on the up and up. *Golf Digest* made it clear from the outset that it wanted contestants to do their best, and Spagnolo says he complied.

One factor behind the integrity of the round was betting. "Friends of a couple of the players put fairly big money on their men to score lowest, although my buddies were pretty restrained in that regard," he says.

But more important was the nature of the game and those who play it. "I never heard of anybody stepping onto a golf course with the intention of playing badly," he avers. "Golfers will understand that."

What made Spagnolo this nation's certified worst golfer was his talent, or, rather, lack of it. He'd played the game some in high school, then took it up again as a young householder here. His awfulness was so apparent that fellow members of a league he played in at the Linden Hall Golf Club near his home demanded a match between him and the league's next-worst member, a 70-year-old beginner who gripped his clubs cross-handed. A videotape of that hilarious duel later was sent to *Golf Digest* to promote Spagnolo's qualifications for its event.

"Actually, I beat the 70-year-old by a stroke, but he was too old for the worst-golfer tournament," Spagnolo notes. "You had to be between ages 25 and 55, play at least 21 rounds a year, which I did, and have a handicap of 36 or above. Mine was a 52."

A 52 handicap translates to an average 18-hole score of about 125 on a typical course, but the TPC at Ponte Vedra is anything but typical. Site of the annual PGA Players Championship, it measures some 6,800 yards from the back tees the fearsome foursome used, has rough and water aplenty, and linoleum-slick greens. If that wasn't scary enough, the group was tailed by a press corps and TV crews recording each shot for posterity.

Any highlight film of Spagnolo's round would linger on hole 17. At just 132 yards, it's a piece of cake for the pros, but to someone who never hit the ball higher than four feet above the ground its wrap-around water hazard "looked like the English Channel." He hit 27 balls into it before giving up and putting over the narrow walking path to the green. Wearied by that ordeal, he lost three more balls, and carded a 22, on the 18th hole.

Once his epic 257 was posted, fame came quickly in the form of newspaper interviews and TV appearances. That sort of thing slacked off soon, but other forms of celebrity have lingered. He's invited to appear at several dozen charity events each year, and accepts as many as he can in July and August, when his sons' baseball leagues have concluded. He heads his own annual charity tourney, benefiting the Multiple Sclerosis Society; it next will be held Aug. 2 at the Nema-colin Woods Resort near Pittsburgh.

Spagnolo has made several commercials, including a recent one for Nike that also featured pros Curtis Strange and Peter Jacobsen. He was flown to Texas, and secreted in a lavish hotel suite, by a man who put him in a tournament as partner to a win-at-any-cost pal. He also taped a "Wacky World of Sports" segment that, he's been informed, recently was shown in Australia.

But the best thing about winning the worst golfer title, he says, is that it no longer applies. *Golf Digest* sent him and the other finalists to an instructional school, and his form, which the magazine described as "grip too strong, stance too closed, visor too low," has improved. He averages about 110 now, and, even, broke 100 once. "I'm no longer terrible, just bad," he boasts.

Unchanged, though, is his love for the game. "I played a tournament recently with a guy who shot 80 but still cursed his way around the course," he says. "I thought, 'What a jerk—99% of the people on earth would be delighted to be where he was and play like he played.' If you can't be happy playing golf, where can you?"

• *June 19, 1992*

The Queue at the 'Q School'

HAINES CITY, FLA.

T
hey had a funny kind of golf tournament here this week. On final-day Monday, while bespectacled Woody Austin was putting on the 18th green to secure victory, most of the spectators were about 100 yards away, watching a man post earlier scores on a large board.

The focus of that bunch wasn't on the leaders but on who would finish 40th or thereabouts. That was because the real prize wasn't the winner's $15,000, but the square pieces of cardboard that went to the top 40 finishers and ties. These are tickets to professional golf's year-around Big Show, the PGA Tour.

The event was the six-day, 108-hole finals of the PGA Tour National Qualifying Tournament. Most call it "Q School" even though its sole classroom component is a session or three on pro-golf logistics, conducted at another time and place.

Everyone calls it nerve-racking, gut-wrenching or variations thereof. A Q School "diploma" means a year of playing manicured courses for shares of weekly, seven-figure purses; flunking means scuffling for a living on a foreign or U.S. minor-league circuit. Many a major-tournament leader has, in answer to the inevitable press question, said the pressures of that role paled in comparison with his Q School experience.

"I haven't really slept all week. My eyes popped open at about 3 every morning, and my mind started churning so fast I couldn't close 'em again," confessed Dudley Hart, a four-year Tour veteran forced back into Q School by a poor money-list showing in the just-completed season.

"Why am I doing this? Because I love the game, although this doesn't seem like a great time to bring that up," wheezed 46-year-old Bruce Fleisher, an ex-U.S. Amateur champion (1969), who battled flu and right-elbow tendinitis here to prolong an up-and-down pro career.

Although there are alternate routes, Q School is the path on which almost all of the gods of golf, domestic variety, started out for the pantheon. Weekly tour spots are allotted according to a lengthy priority list that also includes winners of the four "majors" (the Masters, PGA and U.S. and British Opens) during the past 10 years; winners of regular tour events the past two years; the 125 top money winners the previous year; the top five money winners on the Nike Tour, which is the PGA's official satellite; and players requested by individual tourney sponsors. Most tourney fields number between 130 and 150, so Q School qualifiers, who are near the list's bottom, can't claim space in every event, but they usually can make 25 or so a year.

In the distant past, quite a few event slots were awarded through an open, early-week qualifying round. That number has been pared to four, leading some to assert that the multitude of full-year passes has produced a fat-and-happy attitude that's hurt Americans in the sport's world rankings. Larry Rinker, 37, another Tour vet sent back to Q School by a poor season, disagrees. "There's enough adversity in the game without also making a lot of guys sweat out Mondays [the usual qualifying-round day]," he asserts. "That would be cruel and unusual punishment."

The alternative, the Q School tourney, consisting of 18-hole rounds Wednesday through Monday on the courses of the sprawling Grenelefe Resort near this central-Florida burg, was the last of three qualifying stages that pro-golf novices had to endure to get their Tour cards. The previous two were regional 72-hole affairs that players with better credentials could skip. Still, all of the more than 800 men who participated had to put up entry fees ranging from $2,500 to $3,000, and only the top 46 won them back.

By the time the field was trimmed to 94 for Sunday and Monday's rounds, the tension had become palpable. These were days of deep breaths and distant stares, played out before the large, silent homes that lined the fairways, and galleries consisting mostly of the players' friends or relatives who could stand it. "My wife stayed home. It's bad enough that I'm here," groused Tray Tyner, a trim 30-year-old from Humble, Tex., who was going through Q School for the eighth time.

Tyner's phone call home late Monday afternoon bore glad tidings: Starting the final round in a tie for 13th place, he shot a 6-under-par 66 that not only secured him a Tour card but also won him $7,000 for a third-place tie at 419 strokes. That bested such much-better-known players as Mike Donald, runner-up in the 1990 U.S. Open, and former U.S. Amateur champs Chris Patton (1989) and Sam Randolph (1985), none of whom made the cut for the last 36 holes.

Some who didn't expect to make it were pleasantly surprised. One was Carl Paulson, a 23-year-old May graduate of the University of South Carolina. A collegiate player of middling distinction, he came here hoping for a 41st-through-110th place finish that would have given him a Nike Tour berth. He was one of nine players who tied for 37th-through-46th place at 427 strokes, and will play next year with the big boys. "Anything can happen, and it did," he said, smiling broadly.

Larry Rinker didn't make it, and will play the Nike Tour in '95. So will Damon Green, 34, a sometime freight handler from Orlando who's been through Q School seven times. A bogey on the par-five final hole, after he'd hit his drive down the middle of the fairway, cost him a spot. "Want a sad story?" he groaned later. "You've come to the right place."

Hart made it. So did Fleisher, who tied for third with Tyner. But both—and everyone else—trailed Austin, who strung together rounds of 70, 68, 72, 68, 69 and 67 to win by four strokes. He's a 30-year-old who dreamed of a golf career while working as a teller in a Tampa credit union.

Austin's first living wage in the sport he took up at age 13 came last year, when he won $72,206 on the Nike Tour, but he kept his day job, because, he said, "you never can tell." His next PGA Tour event will be only his second; he made the 1992 Buick Southern Open as a qualifier. "They treated me awfully well there," he recalled of that experience.

After this, a guy could get used to that.

• *Dec. 7, 1994*

A Legend Made in Four Days

AUGUSTA, GA.

Every year the Masters golf tournament invites its old champions back, and every year many come. Some, like Arnold Palmer and Gary Player, still play, and, sometimes, well. Others, such as Gene Sarazen, Byron Nelson and Sam Snead, tee off ceremonially in the early-morning dew of opening-day Thursday, take a bow, and retire to the clubhouse for a breakfast well earned.

Billy Joe Patton never won the tournament, but he comes back, too, or did until this year when Betsy, his wife of 47 years, fell ill. He can wear the green jacket of Augusta National Golf Club because he's a member. In recent years he's been on the club's rules committee at tourney time, stationed at one hole or another in case a judgment is called for. He's recognized by many there, sometimes in surprising ways.

"People like to tell me how they rooted for me to win in 1954, the year I came so close," the 72-year-old says. "From the looks of some of them, they couldn't have been more than three years old at the time."

Patton's performance in that long-ago tournament was the kind that people claim to have seen although they didn't. A lusty-swinging amateur from Morganton, N.C., just a morning's drive from here—making him almost a local boy—he led his first Masters after two rounds, faded with a third-round 75, then roared back into the lead with a subpar front nine on last-day Sunday, including a hole-in-one on the 180-yard sixth.

Patton didn't win, but he established his legend. On the par-five 13th hole, his risky, four-wood second shot spun back off the fringe of the green into a closely fronting pond, and he took a seven. He found water again striking boldly for the green in two on the par-five 15th, and bogied. His one-under-par 71 left him one stroke behind a couple of gents named Snead and Hogan, who played off for the title the next day, with Snead winning. Other amateurs have finished a notch higher than Patton's third in that Masters, but none have missed a crown by less.

He's been asked about that day many times, and his answer hasn't varied. "If I had it to do over, I'd do it the same. Playing safe wasn't my way, and I wouldn't have gotten to within a stroke of Hogan and Snead by changing," he says. He adds: "I've never looked on my showing that year as a defeat. There aren't many things you can do for four days that can give you a lifetime identity."

Patton pondered gilding that identity on the pro tour, but didn't. His reason was money: as a lumber dealer he was earning more than all but the top few professionals of the time, and as a father of three children he felt he should limit his risk-taking to going for par-five greens in two. A lumber dealer he stayed, until his retirement eight years ago.

He admits to having wondered how he might have fared as a links full-timer, but says he has no regrets on that score, either. "I played enough golf to satisfy any man, and had fun doing it," he remarks. "Fun isn't something you hear the pros talk a lot about, is it?"

Besides, he goes on, staying amateur meant he didn't have to stay awake nights worrying about his swing. It wasn't a swing that could stand much thought. Jack Nicklaus called it the fastest he'd ever seen. Charley Price, a noted golf writer of the period, opined that Patton swung "like a drunk at a driving range."

Patton laughs at the characterization. "I learned the game as a kid, caddying for my dad, and I was pretty much self-taught," he says. "I'd just tee up the ball and hit it, and that was that. I served in the Navy during World War II, and didn't touch a club for three years. That gave me time to think, and I thought about trying to be more stylish. I slowed things down my first few weeks back, but hated the results. That was it for experimenting."

Swinging from the heels, Patton compiled a good but not great amateur record. He won the North-South Amateur three times, the Southern Amateur once, and, in 1962, reached the semifinals of the U.S. Amateur.

He played on the U.S. Walker Cup team five times, and his appearance at the '54 Masters came as a result of his being an alternate on that squad. In those days, a large amateur contingent played the tournament, partly in consequence of the desire of Bobby Jones, the many-time U.S. Open and Amateur champion and Augusta National's co-founder, to see an amateur scale the heights as he had. Reflecting today's lopsided professional tilt, only five amateurs teed off here yesterday.

The relationship between Patton and Augusta National was love at first sight; the spacious layout suited his game like no other. Besides his third place against the world's best in 1954, he finished 12th in 1956, eighth in '58 and '59, and 13th in '60.

He played the tournament six more times, and kept right on playing the course after that because he was tapped for membership in 1957. He resigned in 1970 following a dispute with Clifford Roberts, Augusta National's autocratic chairman, that, Patton says, "wasn't complimentary to me or the club." Invited to rejoin in 1984, he did, although he now plays more at his home club, Mimosa Hills, or at the Seminole course in North Palm Beach, Fla. He says he doesn't hit the ball as far as he used to, or putt as well, but his handicap is a respectable 7.6.

If he's of a mind to recall the good old days, though, Augusta National still is the place. "I remember the last round in '54, hitting an iron dead to about six feet of a pin, and listening to a spectator ask Joe Dey, who was walking with us as an official, who I was and how I got there," he says. "Joe told him my name and said I was a Walker Cup alternate. The guy said he'd love to see the fellow who beat me out."

• *April 7, 1995*

A Rainy Weekend at Pebble Beach

PEBBLE BEACH, CALIF.

hatever else might have been said about Bing Crosby, the late crooner, it was certain that he was an optimist. Otherwise, he wouldn't have put the annual professional and celebrity-amateur golf tournament that bore his name on the Monterey Peninsula during a late-January-early-February week.

That's because Mark Twain's line about summer in San Francisco, up the coast, goes double for Monterey in winter. It often rains here this time of year, and, sometimes, it snows. The tourney's most repeated anecdote has Jimmy Demaret, the late pro and bon vivant, waking one morning to find the ground covered with the white stuff and exclaiming, "I know I got loaded last night, but how did I wind up at Squaw Valley?"

The upshot has been that, over the years, the event that has survived Bing, and now is played under the sponsorship of AT&T, has had numerous rounds delayed and postponed, and, on a few occasions, been pared from its usual four-day, 72-hole format to three days and 54 holes. Last weekend, it went that one worse: heavy nighttime rains that created unplayable conditions on the Spyglass Hill Golf Course, one of the three host venues, washed out Saturday's and Sunday's scheduled third and fourth rounds, and the forecast for more rain Sunday night foreclosed a possible Monday extension and caused the tournament to be canceled 18 holes short of official status.

This caused some disappointment, but less than one might expect. Under the cancellation ruling, each pro who played received $5,000 regardless of score, instead of a shot at the $270,000 that was supposed to go to the winner. But Jeff Maggert, whose 68s on Thursday and Friday put him in the lead for that paycheck, evinced little financial chagrin. "I'd give up the money for the Masters berth and Ryder Cup qualifying points" that go with a bona fide PGA Tour victory, said he. "I think a lot of the guys would feel the same way."

It's apparent from the above statement that today's links tourists have a quite different slant on money from those of 1937, when the golf-loving Crosby first gathered some of his pro-golf and show-biz buddies to San Diego for a friendly tourney that carried a $500 first prize. Sam Snead's 68 won it after several days of rainouts (in San Diego?!), and, when handed his check by Der Bingle, Snead said he'd rather be paid in cash. Palship was great, but Sam kept his eye on the ball in many ways.

Professional golf has changed in other respects, too, and the National Pro-Am, staged on the scenic Pebble Beach Golf Links and other Monterey courses since 1947, embodies many of the changes. For starts, there's its title: Bing died in 1977, but his name stayed on the tournament until 1986, when AT&T took it over. Golf tournaments first were named mainly for cities, then went through a phase in which the imprimatur of entertainers such as Crosby, Bob Hope, Danny Thomas, Glen Campbell and Andy Williams was deemed desirable. Now, they're stamped by their corporate sponsors, enough of which are auto brands to make the PGA Tour resemble the Indy 500.

Moreover, the institution of the celeb-dotted pro-am, which the Crosby pioneered, has become a kind of industry in itself, not only attached to (generally preceding) the regular PGA and LPGA stops, but as free-standing events around the land. No ex-ballplayer or TV sitcom performer with any kind of skill in The Humbling Game need pay a green fee again.

It's in this class that the tournament here remains special. That's because the people in its "am" side must pay to play—$3,500 each— with much of the proceeds going to charity. While Bing lived, he picked the field; with AT&T running it, a committee does (naturally). Both ways, the line for entry has been long.

Mainly, one gets in by being somebody or knowing somebody. Big-time sports or entertainment figures, represented this week by such as the actors Clint Eastwood, Kevin Kostner and Bill Murray, and tennis ex-great Jimmy Connors, get first call. After them, in no particular order, are the relatives of golf pros with clout (Jack Nicklaus and Johnny Miller played with their sons, Brad Faxon with his dad), business heavy-hitters, people who sign up for lifetime AT&T long-distance service (just kidding) and Bay Area residents with golfing or other distinction. Sally Krueger, a San Francisco physician and local women's amateur champ, made it on the last such ground. She was the first woman in the field since 1977.

As far as the spectators are concerned, everybody but the golf pros and show-biz types could stay home, and off of Saturday's example maybe even the pros aren't necessary. Even though the wet fairways caused the noon-announced cancellation of regular play that day, the sponsor put up $20,000 and got 12 actor-golfers together for a late-afternoon, five-hole "shootout" at Pebble Beach, and a gallery that was sizable by any standard stood around in the muck for 75 minutes past its scheduled starting time to watch.

I'll leave it to *People* magazine to provide details, but here's the quick-and-dirty on a few of the celebrities' golf games: Kostner's swing looks pretty good, but he often hits the ball sideways, and put shots into greenside bleachers on two holes; actor James Woods is a truly awful golfer with a swing that would fit in a phone booth; actor Andy Garcia takes as long as Jack Nicklaus to line up a putt, but doesn't hit 'em as well.

Murray, wearing bib overalls, won the thing for himself and partner Campbell in a last-hole putt-off. He accepted his winner's check (it went to charity) from AT&T chairman Robert Allen, who said, "I can't believe I'm giving a check to someone on a golf course dressed like you." Replied Murray, "I can't believe I'm taking a check from somebody like you."

Murray's meaning was murky, but he got a laugh anyway. That'll teach Allen to kid with a kidder. The bottom line was that all concerned yukked it up, and nobody asked for his money back. Maybe golf's next wrinkle will be a CGA Tour, the "C," of course, standing for celebs.

• *Feb. 6, 1996*

Jack Comes Back

AUGUSTA, GA.

M y first Masters Tournament, in 1986, began with a disappointment. I'd heard about Magnolia Lane, the tree-lined road leading to the clubhouse of Augusta National Golf Club, and looked forward to driving upon it, but my parking permit was for Lot 4, the press lot, and it turned out to be a big, rutted field whose outlet was the side entrance to the course that many spectators use. Ordinary folks can glimpse Magnolia Lane from the property, and walk on it if they choose. But gliding up it by car during tournament week is, pretty much, the province of members of the club and players.

That shouldn't have come as a surprise; of all the sports that are popular in America, golf is the least democratic. Now and again, major tournaments are staged at public courses open to anyone with the (usually steep) price of the green fee. Mostly, though, they're at private clubs from which the majority of their spectators, as well as most of the news people who cover them, would otherwise be barred on any number of grounds, some of them unsavory.

For me, the initial feeling of alienness was especially strong at Augusta National. It's in the small-city South, and I'm from the big-city North. The club's reputation for starchy exclusivity is well known. To speak with a club official—as I did my first day there, the Wednesday before play was to begin—you go to a white-porched office building just off the main clubhouse, state your business to the uniformed guard on duty, and wait outside while he goes in and asks if you're welcome. I wasn't wearing a hat that afternoon, but if I were I think I would have taken it off and held it in my hand.

I found, however, that it didn't take long for Augusta National to break down my defenses. The warm Georgia sunshine that early-April day was welcome after a long Northern winter, the people I met were pleasant, and the course itself was pure enchantment—so beautiful that they could charge admission to see it even if no one were playing golf. Fretting over social inequities would have to wait for another time, and place.

What's more, the best of that visit was yet to come. In the tournament that ensued, Jack Nicklaus, the best golfer ever, played one of his best rounds, a last-day 65 that enabled him to come from behind to win his sixth Masters title and, it now seems likely, the last of his 20 triumphs in "major" championships. It was the kind of tournament about which those in attendance would tell their grandchildren. The winner figured to do the same, and soon, because he was 46 years old at the time.

Was the 1986 tourney the best Masters? That depends on whom you ask. The 1935 edition, in which Gene Sarazen made up a three-stroke deficit with his 15th-hole double-eagle two and went on to win in a playoff, helped put Bobby Jones's two-year-old invitational on the map. In 1954, the amateur Billy Joe Patton, from just up the road in North Carolina, thrilled the multitudes with his devil-take-the-hindmost shot making, and fell just a stroke behind Sam Snead and Ben Hogan, the two best players of the era, in the 72 holes of regulation play (Snead won the playoff). Any of Arnold Palmer's four victories were special to those who saw them, and so was Nicklaus's win in 1975, when he and one-stroke-runners-up Tom Weiskopf and Johnny Miller traded Sunday-afternoon birdies in a memorable show.

But the 1986 event stood out for reasons that only tangentially concerned the shots that were made. They had to do with the relationship between Nicklaus and the people who witnessed the tournament. Jack might have been the master of the Masters—no one had captured more than his five titles going in—but he'd had the misfortune of winning most of them at the expense of the charismatic Palmer, whom the long-memoried galleries of Augusta National had clasped to their bosoms as no other player.

Oh yes, they knew that Nicklaus's golfing skills were unmatched, and as he aged he cut a trimmer, more-benign figure than did the stocky, phlegmatic young man who'd broken their and Arnie's hearts in 1963, '65 and '66, but the thought of those years still rankled in many. Couldn't he have let Palmer win *one more time?* they thought. Why, with all of Jack's trophies, he'd scarcely miss just one.

In 1986, though, Nicklaus was not only a winner again, but also a hero, and the feelings flowing towards him from behind the gallery ropes were of affection as well as respect. The people cheered his successes and greeted the misfortunes of his adversaries with exclamations akin to glee, although most were quite aware that the Masters's overseers didn't approve of the latter outbursts. It took awhile but he was, at least, Darlin' Jack.

Behind the transformation, in part, was the fact that this Nicklaus triumph was a surprise, both to himself and others. He'd come to Georgia not as the conqueror of the recent past, but as a man struggling with the physical realities of middle age and trying to mix his growing business responsibilities with competitive golf. His last "major" victory had been at the 1980 PGA Championship, and he'd won only two PGA Tour titles since then. In his seven 1986 tourney stops before Augusta, he'd missed the cut three times and withdrawn once. "Sometimes I play as well as I used to, but not for long," he admitted at his pre-tournament press conference.

Still, few were ready to say that he was over the hill, and when a Masters-week article raising that possibility appeared in an Atlanta newspaper, the golfer clipped it as a motivator and taped it to the refrigerator of the house he was renting. Apparently, hinting at it himself was one thing, but seeing it in print was quite another.

Early on, Nicklaus's play justified the doubts about him. His opening-round score of 74 was one of his poorest in the tournament. He was using a new, longer-bladed putter, and it was strange in his hands. About the only solace he could gain from the round was that most of the other players didn't handle Augusta National's slick greens any better on a dry, windy day; the average score was over 75 strokes.

On Friday, another windy day, Nicklaus putted better, and his score came down to 71. "I'm playing pretty well—like that fellow I used to know—but I haven't scored," he said in reference to his former self. His improvement was little noted, however, because Seve Ballesteros was shooting a 68 to go with his first-round 71 to take the 36-hole lead. Augusta National's generous fairways always had been hospitable to the dark-visaged Spaniard, and he'd won here in 1980 and '83. Regarded as the world's best player on courses that accommodated his scrambling style, he was favored by many to gain his third Masters crown two days hence.

Nicklaus had hit approach shots to inside 15 feet of the pin on 23 holes the first two days, but had only four birdies to show for it. On a Saturday in which the breezes abated, however, his mastery of his putter revived, and he posted a 69. Again, though, his round was overshadowed by another—Nick Price's course-record 63—and other players also were getting their putts to drop. Nicklaus's 54-hole score of 214 was good only for a seven-way tie for ninth place, and while he was just four strokes in back of the leader, the jaunty Australian Greg Norman, he found the prospect of catching up daunting. "It's the number of players ahead of you, not the number of strokes," he explained. He said he thought that if he played an exceptionally good round on Sunday he could still win, but it sounded more like a wish than a prediction.

Sunday dawned warm and still—birdie weather—but, it seemed, the round for which Nicklaus had prayed was not to be. Eight holes into it and he hadn't further dented par, and as he stood over an 11-foot birdie putt on nine he heard the roar from the gallery around the eighth green that greeted Tom Kite's holed wedge shot for an eagle three. As Jack was again about to putt, *another* cheer came from eight. Ballesteros also had holed his pitch there for an eagle, putting him eight shots under par, six better than Jack.

Nicklaus usually didn't address his gallery, but this time he did. "Let's see if we can make a roar of our own," he told it. Then he sank his putt to go three under par.

From there, roar after roar followed Jack. He played a back nine to remember, and his gallery, growing with his charge, carried on more like college students at a basketball game than the late-middle-aged or early-elderly sorts most were.

Nicklaus sank a 20-foot putt to birdie the par-four 10th hole, and repeated the performance on 11. He overshot the green to bogey the tricky, par-three 12th, but got that stroke back by reaching the green on the par-five 13th in two and two putting.

After parring 14, he hit his best shot of the day, a wind-aided, 202-yard four iron to 12 feet of the pin on the 500-yard 15th, and holed his putt for an eagle three. On the 170-yard 16th, his five-iron tee shot just missed the hole, and he birdied from three feet. He punched a pitching wedge to 10 feet on 17, and sank that putt, too.

Nicklaus said that as he was playing the 17th hole he heard "a roar that wasn't a cheer." It came from 15, where Ballesteros had sculled his second shot into the pond fronting the green. The resulting bogey deflated him, and his 70 for the day would leave him in fourth place, two strokes back.

Nicklaus parred the 18th hole for his 65 and nine-under-par total of 279, then retired to the television set in a cabin on the grounds to watch his challengers finish. Two of them—Norman and Kite—had chances to catch him.

Kite, then the best active player never to have won a "major," started the day at 212, two strokes behind Norman, and gained momentum with his eagle on eight. The small Texan with the large eyeglasses went eight under par with birdies on 13 and 15, and at 18 put his approach shot 12 feet from the flag. He putted for the birdie that would have tied Nicklaus, and missed by a turn of the ball. He later said he'd hit that same putt repeatedly in practice, but it had never broken left, as it did on Sunday. "I made that putt. It just didn't go in," he said of his effort.

Like Nicklaus, Norman spun his wheels early on Sunday, playing the first 13 holes in one over par, but he birdied 14, 15, 16 and 17 to go nine under, and could have forced a playoff with a par at 18. Alas for him, his four-iron second shot on the finisher sailed into the gallery to the right of the green, and he could get no closer than 15 feet from the pin with his chip. When his putt slipped past the left side of the hole, Nicklaus exhaled in happiness and relief. For one more golden day, the Golden Bear had played—and scored—like that fellow he used to know.

- *April 10, 1996*

SPEED BALLS

•

Part 6

Death at the Races

D anger always lurks on the knife-sharp edge of speed, and sometimes—even when the activity is sport—that edge is brutally crossed. So it was on a sunny Saturday of horse racing that turned tragic as the two best in an afternoon of the best pounded down the homestretch of Belmont Park here.

Go For Wand, a brilliant, three-year-old filly who had won seven of eight starts this year and was bidding to become one of the few of her sex to claim horse-of-the-year honors, and Bayakoa, the six-year-old defending female champ, had turned the $1 million Distaff segment of the 1990 Breeders Cup series into a match race. Leaving the rest of a field of seven far behind, they toured the track in tandem, Go For Wand on the rail and Bayakoa hugging her right hip as the crowd of 51,000 roared like an approaching subway train.

But about 100 yards from the finish Go For Wand stumbled and pitched headlong into the dirt, throwing jockey Randy Romero before her, and the roar turned into a shriek. When she arose, her lower right leg dangled sickeningly. Horses do not survive such injuries. She was brought to ground near the finish line, a screen was thrown up to shield her from sight of the crowd, and she was destroyed by lethal injection.

Romero emerged unscathed, and returned to ride again. Had Go For Wand rolled forward over him, instead of sideways into the rail, his injuries might have been severe.

121

That was the second equine fatality of a day that would be memorable on a number of scores. Mr. Nickerson, a four-year-old colt with career winnings of $600,000, fell while running near the rear of the pack in the $1 million Sprint—two races before the Distaff—unseating his jockey, Chris Antley, and causing another horse, Shaker Knit, to go down. Mr. Nickerson succumbed on the track, but his death was attributed to a heart attack or ruptured artery rather than injuries caused directly by the fall. Antley was hospitalized with a broken collar bone.

An investigation no doubt will be mounted, but officials of the host New York Racing Association said that, as best they could determine, the Belmont Park oval was blameless. "They were different accidents on different parts of the track. Spills are part of the game," said Gerald McKeon, NYRA president.

He added, "[The mishaps] were like a relative dying on your wedding day. It's not the way you'd like a special occasion to be remembered."

Were it not for the spills, Breeders Cup day, the seven-race, $10 million extravaganza that climaxes the racing calendar, would have given the turf sport reasons to rejoice. Fifty-four-year-old Lester Piggott, the great English jockey who had been knighted and, later, jailed for tax evasion, returned from a five-year layoff to ride the Irish-owned Royal Academy to victory in the Mile. The unbeaten Meadow Star breezed home first in the Juvenile Filly event without giving unease to the multitude who bet her down to odds of 1-to-5, the shortest price ever carried by a Breeders Cup winner.

And in the $3 million Classic, the day's traditional main event, Unbridled, who had been all but forgotten since his Kentucky Derby win last May, slipped between British-bred Ibn Bey and New York favorite Thirty Six Red in the final strides of the 1¼-mile run to prevail. The win was worth $1,350,000 to owner Frances Genter and $15.20 to anyone who put $2 on Unbridled's nose.

If there was a pattern in the afternoon's activity, it was for come-from-behind horses to win. No animal led wire to wire, although one early leader, Safely Kept, did rally in the homestretch of the ¾-mile Sprint after being headed by Dayjur, a highly touted colt from England. This race, too, had its bizarre aspect: As Dayjur passed Safely Kept within sight of the finish, Dayjur broke stride by jumping at a grandstand shadow jutting into the track, and jumped at another shadow at the wire.

The antics left Safely Kept a winner by a neck, and Dayjur's jockey, Willie Carson, shaking his head. "I can't believe it. He was the best horse, but we didn't get the money," he said. Safely Kept's backers, though, smiled at their 12-to-1 return on a horse that had won 18 of 23 starts and $1.3 million going in.

Compared with that, the day's other races that weren't accident-scarred were routine. Meadow Star prevailed by five lengths among the fillies, and owner Carl Icahn, of corporate-raider fame, pledged her $450,000 prize, and future winnings, to a group that aids under-privileged children. Fly So Free, a 7-to-5 favorite, won the Juvenile Colts' go by three lengths, installing himself as the early choice for next year's Kentucky Derby.

England-based In The Wings won the $2 million Turf by ½-length. Piggott scored on Royal Academy by a similar margin, and the wisened rider of several thousand winners later said that, no, it wasn't his biggest racing thrill.

Trainer Carl Nafzger attributed Unbridled's Classic victory to the horse's 10-week layoff after his losses in the Preakness and Belmont stakes. "The Triple Crown races took more out of him than I recognized. I haven't pushed him since," said he.

In a season in which the best older horses had their careers ended by injuries, the ungainly looking Unbridled now is a likely horse of the year, but he might not have held that status if Go For Wand hadn't fallen. Her race with the gallant Bayakoa recalled the stirring duel between Personal Ensign and Winning Colors in the same event two years ago, at Churchill Downs. Some called that the best race of the decade.

Go For Wand, a stocky brown, was the 1989 two-year-old filly champ, and had already clinched that honor for three year olds. In her last outing, also at Belmont, she came within a whit of equaling Secretariat's 1⅛-mile track record. "She was going to win today. She took a bad step," said jockey Romero. Bayakoa won by 6¾ lengths.

Fifteen years ago, at Belmont, the champion filly Ruffian broke a leg in a match race with the colt Foolish Pleasure, and was de-stroyed. She's buried in the track's infield. If her owner agrees, Go For Wand will join her there.

● *Oct. 29, 1990*

The Great Dan Patch

SAVAGE, MINN.

efore there was Michael Jordan, or Refrigerator Perry, or Arnold Palmer, or, even, Babe Ruth to serve as sport's gift to the economy at large, there was Dan Patch. And you can still make a case that not only was Dan a better athlete than those other worthies, but that he was a more potent endorser as well.

As some may know, Dan was not a man but a horse, a horse who pulled a buggy. That meant a lot in the days when this century was new, this nation was predominantly rural, and horsepower was something besides an engine rating.

Dan Patch was a pacer, the greatest that ever lived. When two-minute miles by harness horses were rare, the handsome mahogany ran them just about every time out. He set his first world's record, of 1:59, in 1903, and in two years lowered it, in steps, to 1:55¼. That mark stood until 1938, when it was bested by a quarter-second. It would be fully 22 years more before the 1:55 barrier was broken.

Dan ran a 1:55-flat mile once, at the 1906 Minnesota State Fair, but it was disallowed as a record because a pacemaker's sulky had been rigged with a shield to deflect flying dirt, in violation of a rule. His owner, feed manufacturer Marion Willis Savage, was not one to be put off by technicalities, though. He changed the name of his International Stock Food Farm to the International 1:55 Stock Food Farm, and that it stayed.

Savage was a kind of Don King of his day, minus the prison record and funny hair. He'd purchased Dan Patch in 1902 for a then eye-popping $60,000. By the time he'd bought the animal, owners of other pacers had given up running against it, so Dan's subsequent performances—including his record-breaking ones—were exhibitions against the clock.

Savage took Dan on the state-fair circuit for these, with both man and beast traveling in customized rail cars. He insisted on a percentage of the gate, and stationed employees in the fairs' counting offices to make sure he received his due. Crowds of 30,000 or more weren't uncommon when Dan Patch ran; Savage's cut from one appearance alone was reported at $21,500. "Cheapest horse I ever bought," he'd smile.

But the way that Savage really cashed in on Dan Patch—and a main reason the horse has remained a part of Americana—was through the items he authorized to bear Dan's name. Their number and variety put in shade those endorsed by Michael, the Fridge, et al. Besides a multiplicity of Dan Patch products put out and energetically advertised by Savage's Minneapolis-based International Stock Food Co., they included posters and postcards galore, liniment, baking soda, coffee, a soft drink, smoking and chewing tobacco, children's wagons and sleds, cutlery, china plates, billiard-cue chalk, thermometers, clocks, watches, stoves and washing machines.

There was a Dan Patch automobile and a Dan Patch railroad line that ran between Minneapolis and Northfield, Minn., with a stop at Savage, a Minnesota River town 20 miles south of the Twin Cities that changed its name from Hamilton after the entrepreneur's showplace farm and equine training center (it had an enclosed half-mile track and barns topped by minarets) here became a tourist draw. The rail link still is in operation, a part of the Soo Line.

M. W. Savage's farm is long gone, but the Dan Patch heritage lingers in Savage, now a suburb with a population of 11,000 people. There are a Dan Patch bowling center and coin shop here, a depiction of the horse in full flight graces the city water tower, and an oil painting of him hangs in the public library. Several Savage residents have collections of items that bear the horse's name.

The largest of these—indeed, the largest anywhere—was assembled by Joe Egan, who grew up on a farm close to the old M. W. Savage place. He died last June, about three years after the death of his wife, Jean, and his stash passed to his four children. The town wanted to buy all or part of it, with an eye toward opening a museum, but couldn't raise enough money to get the project off the ground. The Minnesota Historical Society, in St. Paul, showed an interest, but backed off from a large-scale purchase. So sometime in late May or early June, the Egan collection will be auctioned off at the Meadowlands race track in East Rutherford, N.J., across the Hudson River from New York.

Some people around here think that's too bad. They include the city administrator, Mark McNeill. "We're a third-ring suburb that's not much distinct from our neighbors except for our history. It's a shame we can't retain more of it," he says.

"We're disappointed," says Del Stelling, who edits the *Savage Review*, the local monthly newspaper. "Dan's memory belongs here."

Jean Johnson, a daughter of Mr. Egan who lives in the nearby town of Eden Prairie, agrees. "We would have liked to have kept the items in the community, but it couldn't be worked out," she says quietly. One reason she's anxious to sell is obvious from a visit to her home; it's stacked with boxes containing parts of a collection whose inventory covers 10 pages of single-spaced type. And that doesn't include the larger pieces, such as a racing sulky Dan Patch pulled, or a sleigh to which M. W. harnessed the amiable animal for winter jaunts.

All is not lost for the locals, however. Mrs. Johnson says printed material that is part of her father's estate will be photocopied for exhibit here, and the Minnesota Historical Society says it intends to attend the auction to bid on individual items to add to its existing Dan Patch memorabilia. The society often lends parts of its collections to state communities for display, and "certainly" could do that for Savage, says curator Marsha Anderson.

Some of the Dan Patch pieces are "quite wonderful—a vivid link with an interesting part of our past," Ms. Anderson observes. "Sports have a way of drawing people into things, don't you think?"

• *April 17, 1992*

The Naming Game

I

f the importance of a sporting event is determined by the number of office pools it engenders, the Kentucky Derby is or is close to being No. 1. Come late tomorrow afternoon, Americans in our millions will be hunched before our TV sets, clutching scraps of paper bearing the names of horses whose success also would enrich us, albeit in a minor way. One of every 15 or 16 will go away happy, a proportion that, at least, beats the lottery.

But even the losers might give their scraps an extra glance before tossing them away. Much of the turf sport's history is contained in the names of its contestants. Much of whatever creativity that sports-entity ownership allows is in them, too.

The experts say that this 120th Derby shapes up as a good one. Holy Bull, a winner of seven of eight starts and the likely favorite, is said to be a potential "super horse," but some of the other steeds in the race may not have read his press clippings. Already, though, it's safe to say that several of the horses' owners have done themselves proud in the naming game. I'd go so far as to call this the best-named field in recent years.

The art of naming horses well is magnified by the restrictions that surround the process. The Jockey Club, which oversees this aspect of racing, has placed 16 categories of labels off-limits, including ones with commercial significance, suggestive or obscene meanings or double meanings; copyrighted materials such as books, plays or songs; and words with more than 18 characters including spaces and punctuation. The names of champion horses, such as Kentucky Derby winners, are retired forever. No horse can be named for a living person without that person's written consent.

The greatest obstacle to creativity is the rule that no Thoroughbred can carry the name of any horse that's performed on the tracks or at stud in the previous five years. This rules out a telephone-book-sized list of some 550,000 names. Until last year, recycling of names employed within the past 10 years was forbidden. Making this resource renewable freed up more than 150,000 names.

Even so, owners sometimes must submit several names before one is approved. This has led to some that can only be called desperate. Jack Dreyfus, the owner of a large stable, once dubbed a foal Fried Eggs Over when he was told, at breakfast, that his sixth submission for the animal had been turned down.

Fried Eggs Over is far from the worst name ever inflicted upon a horse; many have labored under monikers that are inept, inapt or both. The son of Bold Ruler and Somethingroyal, for instance, was Secretariat, a name more suitable for mutuel clerks than the greatest racer ever.

My list of least-favorites is heavy on meaningless, squashed-together names such as current Derby entry Kandaly, the son of Alydar and the mare Kanduit, and silly misspellings such as Barbicue Sauce, the dam of Derby entry Tabasco Cat. "Some owners misspell names intentionally to be cute; others just don't know how to spell," says Buddy Bishop, the Jockey Club's registrar. "We don't care about that as long as our other rules are met. We're not running an English class."

The best names are those that are fresh and stand on their own in addition to fulfilling their instructional function by playing off an animal's pedigree. Just about everyone's favorite is Native Dancer, put together by Alfred Gwynne Vanderbilt from the names of the horse's sire, Polynesian, and dam, Geisha. Vanderbilt was the sport's long-time naming master, witness Splitting Headache for the issue of The Axe and Top O' the Morning, and Query for that of Questionnaire and Pansy.

Vanderbilt's generally acknowledged successor is Cot Campbell, president of Dogwood Stable. He declines the honor, explaining that other employees of the Aiken, S. C., concern, encouraged by the lure of $50 bonuses, also offer their ideas when foals must be named. A committee, headed by Campbell, picks the winners.

Dogwood has distinguished itself in recent years with such gems as Summer Squall (the 1990 Derby runner-up) for the offspring of the sire Storm Bird and dam Weekend Surprise, Oz from Ogygian and Sacred Journey, Hobgoblin from Exuberant and Halloween, and Garbo from Capote and The Private One.

Dogwood's '94 Derby entry is Smilin Singin Sam. He got his name from his sire, Smile, his dam, Earth Song, and the fondness of a previous owner for someone called Sam. "I wish we could take credit for it, but we can't," Campbell admits.

Like most racehorses, many of tomorrow's probable Derby entries bear more pedestrian rub-offs of their sires or dams. Mahogany Hall's sire was Woodman and Southern Rhythm's was Dixieland Band. Blumin Affair's dam was Medical Affair; Powis Castle's was Castle Eight; Soul of the Matter's was Soul Light.

Strodes Creek was named for a stream on the property of his breeder, Arthur Hancock; Lakeway for a residential area of Austin, Texas; Brocco for his owner, the movie producer Albert Broccoli.

Valiant Nature's name is a wish: The son of His Majesty and Premium Win is the brother of Tight Spot, a very good horse, and his owner, Verne Winchell, hopes he'll be just like him. Ulises, the son of Temperence Hill and Joi'ski Too, was named by a previous owner for reasons unknown to present owner Robert Perez.

Smilin Singin Sam is a really good name, I think. The same goes for Tabasco Cat, from his folks, Storm Cat and Barbicue Sauce; and Meadow Flight, from Meadowlake and Cassowary (although Meadow Flightless might have been better). Holy Bull's sire was Great Above; the late Rachel Carpenter, who named him, said that if he were a filly she'd have picked Holy Cow.

My Derby name winner is Go For Gin, owned by Bill Condren and Joe Cornacchia. Go For Gin's mom is Never Knock. To "knock" in gin rummy means to call, which means . . . well, ask someone who plays. But trust me, it's clever.

Trust me, too, and insist on odds if someone wants you to take Go For Gin against Holy Bull straight up. Last time they met, Holy Bull beat him by six lengths.

• *May 16, 1994*

Note: Go For Gin beat Holy Bull in the Derby, and everybody else, too.

What's New, Pussycat?

T
•
here's nothing unusual about people talking to animals. I do it frequently at the horsetrack. "C'mon, you #$%&*, run!" I'll holler at my selection as a race begins. "Why didn't you run?" I'll ask him when it's over.

There is, however, one person who says that animals talk to *her*, although "talk" may not be the right word. Communicate telepathically is better.

"We exchange thoughts, but it's very much like a normal conversation," says Krista Cantrell. "There's an exchange of information and, sometimes, ideas. Animals can be quite expressive if given the chance."

Cantrell calls herself a "cognitive animal behaviorist." Her home is in this suburb on the desert northeastern edge of Phoenix and she shares it with her engineer-husband, Jeff, and several dogs and horses (actually, the horses live outside in the stables).

She functions as an animal trainer and psychologist, and consultant to veterinarians. Some of her patients—er, clients ("I'm not a doctor, so I don't have patients," she corrects)—are race horses, which is why you are reading about her in a sports column. By her own account and that of others, she has helped put also-rans into the winner's circle.

But first, I'm sure, you'd like to know more about Cantrell, who is tall, wide-eyed and 44 years old, and about the power she claims. She says she doesn't know where it comes from, but she knows she's always had it.

"My first memory is of seeing things that looked like waterfalls dripping from my fingers. No one could see them but me," she says brightly. "The substance was sparkly and clear, like water, but it wasn't. It was the internal energy we all radiate. Not much later, I became aware that I could hear animals speaking to me in my mind, and that they could hear me. I understand that this is unusual, but I don't think of it as weird. Some people are gifted musically, others can draw and paint. That's my gift."

It's to her credit, I suppose, that Cantrell has chosen not just to chitchat with passing beasties. As a student at the University of Minnesota, she fashioned a major in what she calls crossparadigmatology, which, by acquainting her with the mind habits of different cultures, clued her into interspecies differences as well. She also became adept at Tai Chi, an Asian exercise form that, she avers, utilizes energy sources beyond the muscular.

Those things proved useful, she says, because, contrary to the widespread human assumption, animals are capable of quite-complex observations and thoughts. And we're not just talking horses, dogs and cats, but also reptiles, rodents, birds and, even, insects, all of which she claims to have tapped. "Brain size doesn't matter; intelligence differences within a species are much greater than those between them," she asserts.

She's fuzzier when it comes to the process by which she plugs into animal wavelengths, likening it only to dialing a mental radio. There are, she acknowledges, human-thought wavelengths as well, but she has chosen to avoid them because they are not her "path." This precludes rough-and-ready tests of her telepathy, but she's resigned to living with the resulting skepticism.

Cantrell charges $75 an hour for her services, which precludes lengthy gassing. Thus, her most frequent questions to clients' pets or livestock are "Where does it hurt?" or "Why do you bite?" However, along the way, she has picked up some general intelligence about our variously legged friends. To wit:

All of them, regardless of country of origin, "speak" English.

Communication between animal species is widespread, both telepathically and by arfs, oinks, chirps and so forth.

Animals think we're deaf because we can't understand what they're saying.

Given racing's competitive nature, it's not surprising that horse trainers are among her clients, and it's at the racetracks that her legend is strongest. Many of the horses she works with race at Turf Paradise, the Phoenix oval. Vincent Francia, a member of the public-relations staff there, took it upon himself last year to chart the performance of 11 less-than-world-beating horses with whom she'd talked. He says that seven of them won their next outings.

"She's pointed me in the right direction in several difficult diagnoses," says Cindy Reynolds, a veterinarian at the track. "She's not right every time, but, then, neither am I."

Trainer Lynn Posen has been a believer since the psychologist, summoned as a last resort, diagnosed one of her animals, apparently near death, as overmedicated, and not only saved her with doses of health-food staples such as yogurt but also returned her to racing. Last week, Posen asked her to talk to Popular Pair, an 11-year-old gelding nicknamed "Bones" whose performances had turned sour after several years as a steady producer in low-level events.

Cantrell began the interview by placing stones at the entrance and wall midpoints of Bones's stall, and waving her hands above his head. This set up an "energy field" that kept other thoughts from intruding, she said.

Steno pad in hand, Cantrell stared intently at Bones. He behaved horsily, nosing about his stall and gazing here and there. After some minutes of wordless note taking, she reported the following: He had a pain in his left cheek, he dislikes the jockey that's ridden him the last few times, he likes to run his own race "without being pulled around," and is grateful for the pain-relieving qualities of Butazolidin.

Trainer Posen took it all down. Afterward, she called in a vet, and he confirmed that a jaw dislocation might have caused the animal's left-cheek pain. Popular Pair, armed with "bute" and a different jockey who'll be given instructions from the horse's own mouth, is scheduled to run in the ninth race at Turf Paradise this afternoon.

Don't say I never did anything for you.

• *Feb. 2, 1996*

Note: *Popular Pair ran eighth in a field of 11.*

PRO BALL

•

Part 7

A Day at the Baseball Bazaar

HARVEY, ILL.

A. t 10:10 a.m. last Sunday, a tall, tanned, thick-bodied man wearing a fur-collared jacket entered the exhibition hall next to a Holiday Inn in this southern suburb of Chicago, and began making his way past tables stacked with baseball cards and memorabilia.

"He's big, isn't he?" said one browser as he passed.

"Not much gray hair, either," said another.

By the time the man had half-traversed the long floor he'd been noticed by most, and applause began to follow his progress. Pleased, the 70-year-old Ted Williams smiled broadly, and waved. That was something he rarely did in his 19 seasons as a peerless, and ofttimes peevish, batsman for the Boston Red Sox.

But that was baseball, and this is commerce. The former Splendid Splinter is being paid $20,000 to sign autographs for four hours here at $20 each. At that price, a little P.R. is in order.

As you no doubt have read, "card shows"—actually, bazaars at which collector-investors buy and swap all manner of artifacts connected with baseball—have replaced hot-stove chitchat as the summer game's winter staple, much to the profit of many concerned. It's as if the fans, reacting to their heroes' seven-figure salaries, have decided to grab for a few dollars themselves. On any winter weekend, thousands descend upon dozens of such marts around the land, usually featuring active or former star players.

135

Some children attend these affairs, but the real action is decidedly grownup. A Ty Cobb autograph, nicely framed beneath a portrait print of the Detroit slasher, bears a tag of $390, while $1,000 is asked for a faded autographed photo of Babe Ruth with the vendor's assurance it's a bargain.

The card-show auction is as volatile as the Taiwanese stock market and as quirky as the one for antiques. When New York Giant slugger Bill Terry died recently, the price of baseballs he'd signed jumped from $60 to $125. Remnants of a batch of current cards of Baltimore Orioles second baseman Billy Ripken that were yanked from stores when it was discovered that a written obscenity was visible on the butt of his bat were being hawked Sunday for $35.

Prices for card-show autographs vary with the signer's past or present diamond eminence. Mickey Mantle and Sandy Koufax pull $18, Johnny Bench $12, Bobby Doerr $6. Among active players, Oakland A's strongboy Jose Canseco commands a top of $15. The list drops to $4 for 1988 U.S. Olympic team members such as Ty Griffin and Tino Martinez, who aren't Major Leaguers yet. The two were supposed to appear here with Williams, but didn't make it through the snow.

Like any other commodity, availability also plays a role in signature value. The Detroit Tigers' Fred Lynn can sell his for $10 at shows partly because he rarely gives them away. Among the late-greats, the most valuable plain autograph—worth about $500—is that of Hall of Famer Rube Foster, a Negro League pitcher and manager of 60 years ago. "He didn't sign many, probably because few people asked," explains dealer Ken Peck.

As they were when they played, the kings of the circuit are Williams and his New York Yankees' contemporary, Joe DiMaggio, now 74 years old. Each commands a guaranteed $5,000 an hour at the table, which leaves promoters a fair-sized profit for the 300 to 400 signatures each ex-ball player inks hourly at $20 each.

Both Williams and DiMaggio play the scarcity game, making only a half-dozen or so show appearances annually. DiMaggio reportedly has tightened the screws further by lately refusing to sign "round" objects such as bats and balls. Of the two, Williams is said to be the more accommodating, no small feat for a man John Updike once described as wishing "to sever the game from the ground of paid spectatorship and publicity" because they interfered with his "perfectionist's vacuum" afield.

"DiMaggio signs without looking up," says George Brown, a Merrillville, Ind., steelworker, autograph collector and cardshow vet who paid $220 for 11 Williams signatures on a variety of objects Sunday. "Ted'll answer a question if you ask one, if there's time."

On this day, though, there would be little time for conversation. A throng of several hundred, all of whom had purchased their autograph tickets in advance and paid a $3 admission charge to boot, awaited Williams's entrance, arrayed in Disneyland-style lines separated by chains on stanchions. That number held steady throughout the day.

Williams sat flanked by two show officials. One fed him objects to be signed, the other returned them to the customers. Off-duty Harvey police, hired for the day, verbally prodded people to keep them moving. Rules for the session were posted behind the table: "No personalized autographs. No smoking in line."

"Get your items out. Get 'em ready," barked Jacques Audette, the barrel-shaped card-shop owner who staged the show.

At $20 a pop, people do not shove scraps of paper in front of a celebrity. They mostly brought bats, balls and photos, items for which there's a ready resale market. Some brought shiny metal signs advertising "Ted's Creamy Root Beer." The vendor selling the signs for $12.95 each explained that the product went off the market 30 years ago after a short life, but an Ohio firm still makes the signs for events like this one.

Williams, wearing tan cotton pants and a blue cardigan sweater over an open-necked white golf shirt, signed steadily, his signature as clear and bold as his old batting stroke. At 12:10 p.m. he broke for lunch, and at 1:10 he returned. At 3:10, he signed the last of 1,600 autographs, and rose to leave.

In answer to a question, he gave his view of the card-show phenomenon. "It's amazing, but it shows the way people feel about baseball. People who object to the prices don't come. I've had no complaints."

A blond woman, a friend of the promoter, posed for a photo with Williams and clung to his arm well after the flashbulb popped. A man in a Red Sox uniform shirt handed him a baby and fired away with an Instamatic. "Will you go fishing with me sometime?" a boy of about 11 called out. "Sure," said Williams, striding away.

• *Feb. 10, 1989*

Athletes Out
of Control

S
•

ome friends, knowing what I do for a living, have asked when I'd be writing a column about Magic Johnson. Hadn't everyone else?, they said.

I shrugged and replied that I didn't think there was much to say beyond expressing the hope that medical science would find something to help the poor guy, and others in his situation, before they got really sick. I guessed I also could grope for a silver lining and say that his example might convince people that sexual promiscuity has become a form of Russian roulette in the era of AIDS, but that's more a wish than an expectation.

But pretty quickly the thought occurred to me that we have been getting a lot of terribly bad news about our athletic heroes lately, and that the HIV virus may not be the only bug going around in the circles in which they move. Oscar Wilde's line that we'd better be careful what we wish for, because we might get it, seems to have gained new currency.

Consider the plight of three other men whose careers at least equaled that of Magic. Mike Tyson, who if not for one bad fight in Tokyo would be rated among the greatest boxers ever, faces trial in Indianapolis on rape charges. Pete Rose, baseball's most prolific hitter and its most distinctive personality of recent years, is banned from his sport for gambling and just out of prison on a tax-evasion conviction. The once-jaunty Muhammad

Ali, who may have achieved his boast of being the world's most famous person, is old before his time and ill, a figure of pity instead of admiration.

What the very different current circumstances of these quite different people have in common, I think, is that they followed a kind of success that appears to be a distinctly recent phenomenon. Sports heroes long have been lionized, of course, but the adulation has grown to a point where it seems to me to be something new under the sun.

It includes wealth so great that, probably, it remains an abstraction even to its recipients; Rose enjoyed a seven-figure annual salary in the last years of his lengthy career, while the reported yearly earnings of Johnson, Tyson and Ali are or were well into eight figures. It includes a television-based celebrity that has placed big-time athletes among our most recognizable figures at a time when recognition alone can open just about any door. Who has not seen the sea of a crowded restaurant's waiting room part for a local-TV weatherman, for heaven's sake?

And it includes a sports-crazy populace's willingness to overlook any number of transgressions as long as their perpetrators can put points on the board, or some-such. For the obviously talented, that sort of destructive forgiveness begins in high school, or sooner. A lot of athletes today behave as if they've never heard the word "no."

This certainly seems to have been the case with the 25-year-old Tyson. His biographers, of whom there have been many, portray him as a preteen hard case who used his fists to get his way on the streets of Brooklyn. He was plucked from a reformatory at age 12 by men who saw him as a future boxing superstar and proceeded to use their influence to help him avoid the consequences of his later forays into truancy and schoolyard bullying. Once an adult, Tyson's behavior turned toward manhandling women who resisted his advances, along with the occasional boyfriend who attempted their rescue; it's been reported that his own, boxing-spawned wealth has smoothed over possible difficulties there. It remains to be determined if he's a rapist, but if he's convicted he'll forfeit both his freedom and his career.

The biography of Pete Rose is less dramatic than that of Tyson, but similar nonetheless. He cracked a windowpane with a batted ball at age three, but instead of replacing it his parents kept it as a shrine to his prowess and, much later, offered it to the Smithsonian. His mother paid him 50 cents for every Little League hit, making him a child "pro." And if he did poorly in school it was all right, as long as he kept his batting average up.

The adult Rose gambled both unwisely and unwell. According to Michael Sokolove in his book *Hustle: The Myth, Life and Lies of Pete Rose*, he shoveled money to the bookies on team sports, and as much as $30,000 a day through the windows at the horse and dog tracks. Flunkies ran or called in his bets, sometimes from the telephones in baseball clubhouses. One dog track let him write checks. Sportswriters, teammates and baseball executives knew of his habit, Sokolove writes, but few thought much of it until, finally, it became a public issue.

Like Rose, Ali surrounded himself with sycophants who could be counted upon to tell him what he wanted to hear and no more. What he didn't want to hear—and thus rarely did—was that his skills were failing. He continued to fight long past the time he should have stopped, and as a result suffered irreparable physical damage. Ali's downfall seems to have been fame itself; he said he was "the greatest" so many times he believed it himself.

And so we come to Magic Johnson, who stands out even in the preceding company. This was an athlete of superlative talent and a disposition so sunny that he was liked by foe as well as teammate. At 6-feet-9-inches tall, he could handle the ball like a guard or go inside like a center. Nobody else could do what he could on a basketball court.

Apparently, few could do what he did off the court, either. "I was the one most NBA players looked up to when it came to women," he said in a recent *Sports Illustrated* article. "I lived the kind of social life that most guys in the league wanted to live . . . I'm no Wilt Chamberlain [who has claimed 20,000 sexual conquests] but I was never at a loss for female companionship. I did my best to accommodate as many women as I could—most of them through unprotected sex."

It's hard to believe that, in this day and age, anyone with that kind of "social life" would eschew AIDS precautions, but Magic did, and it cost him.

Did anyone tell him that what he was doing was a bad idea? And if anyone had, would he have listened?

• *Nov. 22, 1991*

Is There Life After Sports?

I 'd heard rumors that Michael Spinks, the boxer, was contemplating coming out of retirement, so I gave him a call. The last time he'd been in a prize ring, on June 27, 1988, he'd been flattened by Mike Tyson in just 91 seconds, and the experience convinced him, reasonably enough, that his future lay elsewhere. Five years later, at age 36, he was said to be having second thoughts.

I was hoping Spinks would say it wasn't so. I'd spent a couple of days in his training camp in the Catskill Mountains before that bout, and found him to be a pleasant and introspective man, a rare famous athlete who could discuss something other than himself. Despite his one-sided loss to Tyson, he'd been a skilled and courageous fighter, an Olympic gold-medal winner and professional champion of two divisions (light heavyweight and heavyweight). He also understood what A. J. Liebling called boxing's "scientific" side, and turned his natural awkwardness into an asset.

He'd seemed, moreover, to be an unlikely person to succumb to the addictive aspect of his brutal sport. After his 1976 Olympic triumph he returned to his native St. Louis with the intention of joining the workaday world, and had to be enticed back into the ring by promoter Butch Lewis, with whom he's still associated. "Fighting another man is like having all 32 of your teeth pulled,"

Spinks said as he prepared to face the destructive Tyson. "Anyone who tells you he enjoys it is crazy."

But that was then and this is now. And now, Spinks admits that boxing is pulling him back. "I'm still around the gym, you know, working with Butch's fighters and helping with the promotions, so I know who's out there. And I know there are a lot of guys I can still beat," he said from his home in a suburb of Wilmington, Del. "I've talked it [my comeback] over with some of the older fighters like Archie Moore and [Muhammad] Ali, and they told me that, if I had the desire, I should go ahead and do it."

Spinks said a couple of things stand between him and a comeback announcement. One is a knee injury from his fighting days that hasn't gone away; surgery probably will be required to clear it up. The other is a need to "fall back in love" with training.

"I didn't love everything about boxing, but I used to enjoy the gym work, the being with the other guys, the pushing myself," he explained. "That part really had little to do with the actual fighting and none with the money side, and it still doesn't. I earned about $24 million in my career, and even after taxes and expenses I'm so well fixed I'll never be in need. But I miss having a goal, working hard, trying to be good at something. I'm still a young man. There's no reason I can't have that again."

Those last lines were, I thought, sad, and explained much about the postretirement behavior of athletes who have been raised high by sports in recent years. The absence of economic necessity, it seems, has done little to ameliorate the plight of men and women who have devoted themselves to careers that must end at a time when those of their contemporaries are just beginning. For too many of them, the question of what to do next isn't asked until it must be answered.

So we see the dreary succession of comebacks that we—and, maybe, the athletes involved—know are doomed before they begin, such as those of baseball pitcher Jim Palmer, swimmer Mark Spitz and gymnast Kurt Thomas. We see athletes who made a mark in one sport grasping pathetically for a foothold in another, such as Mark Gastineau, the football player turned boxer.

And we see developments that seem sure to result in even worse future predicaments; in the "country-club" sport of tennis, for example, competitive demands force children in their teens to choose between their schooling and athletic careers. Pete Sampras, the Wimbledon champ, is a high-school dropout, and girls such as Jennifer Capriati catch their book-learning when they can amid their tennis wanderings.

Yes, the money today's top athletes earn can cushion the inevitable bump, but it can't solve the problem of filling the empty hours. This came home to me a few years back, when I was in Las Vegas to cover a boxing match and staying in the same, off-the-Strip hotel as the boxer Sugar Ray Leonard. Leonard, in the first of his retirements, was on hand to help with the bout's telecast, yet he was playing tennis on the hotel's courts when I left on my rounds in the morning and was still at it when I returned some six hours later. "The man's bored," I recall thinking, and wasn't surprised to hear shortly afterward that he was risking losing the sight in a surgically repaired eye to return to the ring.

I told that story to Ralph Cindrich, and he nodded in recognition. Cindrich is a former National Football League player turned Pittsburgh lawyer and player agent. His clients number over 100, and he's seen similar things.

"Relatively few pro athletes are ready when their careers end, educationally, psychologically or, sometimes, financially," he said. "Even when they say they are, they aren't. These are guys who think they're invincible. They've always made the cut and beat the odds, and believe they can continue to do so.

"In football, we're talking about people who've been to college, but often they still don't understand how different from sports the 'real world' is. There are no crowds cheering or people telling them how wonderful they are, and few clear-cut results like they got in their games. And the transition is so fast—almost overnight—that it can be, literally, stunning.

"I tell my clients it's OK to goof off and have fun after their first pro season, but after that I want them to take an offseason job," Cindrich went on. "It can be in sales, construction or anything. It doesn't have to lead to another career. But it'll give them a taste of what things will be like the rest of their lives, so at least they won't come as a shock."

And do they do it?

"Sometimes."

• *July 16, 1993*

Supporting 'Our' Teams

ST. PETERSBURG, FLA.

T
•

he thought that unpleasant truths are slow to penetrate some minds hangs in the air here, as the celebrations surrounding last week's awarding of a Major League baseball franchise to the winter-resort cities lumped under the name of a body of water wind down.

In St. Pete and other sunny burgs around Tampa Bay, Fla.—as well as in and around Phoenix, the other newly dubbed franchisee—troops of marginally qualified strikebreakers carry out a charade of spring training that should remind the populace of how the masters of the game regard their customers. Yet people here are rejoicing that "they" finally got the team they've so ardently desired.

Just in case stray particles of reality might mar the festivities, an executive of a local television station, appearing as a news-program editorialist, was on hand to administer a preventative. "We can't let down now that we have a team," he intoned on Thursday, the day of the announcement. "It's our obligation to support it."

Any other business seeking such an endorsement probably would be laughed out of the studio, but when it comes to baseball (or our other big-time professional team sports) different rules apply. No matter how well or poorly the teams perform on the field, or conduct their corporate affairs, they're regarded as civic treasures and expect public handouts as their due. Moreover, John Q. is supposed to cheer as he comes across.

Major League Baseball's latest expansion, to 30 teams when the new clubs take the field in 1998, underlined how much these private enterprises depend on public treasuries, and on how one-sided such transactions can be. The Arizona Diamondbacks will play in a $238 million, retractable-roofed stadium to be financed by a quarter-cent county sales-tax increase due to take effect April 1. Those who follow non-sports news may recall that Maricopa County, the entity involved, has been so strapped for funds that it's threatened to cut off the coffee rations of its jail inmates.

Boosters of the new Phoenix ballpark put a proposal for an earmarked property-tax boost on the local ballot in 1989. It was defeated. They then persuaded the Arizona legislature to turn the Maricopa County board into a special stadium district beyond the voters' immediate reach. In February 1994, despite polls showing continued opposition, this body OK'd the sales-tax hike contingent on Phoenix landing a team. The Diamondbacks have yet to negotiate a lease with the county, but they're not expected to kick in for java for the jailbirds.

Tampa Bay's baseball odyssey has been longer and stranger. Some say its bid finally succeeded as much because of its past travails with the game as because of its intrinsic charms. Since 1986, when St. Petersburg used county-backed bonds and funds from a hotel-motel tax to start building a 43,000-seat, $130 million domed stadium on spec, it's been used as the "or else" by teams seeking more and better concessions from their home cities.

Nobody strummed that chord more skillfully than Jerry Reinsdorf. He's the owner of the Chicago White Sox and, by all accounts save his own, the owners' chief hard-liner in negotiations surrounding the current seven-month-old players' strike. In 1988, he used a threat to move to St. Pete to get a new, state-financed stadium in Chicago in a deal that included such goodies as a state pledge to buy White Sox tickets if sales fell below a certain level.

In 1992, baseball opened the bidding for the San Francisco Giants, and a group headed by Vince Naimoli, representing Tampa Bay, came in high. That prompted a San Francisco bidder to up his proposal, which was ultimately accepted by the National League despite being lower than that of the Naimoli group. Naimoli sued everyone in sight, and the dropping of those actions was part of the arrangement under which a group he heads got an expansion nod.

Meantime, the building of the stadium here—first called the Suncoast Dome, then renamed the (ugh!) Thunderdome—didn't get the taxpayers off the hook. The city has helped pay the operating expenses of the baseball-less facility, and will be asked to pay a reported $30 million more to get the place ready for 1998. Local officials have admitted that subsidies won't necessarily end when the new team, the Devil Rays, begins play, but, they say, baseball's worth it.

Worth what, precisely? you may ask. "VIP box seats" for Ray games will go for a whopping $50 per, with most of the rest of the house in the $20-to-$10 range. That's on the high end of the Major League scale. Some 32,000 people have paid $50 each for a chance to buy season tickets, some as long as six years ago. If they said their money could be used to press Naimoli & Co.'s former lawsuits, and don't elect to buy tickets, they won't get their $50 back.

It may be consolation to some that the baseball moguls treated their new partners much as they treat their ordinary customers. This is an industry that claims it can't survive without major employee concessions, yet the talking price for the two new entries was $140 million each, against the $95 million that the Colorado Rockies and Florida (Miami) Marlins put up to get in two years ago and the $7 million (!) that the Toronto and Seattle clubs paid in 1977.

The moguls gave preliminary approval to Tampa Bay and Phoenix last Tuesday, allowing local hopes to soar, but retained final OKs until after the charges were worked out. That's like promising a kid a new mitt but not telling dad the price. The "fee" turned out to be $130 million, but the new teams also had to agree to accept $5 million a year less than the existing 28 in national TV revenues for their first four years of operations. That adds up to $150 million but, at that point, you couldn't disappoint sonny.

The other issue in the expansion was its probable impact on the quality of the game. Everybody knows it'll be negative, stretching already thin talent thinner. Last week, though, thinking about anything that smacked of real baseball would have spoiled the party.

• *March 14, 1995*

Squeeze Play in Cincy

R

oxanne Qualls is the mayor of Cincinnati, so she knows
the meaning of the word "politic." When asked if she's
been feeling whipsawed lately, she avoids a direct response. "I wouldn't say that," she says. "It's a unique set
of circumstances, but we're doing our best to manage."

She left no doubt, however, that she finds her city's
situation to be less than comfortable. "The realities have
changed, and it doesn't matter whether we like them or
not," she remarks.

The "realities" to which Qualls refers are those surrounding her city's two major-league sports franchises,
the baseball Reds and football Bengals. Each wants its
own new stadium, pronto, and it doesn't matter if the
place they now share, 25-year-old Riverfront Stadium,
not only isn't paid for yet, but still smacks of newness.

The Reds so far have resisted playing the familiar
"or elsewhere" card—the threat to move—in its stadium
dealings with Cincinnati-area governments. The Bengals
have not; they've been carrying on talks with officials of
Baltimore these past few weeks, and the name Los Angeles also has been dropped.

Asked to assess the chances of both teams remaining in the only town they've ever called home, one
knowledgeable local only shrugs. "Pretty good for the
Reds, not so good for the Bengals," says he.

But several things are quite clear about the double whammy that the pro-sports big-timers are applying to a city that's "small-market" by any current definition. One is that the price tag for new stadiums generally has soared since the good people of Hamilton County, Ohio, backed the bonds that built Riverfront Stadium in 1970. That place cost $44 million, while the current ballpark figures for new ballparks are $150 million for the open-air variety and $220 million for a dome. That's without land-acquisition costs and millions of dollars more for what the politicos call the "infra-structure improvements" that go with such projects.

Another is that the leases the Cincinnati teams signed at their present domicile have little power to hold them. The Reds' lease at Riverfront runs until 2010 and the Bengals' until 2000, but in the new world of stadium financing, paying off old lease obligations and remaining bond indebtedness ($23 million in Riverfront's case) are just other cost lines.

A third certainty is that the public at large will be asked to kick in for a large part of any tabs, in the form of credit guarantees, increased taxes or both. That's the way things are done these days.

That last point is rich in irony. At a time when recently strikebound Major League Baseball is operating under an unofficial fan boycott that has cut attendance by more than 20% from last season's levels, Gene Budig, president of the American League, has been able to boast that six cities in his circuit—Anaheim, Boston, Detroit, Milwaukee, Minneapolis and Seattle—have new-stadium plans in the works.

More ironic is the fact that the structures for which the taxpayers would be tapped would advance the gentrification of the sports arena that is pricing some of them out of the ticket market. The main engine of team owners' new-stadium pushes everywhere is their desire to install more so-called luxury boxes and club seats for which they can gather large premiums from well-heeled patrons, whose enthusiasm for such things seems boundless. Riverfront Stadium, for instance, has only 20 luxury boxes, while the new facilities under discussion for Cincinnati each would have about 100. Other teams have 'em, so they must, too, the Reds and Bengals chorus.

"The problem with most existing stadiums isn't with their functionality, but with their revenue-generating capacity, and the availability of premium-priced seats is a big part of that," affirms Mitchell Zeits, senior managing consultant at Public Financial Management

Inc., the Philadelphia firm that Cincinnati-area governments have hired to delineate their stadium options.

Building stadiums to accommodate more fat cats isn't the way such deals are presented, of course; their advocates always hype the supposed economic impact on the community as a whole. But most jobs in stadiums, new or old, are part-time and low-paid—ushers, ticket-takers, food-service workers and parking-lot attendants—and a stack of studies call into doubt the magnitude of the trickle-down effect a sports facility can have on other businesses.

Under scrutiny, the new-stadium case usually hinges on more-nebulous arguments. "Cities want to be regarded as big league or first class. Major league baseball remains a significant factor in the quality-of-life equation," Mr. Budig recently opined. In case anyone missed his point, he put it another way: "No community today wants to lose a franchise."

Cincinnati has rallied bravely to prevent such a catastrophe. Reasoning that no city of its population (about 400,000) can feed two hungry vultures at once, it has combined with neighboring entities to forge its strategies. Its current plan, unveiled two weeks ago, calls for a new park for the Reds near the Riverfront site, and rebuilding the present stadium from the skeleton out to accommodate the Bengals. Both units would be domeless.

Total construction costs were estimated at between $240 million and $335 million, and that would be only part of the bill. The *Cincinnati Enquirer* reported that no financing plan had emerged, but that a county sales tax was being considered, among other things.

Neither the Reds nor the Bengals leaped to endorse the proposal; indeed, the next week, Bengal President Mike Brown was talking again with the Baltimore people. Mayor Qualls could only shake her head.

"That's the nature of the game right now. You have to play it or lose," she says.

It's also possible to do both.

• *June 16, 1995*

Note: Cincinnati later agreed to build new stadiums for both teams, and passed a tax hike to pay for them.

The Calendar Glut

Notional Basketball Association players were scheduled to complete their balloting yesterday on whether their union should be decertified, with the results to be announced on Tuesday. If most voted for decertification, the new labor contract the union has negotiated with team owners would go down the tube. That would set owners and players upon a voyage through uncharted legal waters with no sure destination. League Commissioner David Stern, the owners' man, says the start of the 1995-96 season almost certainly would be delayed, and that, with no agreement, the entire schedule could be in jeopardy.

Losing all or part of an NBA campaign would be unfortunate; pro hoops is a good game well played. Few fans, however, would weep too long over such an occurrence, if only because they don't have the time any more. Our sports calendar has become so full and deep that three months of Major League Baseball and almost four months of the National Hockey League disappeared from it with hardly a ripple. The same fate could befall an idle NBA.

Indeed, the crowded calendar has become the central fact of sports in these United States. On television and "live," sports today are wall-to-wall and floor-to-ceiling, and squeezing out the windows as well. As the example of baseball has shown, an entity that relinquishes any part of its space risks losing part of its audience for an indeterminate length of time.

For my money, the most important date in the modern world of Sportsbiz was Sept. 7, 1979. That was the day ESPN, the first national round-the-clock, all-sports television station, began broadcasting. In its early days, ESPN often found itself stuck for programming; station old-timers tell of asking colleges within driving distance of their Bristol, Conn., studios to tape their hockey games so the station could air them the next day or the day after. By 1993, though, the number and kinds of events available to the cameras had grown so much that ESPN launched a sister entity, ESPN2.

A few statistics give a hint of the sports-entertainment explosion. ESPN, which keeps tabs on such things, reports that in 1979 the three major over-the-air TV networks—CBS, NBC and ABC—offered viewers a total of 1,288 hours of original sports programming, and that was about all there was nationally. By last year, those three, plus ESPN and ESPN2, had upped the figure to about 9,900 hours. Add in Fox, now a National Football League regular; the Turner stations, which carry the Atlanta Braves and NBA and NFL games; USA (boxing, golf and U.S. Open tennis); WGN (Chicago Cubs, White Sox and Bulls) and HBO (Wimbledon tennis and boxing), and the total is a good bit higher.

That tells only part of the story. In 1979, there were three regional cable-TV networks devoted exclusively to sports; now there are 25. All-sports radio stations weren't with us 16 years ago; approximately 75 now exist, and almost every large city has at least one.

The Big Three spectator sports—professional baseball, basketball and football—all have expanded their seasons over the past couple of decades to where they overlap by months, not weeks, and entire new sports, such as arena football and beach volleyball, have sprung up. A typical week's TV menu also includes such *nouvelle* items as men's and women's bodybuilding, in-line skating, roller hockey, sky diving and the several varieties of crazy business that go under the heading of "extreme games."

Should the NBA decide to take the year off, our institutions of higher learning will be there to appease our basketball appetites. Every major collegiate men's conference has a regular-season national TV contract with one network or another, there are local game telecasts galore, and the National Collegiate Athletic Association women's and men's national tournaments, 63 games each, pack the screen in March.

One can argue whether the above-named new sports, and others, would be around without TV to nurture them. Steve Bornstein,

ESPN's president, insists they would be. "A sport has to exist on its own merits. TV can only complement it," he avers. It's not important whether he's right or wrong, though; the games are there, people pay to watch them, and in a country the size of the U.S., all those TV ratings of 0.2% or 0.4% add up to a lot of viewers.

In such a context, the answers to some perplexing questions become clearer. Many observers, for instance, failed to foresee the precipitous drop-off at the gate that accompanied the return of baseball after the 1994 players' strike, because their point of reference was the attendance-record-setting 1982 season that followed the 50-day walkout of 1981. It may be true that baseball's accumulated history of labor strife finally caused fans to choke, but it's also obvious that the increased number of spectating alternatives has given the game's usual customers more places to turn.

Similarly, the answer to the question of why the sports fans of the vast Los Angeles area voted with their feet to let their two NFL franchises leave town could be another question: Who wants to pay to watch a couple of mediocre football teams when there's better stuff on the tube?

The failure of soccer to gain a permanent U.S. foothold in the wake of the smashing success of the 1994 World Cup on these shores traces mostly to its inability to carve out a satisfactory calendar niche, I think. Surely, that's better explanation than the one about the U.S. being populated by people who inherited antisoccer genes from forebears who fled their Old Country homelands to escape the sport.

So while NBA moguls, players and agents have done their best —or worst—and only the ballot-counting remains, the rest of us might begin thinking about a winter without that league. Who knows, we could get to like women's bodybuilding so much, we might never go back to the hardwoods.

● *Sept. 8, 1995*

COLLEGE BALL

Part 8

How Coaches
Rake It In

MEMPHIS, TENN.

I was told that if I wanted to understand the business of
big-time college coaching, I should go to Memphis and
look up the papers on the tax-evasion trial of Dana Kirk.

Kirk coached the men's basketball team at Memphis
State University between 1979 and 1986. His annual
university salary in that span ranged from $35,000 to
$62,500, but the government placed his total earnings
for two of those years—1982 and 1983—at $453,000,
and charged he didn't pay taxes on $162,000 of that.

Kirk's trial ended on Nov. 16, 1988. He didn't tes-
tify; his lawyers affirmed he didn't report some income,
but said he was guilty only of sloppy record-keeping and
of regarding some taxable items as gifts. After hearing
eight weeks of testimony touching on the coach's financial dealings into 1986, a jury disagreed, finding him
guilty on four of six counts of tax evasion, and one of
three counts of obstructing justice by seeking to intimi-
date witnesses against him. He was fined and ordered to
satisfy the tax man, and sentenced to a year and a day in
prison. He served four months of that term, and was released in August, 1989.

Before proceeding, a few points seem in order. One
is that 1982 and '83 figures don't do justice to what high-
profile college basketball and football coaches can earn
today. Another is that while Kirk was successful, guiding
teams to five NCAA tournament berths and one (1985)

155

Final Four in his seven seasons at MSU, he didn't nearly rank with such coaching icons as Dean Smith, Bobby Knight, Jerry Tarkanian, Denny Crum or John Thompson.

A third point is that nothing that follows should suggest that the coaching fraternity is populated by lawbreakers. Indeed, according to Murray Sperber, associate professor of English and American studies at Indiana University and author of the book *College Sports Inc.*, which explores the financial underpinnings of college athletics, that's exactly the point.

"Kirk didn't do anything illegal or very unusual in gathering his outside income. It was just that he didn't pay his taxes on some of it," Sperber says. "Coaches not only are permitted to scrape up every dollar they can, they're expected to, and it's okay if they employ their universities' names in the process. It's routine for coaches to use their schools' seals or emblems as props in product endorsements. No other university employees are allowed to do anything remotely like that."

Sperber estimates that at least 50 current college basketball or football coaches earn $250,000 a year or more, and that a dozen or so top the $500,000 mark. That's quite a lot for overseeing programs involving as few as a dozen athletes, and for athletic departments that are apt to wind up the year in the red. Institutional salary rarely accounts for more than $100,000 of that. Most comes from athletic-shoe contracts, summer camps, radio-TV deals, booster-club gifts, perks such as the free use of autos and speaking and coaching-clinic fees.

Some of the latter can be no more than thinly veiled kickbacks for bringing teams to games or tournaments: Kirk received $10,000 for participating in "press conferences and/or clinics" connected with MSU's appearance in the 1983 Winston Tire Classic in Los Angeles, and $5,000, in 1985, for playing in the San Diego Holiday Bowl tournament. Government investigators quoted a Holiday Bowl official as saying that coaches typically collect between $2,000 and $15,000 for such dates, depending on the "name recognition" of their schools.

In some ways, Kirk wasn't as inventive as his fellow basketball coaches. His MSU contract didn't include the attendance or won-lost performance bonuses negotiated by Bill Frieder at Arizona State, or the 10% cut Tarkanian gets of Nevada-Las Vegas's share of NCAA tourney revenues (that was worth $100,325 to him last year, when UNLV won the national title).

Moreover, Kirk got some jobs because his fees were considered reasonable. A meat-packing group said it hired him as a meeting speaker, for $750, because the fellow it wanted, Notre Dame football coach Lou Holtz (then at Arkansas), asked for $2,500.

Nonetheless, his trial revealed both a total and detailed income picture made rare by the reluctance of his erstwhile colleagues to discuss theirs. For instance, when Georgetown's Thompson in June turned down a reported five-year, $3.5 million offer to coach the NBA Denver Nuggets, it was widely speculated that that would have amounted to a pay cut for him. In response to a call asking Thompson to talk about his income, a school spokesman said the coach regarded it as a "private matter." He added: "I wouldn't hold the presses waiting for him to change his mind."

According to trial testimony and related documents, the government claimed Kirk earned $171,707 in 1982 and $281,338 the next year. By one witness's count, the coach had 23 sources of income in addition to his MSU salary.

Kirk's summer basketball camps, which utilized MSU facilities at little cost to him (he paid $100 a week for gym rent), took in an average of $37,000 a year between 1980 and '83. His three-year TV contract with a Memphis station, ending in 1986, paid him $50,000 annually, and he added about $21,000 a year for a radio show. His shoe contract, with Nike, was worth up to $36,000 a year during the period covered in the trial.

In 1982 and '83, he received $10,000 "bonuses" from the Golden Tigers Club, a boosters' group. He got $500 a month, plus the free use of two cars, from local Ford dealers. Two commercials for a local paint company netted a $3,000 paint job on his home.

He did not disdain small stuff: For allowing a song titled "I'm a Big Blue Fan from Tigerland" to be played on his TV show and at halftime at MSU basketball games, he received $500 plus a $1 royalty on each record and tape sale. He sold, for $1 each, some of the 10,000 Cokes donated to his summer camp by a Coca-Cola bottler.

He didn't lack for chutzpah: He sold a pair of complimentary season tickets to a booster for $1,000, and pocketed the $5,000 Holiday Bowl fee, *after* he'd been informed a grand jury was looking into his finances.

And he still doesn't: On his release from prison, he announced he'd seek a presidential pardon.

• *Dec. 14, 1991*

Horning in on the Shoe Bonanza

I

n college sports, the players come and go but the coaches linger on. Thus, they're the stars, for better or worse. There's been a lot of the latter in the college basketball season that climaxes with Saturday and Monday's NCAA Final Four in Charlotte, N.C.

You had coaches leading a retrograde movement to erase many of the academic reforms so painfully grafted onto their turf over the past several years, and plotting boycotts if they didn't get their way. You had coaches exchanging nasty words on court and hurling threats of mayhem off of it. You had one petty tyrant—guess who?—kicking one of his players and head-butting another during tirades. The kid he kicked was his son.

It all cries out for an antidote and, fortunately, there is one. It comes from the University of St. Thomas, a large (enrollment 10,000) small school in St. Paul, Minn., not to be confused with the University of St. Thomas in Houston, St. Thomas University in Miami or St. Thomas Aquinas in Sparkill, N.Y. Its focus is the big-bucks athletic-shoe contract, that most egregious of coachly excesses.

Paul Alper and Robert Raymond, associate professors in the department of quantitative methods and computer sciences at St. Thomas, have wondered why the sideline ranters should sop up all the campus shoe gravy, especially since the players' feet, not the coaches', are the showcases. Last fall, the two pitched Nike, Inc., a prominent gravy dispenser, with the proposition that ordinary Mr. Chips types like themselves be given the chance to function as sole models.

They proposed an experiment under which they'd wear shoes Nike furnished in one class each taught and "ordinary street shoes" in another, conduct before-and-after surveys of their students' shoe-buying behavior in both, and share the results with the concern. Nike bit, making Alper and Raymond probably the only non-coaching college-faculty members in the land to have their own shoe contracts. The test is underway, and the world awaits the results.

If you detect one or more tongues in one or more of the cheeks mentioned above, you're correct, although, when asked, the profs are cagy about identifying whose is where. "He [Raymond] is in it for the free pair of sneakers. I'm on a crusade to show how absurdly over-blown the college sports-entertainment scene has become," maintains Alper, a squash-playing, 58-year-old size 10. "Only in the United States of today would the typical university student be able to flawlessly pronounce and spell Krzyzewski and yet be unable to distinguish Socrates from Sitting Bull, not to mention a median from a standard deviation."

"I'm in on this because my office is right down the hall from his [Alper's], and he tries to drag me into all his nutty schemes. This is about the least-inflammatory thing he's come up with," retorts Raymond, a sedentary, 50-year-old size 7½. He adds: "At least I'm actually carrying out the experiment. He's been busy asserting his integrity."

(Krzyzewski, of course, is Mike, coach of the Final Four-perennial Duke Blue Devils and possessor of a shoe pact, with Nike, whose payout contains more figures than the Elgin marbles.)

Nike is unfazed by such revelations. "We get so many requests for sponsorship—everyone from preschool rope jumpers to 70-year-old marathoners—that we have to turn down most of them, but this was such a novel suggestion we couldn't resist," says Douglas Stamm, who carries the title of divisional sports category manager at the Beaverton, Ore., company. "We thought the test results would be worthwhile on a cost-benefits basis even if they're less than conclusive. We're giving those guys a lot less than we're paying Michael Jordan, you know."

Nike has a goodly number of notable college basketball coaches on its endorsement roll. Besides Krzyzewski, they include Lute Olsen, whose Arizona team will be a contestant at Charlotte; Dean Smith of North Carolina's 1993 national champions; John Thompson of Georgetown; Bobby Cremins of Georgia Tech; Steve Fisher of Michigan; Bob Huggins of Cincinnati; and Stu Jackson of Wisconsin. Some coaches pocket annual payments from the company, or other shoemakers, that exceed their institutional salaries. Nike, however, doesn't wish to debate the propriety of that practice.

"Sometimes we negotiate fees with individual coaches, sometimes with university athletic departments; the schools call the shots on that, not us," says Stamm. "It's they that must determine what's fair compensation for the people who work for them. The impetus for any changes in the disposition of endorsement money also must come from them."

Meantime, back at St. Thomas, an NCAA Division III school that doesn't give athletic scholarships, the Great Shoe Experiment hasn't proceeded without merriment. The word around campus is that Reebok is behind the whole thing, paying both men to sport its competitor's products.

Alper avers that Nike already has got more than its shoes' worth from the publicity the stunt has generated. *The Aquin*, the university's student newspaper, ran a front-page story about it, right under a piece headlined "Student Suspended For Ear Biting" (what's going on at colleges these days, anyway?!), and it's been featured on a local television station's evening news program. "I didn't see the TV bit because I haven't owned a set since 1958. But my mom saw it, and was very pleased," he says.

Raymond notes that, in light of the "before" survey of the class in which he's wearing his Nikes, it'll be difficult to show that his influence over his students has been positive. "Fourteen of the 18 said they'd already bought at least one pair of Nikes during the past year," he notes. "I don't know how I could top that."

He continues: "Maybe we professors could do like the farmers do, and get shoe companies to pay us *not* to wear their shoes." But he pauses and adds: "I guess, that would be blackmail, wouldn't it?"

• *April 1, 1994*

NCAA Gender Wars

T he old joke has it that "incongruous" is the place where they make the laws, but that's been no joke when it comes to the National Collegiate Athletic Association, which regulates much of college sports in this land. That group will meet in convention for five days beginning tomorrow in San Diego, as often amid conflicting currents.

On the one hand, delegates will be applauding their leadership's latest television coup, the deal with CBS Sports that will add $1.725 billion (that's right, *billion*) to their coffers from this academic year through 2001-2002, mostly for the rights to televise the men's 64-team national basketball tournament.

On the other hand, they'll be voting on a measure that could sound the death knell for one men's varsity sport—gymnastics—and, possibly, prepare the way for other such actions.

The item that affects men's gymnastics is No. 104 on the group's lengthy agenda. No. 104, if passed, would extend for two years a moratorium on the requirement that the participation of 40 member schools is necessary for the staging of a national championship in a sport. Gymnastics, down to a current 32 schools, fell below that limit several years ago, and its tournament has been given reprieves since. If 104 fails—and it is opposed by the NCAA's executive committee—the 1995 meet in Columbus, Ohio, will be the last.

"If that happens, I think we'll lose 10 or 12 more teams quickly, and you can pretty much kiss the sport goodbye at our level," says Richard Aronson, the former coach at the University of Massachusetts-Lowell and executive director of the National Association of College Gymnastics Coaches. He adds: "The real pity is that this doesn't have to happen. It's a good sport and the money for the [national] competition is there. If it weren't for other things that are going on, I don't think we'd be in this bind."

Ask the supporters of other men's "minor" (i.e., non-revenue-producing) sports about those "other things," and many mince no words. Their team numbers also have dwindled, and they blame it at least partly on the drive for gender equity in the distribution of college athletic funds.

"Every men's sport except football and basketball is feeling the pinch—schools are making their gender numbers look better at our expense," declares T.J. Kerr of California State-Bakersfield, president of the National Wrestling Coaches Association. "I don't think that's what people had in mind when they started pushing for gender equity in sports. I also think there's some irony involved. When you talk about student-athletes, you really mean the minor-sports kids, who compete for the love of it instead of as a means to a big-money pro contract. We're what college sports are supposed to be about."

The gender-equity effort stems from a provision of federal education legislation passed in 1972, the so-called Title IX. Nothing much happened until women began taking schools to court on the matter about a dozen years ago. Prodded by adverse rulings, many schools have responded as much by eliminating men's sports as by adding women's programs.

NCAA officials maintain that dropping the national championship in men's gymnastics shouldn't be lumped under that practice. They note that insurance problems have caused the sport to wane on the high-school level, thinning an already spare recruiting base, and that keeping the national championships hasn't checked its decline among the colleges. "At some point you have to decide there are better places to use your funds," an NCAA spokesman says.

Gymnastics boosters counter that football, too, has insurance problems, and that, in any case, their sport's plight isn't unique. Indeed, if the 40-schools requirement is upheld, national championships in men's fencing and water polo seem in imminent danger. Fencing participation now stands at 42 schools, down from 48 in 1990 and 71 in 1982; water polo has dipped to 41 from 55 four years ago.

Wrestling, with 104 participating institutions in Division I alone, faces no such immediate threat, but its decline has been no less alarming in terms of sheer numbers: 136 Division I schools had wrestling programs in 1982, 112 had them in 1990.

When a school eliminates a sport, it usually blames budgetary considerations. No surprise there, but there's often more to it. For instance, when Princeton dumped wrestling in 1993, blame was pinned to financial retrenchment, but when alums came forward and offered to underwrite the activity, they were turned down on grounds that the university reserved the right to order its priorities.

"It'd be fair to say that gender equity was one of the factors in our dropping of wrestling. That's part of every athletics department decision these days," says Gary Walters, who became Princeton's athletics director after the move was carried out.

It's notable, I think, that the carnage among the men's minor sports is decried by some on the supposed "other" side of the gender-equity issue. One such is Donna Lopiano, executive director of the Women's Sports Foundation and former director of women's athletics at the University of Texas. Says she: "The point of any civil-rights law is to bring the disadvantaged up to the level of the advantaged. It's unfortunate that so many colleges have turned that around."

Ms. Lopiano believes that if cuts must be made they should come from the fattest sport. That would be football, of course, where the care and feeding of 85 full-scholarship players at the typical Division I school is the main obstacle to the sporting equality of the sexes on campus. Cut that number to 60 or so—or, better yet, base its room-and-board scholarship component on need—and "most of the problem would go away," she says, adding, "If everyone did it, competition would be maintained, and the revenue flow would continue."

Ms. Lopiano continues: "The way the courts have been ruling, it's not so much a question of if football will be cut, but when. Why shouldn't the schools get ahead of a crisis, for a change?"

There's a thought that should warm things a bit this weekend in San Diego.

• *Jan. 6, 1995*

It's the Core
That's Rotten

I n matters of morality, we're told to hate the sin but love
the sinner, but when big-time college sports are involved,
the temptation is to turn that proposition on its head.
Thus it is that lovers of football can rejoice that another
college season is scheduled to begin tomorrow when Virginia travels to play Michigan, but should lament the circumstances of the engagement.

The game is dubbed the "Pigskin Classic," but it is
classic only in terms of its commercial underpinnings.
Some of its proceeds will go into a football coaches' retirement fund, some to the College Football Hall of
Fame, a much-traveled entity of dubious antecedents
that's about to reopen in South Bend, Ind. Mostly,
though, it gives the participating schools a dispensation
from the powers-that-be to expand their regular seasons
to 12 games from the standard 11. That means they get
an extra week's work out of their players and an extra
payday, guaranteed to come to at least $650,000 each.
And so what if classes at the host University of Michigan
don't start until Sept. 5.

It's enough, by itself, to choke a horse, but if the
horse had been paying attention, he probably was gag-
ging already. The summer docket has been filled with entries that attest to the corruption spawned by the
competition among the college-sports heavyweights. Offenses included, but weren't limited to, illegal loans and

payoffs to players, the ignoring of positive drug tests, and attempts at institutional coverups of same.

As usual, of course, more schools are out of official trouble than are in it. This allows their officers and alums to opine that the "system" is sound but that a few bad apples are spoiling the barrel. It's apparent to all but the willfully obtuse, though, that the system *is* the problem, that corruption is the rule, and that the payoff allegations that most occupy college sports' regulators are the least of it.

The real issue—the way the quest for success in the revenue-producing sports of football and basketball is undermining college's academic missions—emerged in a case involving Baylor University. The forum was not the National Collegiate Athletic Association, but a federal court in Waco, Texas. It sentenced two former Baylor assistant basketball coaches to probation for wire fraud in connection with a scheme in which correspondence-course tests were falsified in an attempt to secure the Baylor eligibility of five junior-college recruits.

The institution that offered those courses was Southeastern College of the Assemblies of God, in Lakeland, Fla. It allowed correspondence students to gather credits by passing exams that could easily be taken by stand-ins. In its Aug. 7 issue, *Sports Illustrated* magazine reported that investigators had found that 55 NCAA schools had enrolled athletes who'd beefed up their transcripts with questionable credits and grades from Southeastern, which it called a "genie-in-the-bottle" for rule-skirting coaches.

Even without such hanky-panky, many colleges stretch their admissions standards to sign up jocks, then ease their way through school with "gut" courses and appeals to sympathetic faculty members for grade leniency. Besides taking up space that could be used by better-qualified students, these practices devalue the diplomas of athletes who surmount the burdens imposed by their sports and manage to get an education worth the name.

"Far too often, jocks pretend to go to school, and the schools pretend to graduate them," says Jon Ericson, professor of communications and former provost at Drake University, and a long-time critic of college-sports practices.

There's a widespread belief that, whatever their defects, high-powered sports programs generate money that helps the rest of a university. Often, that's not true. The last time the NCAA looked, in 1993, the athletics-department budgets of 24% of the members of its football Division IA—the big-timers—finished in the red, and 4%

more only broke even. Those figures would have been considerably higher if gifts to athletics departments, for which those entities compete with the broader university, weren't included. They made up 15% of sports revenues that year.

Similarly, the view that schools with successful teams draw more general alumni and corporate support than those less favored has been debunked by a number of studies, including one by a couple of faculty members at the University of Notre Dame.

College officers, teachers and alums who care about more than sports bragging rights could begin to correct the situation by campaigning for their schools to eliminate the core of the problem, the athletic scholarship. This isn't the radical step it may appear to be: That's already the stance of the NCAA's largest football-playing membership category, which it calls Division III.

I've been to Division III games, and can report that they look, sound and smell like the games the big-timers play. I take that back; they smell better. Naturally, they sell fewer tickets, but that's okay because they don't have elephantine programs to support.

After that, schools could do other sensible things, such as reducing the football season to between Labor Day and Thanksgiving, and the basketball season to between Dec. 15 and March 15. Limiting road trips to four-hour bus rides also would be nice.

About 10 years ago, I expressed those opinions at a forum on college sports, and was approached afterward by a man who identified himself as the alumni director of a Big Ten school. He said he agreed with everything that I, and several of the other panel members, said on the subject, but lamented the possibility of ever seeing real change. "It's like the arms race—if the U.S.S.R. does something that may help it win, the U.S. has to do it," he said.

But, hey, the arms race ended, didn't it? And so did the U.S.S.R.

• *Aug. 25, 1995*

So Long, It's Been Good to Hate You

DALLAS

T he weather was fine here on Saturday morning, and the prospect of another renewal of an old football rivalry might have been expected to light up the midway of the Texas State Fair, next to which the Cotton Bowl stands. But this 73rd meeting between the teams from the University of Texas and the Dallas-based Southern Methodist University would be the last for the foreseeable future, and made the occasion bittersweet at best for many fans.

"I think it's a real shame things couldn't have continued the way they were. It was good for the schools and good for the state of Texas," said Blackshear Jameson, SMU '42.

"I'm going to miss the rivalries and the convenience of being able to see the state schools play so many games so close to home," said Sid Gibson, Texas '56. "It's too bad things had to come to this."

The tectonic plates of college sports are shifting, however, and the Texas-SMU rivalry got swallowed up in one of the resulting holes. Schools such as Arkansas, Penn State, Florida State and Miami have joined conferences or changed affiliations during the last few years. Now, the entire 81-year-old Southwest Conference, all eight of whose members are domiciled in Texas, will break up after the current school year, its pieces scattering hither and yon.

Four of the SWC schools—Texas, Texas A&M, Texas Tech and Baylor—will turn the Midlands-based Big Eight Conference (Nebraska, Oklahoma, Colorado, et al.) into the Big 12. Smaller SMU, Rice and Texas Christian will join the geographically vast Western Athletic Conference, while Houston will take its business to a new amalgam called Conference USA, whose strong suit will be basketball. Starting next season, you won't be able to tell the conferences without a program, much less the players.

In this changing panorama, though, the story of the SWC's demise stands out. Like many a Texas tale, it involves money, blood and other juicy stuff. Further, and predictably, it should only accelerate the commercial bent of the games our institutions of higher learning conduct.

The reason for the split was the lack of network-television salability of a one-state athletic conference. The league's main internal division was between its big schools (Texas's enrollment is about 48,000) and small ones (Rice's is about 2,600). But those things were exacerbated by athlete-recruiting battles that left emotions, and an occasional knuckle, raw from the Panhandle to the Rio Grande.

"Having so many close-together schools competing against each other for pretty much the same kids led to hard feelings and negative recruiting, and some whistle-blowing," confirms Kyle Kallander, the league's commissioner. "It got to where schools were saying that if they couldn't land a kid, nobody else in the conference would, either."

The upshot was a rap sheet for recruiting violations unmatched in college sports: Every SWC member save Rice has been sanctioned for same by the National Collegiate Athletic Association. SMU's violations were so blatant (Ron Meyer, its football coach from 1976 through 1981, used $100 bills as calling cards) and deep-seated (scandals involved an athletics director, several school trustees and the regimes of two head football coaches) that its football program is the only one to receive an NCAA "death penalty," which cost it the 1987 and '88 seasons.

SMU alums are quick to assert that their school didn't do anything its rivals hadn't done. They and others blame the conference's breakup on the desire of the University of Texas, the league's 600-pound gorilla for most purposes, to strut upon a larger stage. It's no accident, they say, that rumors of Texas going alone into the Big Eight, PAC 10 or Big 10 have been widespread for years.

UT officials deny causing the split. "Anybody who thinks we could leave the conference alone doesn't understand Texas politics—the legislature would never permit it," says Christine Plonsky, the school's associate athletics director. "The fact is that, with conferences now having to make their own TV deals, there aren't enough TV sets in our state to justify a good one, and the SWC couldn't survive without one."

The Big 12-bound group should have things easier than their erstwhile confreres. Texas, for instance, will be able to maintain its two annual football "big games"—with Oklahoma and Texas A&M—while *it* always has been the big date for SMU, Rice, TCU and Houston. Moreover, by moving to a 16-school WAC, which will cover some 1,500 miles east to west without counting the University of Hawaii, SMU's athletic travel bill will increase by between $250,000 and $300,000 a year, according to athletics director Jim Copeland.

"I think if you took a vote of our alums they'd favor keeping the SWC as it is; there's sadness over losing the old rivalries," says Copeland. But he adds: "We're excited by the WAC and the possibilities it offers."

There also might be excitement at SMU about the prospect of winning more football games; the school hasn't had a winning season since it resumed the sport, and had lost three of four this year going into the Texas game. It also carried a 22-46-4 won-lost-tied mark in a series that began in 1916 and has been populated with such as Doak Walker, Kyle Rote, Bobby Layne and Tommy Nobis.

The loss side of both those ledgers grew by one on Saturday as a result of a 35-10 Texas victory. The game was witnessed by just 26,921 people in the 68,000-seat stadium, indicating that, maybe, nostalgia ain't what it used to be.

Even among the young, however, there was a sense that something important was ending. "I'll be sorry we won't be playing Texas any more. I read about the SMU-Texas games as a kid, and hoped to be a part of four of them," said SMU's sophomore quarterback from Arlington, Tex., David James, after the fray.

He continued: "A couple of my high school buddies play for Texas, so they got bragging rights on me the last two summers because they beat us. It'll be a shame I'll never be able to get them back."

• *Oct. 2, 1995*

WORLD BALL

Part 9

Fighting for Fidel

SANTA CLARA, CUBA

J.

ust outside this provincial capital of some 250,000 residents, tourists lounge in the sun beside the pool at Los Caneyes, a resort built to resemble a Polynesian village. Competing with the Latin music coming over the complex's sound system, however, is the thump of artillery fire from a nearby military installation.

At Sala Amistad, the local sports arena, the press room bristles with telex and photo-facsimile machines, paraphernalia of modern journalism. But the place's communications system begins with Soviet-made, hand-cranked telephones, updated versions of the kind that disappeared 50 years ago in other countries.

Such incongruities also extend to the goals of Cuba's sports establishment and the current policies of the Castro government. Cuba's sports program, like those of its one-time Soviet and East European mentors, is geared toward advertising politics through the winning of medals in international showcases, the showiest of which is the quadrennial Olympic Games. But while Cuban athletes prepare for Seoul in 1988, officials tell visiting journalists that they probably won't be making the trip.

"If the Games are not equally divided between North and South Korea, Cuba won't participate," said the government guide for a small American press group that came here for a U.S.-Cuban boxing dual meet Saturday. Reminded that the stand goes well beyond what most other communist countries are seeking for their North Korean confreres, the fellow merely shrugged. "They may participate if they wish, but we won't," said he. "We are definite about this."

The fact that Cuba feels it can stand alone on matters of sport—or, at least, say it will—reflects its growing prominence in the field. Pound for pound of humanity, this nation of 10 million souls ranks with the East Germans at the top of the medal-collecting heap. It won 20 of them, including eight golds, at the 1980 Olympics in Moscow, the last in which it competed. Its gold-medal haul there was the fourth highest of any nation, and topped that of Great Britain, France, Poland and Hungary, among other more-populous places.

At last summer's Pan Am Games in Indianapolis, Cubans took home 175 baubles, second only to the U.S.'s 369. On a per-capita basis, its count was 11 times that of the U.S.

Those are impressive numbers, to be sure, but there is a tendency among Americans, including American sportswriters, to make more of them than they deserve, and to ascribe them to superior knowledge. A visitor to Cuba sees rundown housing similar to that of other Caribbean countries, and roads filled with pre-1959 Chevys and Fords, stuck together with spit and gum. Yet we believe our own popular fiction and prowl the sports complexes in search of Rocky IV-type technology. Our failure to find it only reinforces our conviction that it exists, hidden.

Our hosts, on to us, smile and give us ideology instead. Cuban officials insisted, repeatedly and with straight faces, that their country's new-found sports prominence stems from the regime's shucking of the capitalist professional-sports mold and making athletics the right and joy of "the people." All those people running around all day in sweat suits are, really, students or "workers" rounding out their socialist personalities, they said.

The fiction extends to athletes past as well as present. One focus of journalistic curiosity here was the whereabouts of Teofilo Stevenson, Cuba's three-time Olympic heavyweight boxing champion and one of the nation's sports idols. He had fallen from public view, reportedly after an accident in which a motorcyclist was killed by an auto he was driving.

Yes, there was such an accident, but Stevenson was absolved of blame after a trial, we were told. We were further informed that this giant man, known for his taste for the good life, is, as before, an undergraduate student of physical education in his hometown of Las Tunas. He is 36 years old, and one can only hope he will get his degree soon.

In fact, Cuba's sports program differs little from those of communist Eastern Europe. It identifies promising athletes young, gives them special training, and filters them through local and national age-group competitions. Survivors are rewarded with whatever goodies the government can muster, including the prized ability to travel abroad.

Cuba has applied this system most successfully to boxing, a sport in which it was strong, albeit haphazardly, in pre-Castro days. At Inder, the national sports governing body in Havana, Raul Villanueva, Cuba's boxing chief, happily spouts statistics: 494 coaches now against 50 in 1960; 185 gyms against 35; 19,300 boxers currently in serious competition. Reporters press him on training techniques, especially weightlifting. "It's perhaps an element in our success, but not the main thing," he says.

In Santa Clara, the Cuban boxers go through final preparations for their bouts with the Americans, of which they would win nine of 10. They skip rope, smack punching bags and spar, just like boxers everywhere, and in a typical, spartan gym. How about weight training or more exotic techniques? Alcides Sagarra, the longtime coach of the nation's world and Olympic championship teams, isn't impressed. "We have natural qualities for boxing—speed, rhythm and courage. We train hard. We want to win very badly," he says.

And, of course, it's the only game available for the same kind of tough, hungry young men that boxing attracts elsewhere. That's unlike the U.S., where the amateur ranks empty into the pros after every Olympic year.

Rangy Felix Savon, Cuba's world champion 201-pounder, is asked about his goal in the sport. "An Olympic medal," he says without hesitation. And if there is to be no Olympics for his country? "Then I fight in the World Cup, World Championships, wherever the team goes," he says. "If you are a fighter, you fight. Isn't that right?"

• *Dec. 18, 1987*

Going for the Goldeye

A fter a series of events too complex to recount here, a sensitive, bewildered Ugandan teen-ager finds himself fostered out to a family in a small town in Western Canada. In keeping with the custom of the country, he is sent off to learn to play hockey. His first lesson at the local rink is in the manly art of body checking.

"I am against violence! It is against my principles!" he protests to his coach.

"This isn't violence. This is sport," the coach tells him.

In fact, it wasn't sport, it was art—theater to be exact. The scene was from the play "Welcome to the NHL," presented by the Alberta Theater Project as part of the Olympic Arts Festival, which began three weeks before the Winter Games here and will run to their conclusion Sunday.

The Olympic charter requires that Olympic host cities give visitors something to do at night by providing "cultural" attractions "of equal standard" to the Games' sports events, and Calgary has busted a gut to comply. It declares that its festival, featuring scores of offerings in theater, dance, music and the visual arts, is the largest ever associated with a Winter Games, and one can only believe it.

Almost nightly, those with the wherewithal can choose from a smorgasbord of entertainments as well as from actual smorgasbords, Swedish cuisine being one of the many available at restaurants here. A little box-office pull helps, too; some 70% of the performances have been sold out, so getting tickets can be tough.

Even more difficult is determining what is "Olympic" about this Olympic Arts Festival. Local sponsors apparently have given the matter some thought, because they have decided what is not Olympic. When the Banana Maxx Lounge downtown announced its intention to hold a "Nude Miss Olympics" contest, it was visited by local Olympic committeemen and told it couldn't use the Olympic label. Not wishing to tangle with the organization's legal talent, it relented and changed the name of the pageant to "Nude Miss O-word."

The Joffrey Ballet had no such problem, nor did the Julliard String Quartet. Trouble was, both did their things and left before the beginning of the Games. Other prime attractions, like the Calgary Opera Association's production of "Porgy and Bess," overlapped the athletic action (and got raves). But let's face it, you can see "Porgy" anywhere.

So this Olympic visitor, his schedule circumscribed by the need to watch a bit of O-word sports, decided to do some editing and seek out events that had a Canadian, winter or Olympic tie. Since I set aside abundant time for eating in any venue, a quest for the local cuisine also was included.

The most rewarding of these pursuits has been in the visual-arts area; just about everywhere you turn here, you see works of merit with an Olympic twist. Of these, two stand out: the Arts Festival's advertisement showing four bobsledders crouched in a pink ballet slipper, and an exhibition in the concourse of the Saddledome, the primary arena for hockey and figure skating, of masks used by the strange and primitive tribe of hockey goalies. The poster of the bright and ferocious masks has become the Games' bestseller.

At Prince's Island Park near downtown stands art of a different scale, the fruits of the Olympic International Snow Sculpting Competition. The two dozen 20-feet-high works have become a mecca for small children and their moms and dads. It's one of the few festival events that's also a contest, and Finland won first prize for the sort of abstract creation judges generally favor. The people's choice, though, was New Zealand's carousel of circus animals. "I want to go *in* that," announced one toddler, awarding it his personal gold medal.

The show on the boards has been more uneven. The Olympic Theatersports Tournament purported to match teams of actors from various locales in an evening of improvisional comedy, but the teams from England and Denmark turned out to be almost identical, and, anyway, how funny can a sketch about a guy who caught pneumonia waiting to see the pope's appearance in Halifax be?

"Welcome to the NHL" was cute, especially the performance of the Uganda-born lead, George Seremba. But—wouldn't you know it?—the "kid" circumvents his moral aversion to rough stuff by playing goalie, and ends up liking hockey.

Most testing of all has been my search for a unique Western Canada cuisine. I asked around, and was told to forget it, that this was a steak-and-potatoes town, and that folks weren't all that crazy about potatoes.

But I persisted. At the Mt. Royal College cafeteria, my usual breakfast venue, I spied "Egg McBeaver" on the menu board. It turned out to be the same egg, cheese, ham and muffin concoction peddled by another McOutfit. Wincing about my waistline, I tried the brown gravy that always accompanies french fried potatoes here. I sought, but did not find, Winnipeg Goldeye, a smoked fish that's reputed to be almost as good as smoked whitefish.

Then, success. A call to Canada Safeway, food purveyor for the athletes' village, revealed that the local game delicacies of buffalo and rabbit were being scarfed there in fair quantity. "If we have a local cuisine, that's it," a Safeway spokesman said.

A few more calls led me to Hunter's Horn, a downtown restaurant specializing in game. There I met chef George Kuban, a native of Czechoslovakia, who told me what to expect. "Buffalo tastes like beef, only leaner and denser," he said. "Rabbit tastes like chicken, only heavier." He served me both and was right, except that he omitted the small bones that I kept finding in my rabbit. The highlight of the meal was Mr. Kuban's tangy buffalo sausage, which, he confided, included some beef for binding.

Game food would be more plentiful here if it weren't for unreasonable state regulations, Mr. Kuban said. "Elk is raised in Alberta, but they have to sell it to a wholesaler in Saskatchewan and I have to buy it from him," he noted. If Alberta would get with it, he went on, game food might be as popular here as in his Czech homeland. "That's where I learned to cook it," he said. "It's the national cuisine."

• *Feb. 23, 1988*

Putting on the Dog

SEOUL, KOREA

T he South Koreans value the world's good opinion, and on the bus coming back from a tour of the North-South truce line at Panmunjom, a guide passed around a questionnaire for visiting journalists. It asked about our impressions of Korea and Koreans, as well as some specific items about press accommodations here.

I completed my form, and handed it to the guide, a young Korean woman who spoke some English. She wanted an oral report as well. "What do you think of our Games?" she asked.

I mumbled a few compliments, and she lit up. "Yes!" she said. "The Games are very *big*, don't you think?"

I'm not sure whether her expression was meant to be taken literally. "Big" could have meant "wonderful," or some such. But on reflection, I concluded that maybe a literal interpretation was best. Seoul has put on what Ed Sullivan would have called a "really big show" (or, as Ed would have pronounced, it, "shoo").

Most of the facilities here come in one size, extra large, and so do the cultural attractions that, as an Olympic host, this city is presenting along with the running, splashing, punching and pedaling.

For music, we have had the Moscow Philharmonic. A Japanese troupe presented five-and-a-half hours of kabuki *sturm und drang*. An exhibition of sculpture at Olympic Park, the 530-acre layout that is one of the

Games' two, five-stadium centerpieces (the other is the Seoul Sports Complex), features a steel crescent longer than Reggie Roby can punt. All across the city, huge Olympic flags are held aloft by huge balloons. Nowhere in Seoul is one of them out of sight.

That industrious Korea is out to impress the world through these Games is no secret and, as a newly rich nation, it's no surprise that its tastes run to the grandiose. Moreover, much of the big stuff succeeds, even spectacularly. The 70,000-seat Olympic Stadium, at the Seoul Complex, is a work of art itself with its curved roof and undulating exterior lines. The adjacent baseball stadium, also new, would look good on the South Side of Chicago, and has a real-grass field to boot. The lights of the Velodrome at Olympic Park shine at night like a carnival ride. Just the look of it was enough to entice me to sample bicycle racing, a strange, stylized sport.

Seoul, an immense metropolis of 10 million souls, is itself something special. It's perhaps the cleanest big city on earth, and the freest of graffiti. To see the latter, you must peer from Panmunjom into North Korea, where the Korean-language symbols meaning "reunification" are mowed into one hillside, and others saying "We are anti-American" decorate another.

Whatever the intentions of its organizers, though, the Olympics aren't all pomp and polish. It's not clear whom to thank for this; probably not the government that, even in its new, democratic form, still takes a dim view of pointed humor.

For example, the Foreign Correspondents' Club, in an effort to woo visiting writers to its downtown bar, made some posters showing a reporter in a gas mask tapping on a lap-top word processor, in need of liquid succor. The gas mask, of course, was a reference to the way police here have dealt with student anti-government demonstrators. Censors killed that effort, and the club's come-on instead pictures a chubby, sweaty guy in glasses staggering under an Olympic torch.

The powers-that-be, however, either didn't get or ignored the implication of one of the Olympic Park sculpture exhibits, a 19-foot-tall thumb by the French artist Cesar. It has been labeled "Going My Way?" by tourists who've spent a half-hour or more trying to flag a taxi in the Itaewon entertainment district.

Funnier yet (and more subversive) is the sculpture "Dog's Own World," by Mark Brusse of the Netherlands. It depicts, in stone, a pooch at the bottom of some steps, looking upward at a square hole in a large slab that resembles nothing so much as a guillotine.

The work should have touched a nerve here because of the Korean government's effort to hide, for the duration of the Olympics, a popular variety of Seoul food—namely, dog meat. Stories of dog restaurants being shooed from areas tourists frequent filled the foreign press in pre-Olympic days. Not only didn't the campaign succeed, it served to whet the appetites (and wits) of visiting writers. More than a few tried the dish, and lived to write about it. A few days ago, I joined their number.

Before I proceed, I think a word about the cultural relativity of food tastes is in order. Moslems and many Jews abhor pork. Hindus aren't crazy about beef. The French fancy horse meat.

There is, moreover, a strong Korean notion that many foods have medicinal value. Drinks made with ginseng, a local root, are touted for their rejuvenating effects. Dog meat has the same rep. "I ate it for the first time last year because I was feeling tired and getting colds," a young college grad told me. "I haven't had a cold since."

Curiosity got the best of me and, guided by Susan Moffat, this newspaper's resident reporter here, I visited a local hot-dog stand. In accordance with the recent edict, part of its sign had been blacked over, replaced by the catchy euphemism "four seasons stew."

Dog meat is gray and stringy, resembling turkey dark meat. It was served in a stew with local greens. It had little taste. We didn't dog out, we nibbled. I didn't particularly like it. I won't try it again. But I'll tell you this: I haven't had a cold since I ate it.

• *Sept. 26, 1988*

It Rhymes
With 'Clonk'

PARIS, FRANCE

At the last football Super Bowl, I sat next to a writer from a French newspaper. He took in the extravaganza at Miami's Joe Robbie Stadium with a mixture of bemusement and, I thought, envy.

"In France," he said, "something like this would be impossible."

"Why?" I asked.

"French people are not so sports-minded as Americans," he replied. "We have football [soccer], but most people only care about the occasional big international match. Bicycle racing is important for a few. Tennis is popular for two weeks, at the Open. Track and field is not much."

"What about sports participation?" I asked.

"Ha! The same!" he exclaimed. "Most French don't like to sweat, so they don't participate."

"Not at all?"

"Well," he said after a moment's thought, "there's *petanque* . . ."

"Petanque?"

"Yes. It rhymes with 'clonk.' That will help you remember."

Remember I did, and when planning my trip to this dirty, beautiful city for the French Open tennis tournament, I telephoned the French consulate in Chicago to inquire about the native game. I was put in touch with

Jean Budan, the vice consul. His voice rose at my mention of the subject.

"You have come to the right man about petanque!" he said. "I am ranked No. 4!"

"In France?" I asked.

"Oh, no. In the U.S.," he laughed. "In France, I am not so special. There are very many good players."

I suggested lunch to discuss petanque, and at a restaurant of his choice (an Armenian one) he explained the game to me.

"There is a little white ball, called the *cochonnet*, or jack," said M. Budan, a wiry man of middle age. "The game starts when one player throws it out about six to 10 meters [20 to 33 feet]. Then the players take turns throwing their balls, trying to get them closest to the cochonnet. If you toss your ball high in the air, that is called a *plomber*. If you roll it, it is called a *rouler*.

"You can play one against one, two against two or three against three," he went on. "In singles, each player throws four balls. In doubles it's three, and in triples two. If you have one ball closer to the cochonnet than your opponent, you get one point. You get another point for each other closer ball. A game is 13 points."

I pondered that for a moment.

"Sounds like boccie, an Italian game. I played it in my backyard with my children," I said. "It also sounds like lawn bowling, which I saw on television in England."

"Petanque is different," said M. Budan. "We play with metal balls instead of plastic or wood, as in boccie or lawn bowling. We play on dirt instead of grass. And a *petanqueur* must throw with his feet together, from a little circle drawn on the ground. That takes skill! It is the main thing that makes petanque unique."

I observed that petanque sounded like a sedentary game. M. Budan demurred.

"When I was stationed in Los Angeles, we had a petanque club, and we worked it out," he said. "We calculated that if you play petanque for an hour you will walk one kilometer, throw 40 kilograms [88 pounds] of steel and flex your knees about 30 times in throwing and picking up balls. That's good exercise!"

It didn't sound very strenuous to me, but I let the point drop. Was there anything more I should know about petanque? I asked.

"Yes, Pernod," he replied.

"Pernod?"

"Yes," he said. "Many Frenchmen drink it when they play. I do."

I promised to keep my eyes open.

In my two weeks in Paris, I failed to see anyone drinking the anise-flavored liqueur while playing petanque, but I did see plenty of the game. Petanqueurs of all ages, physiques and levels of skill play in the Jardin des Tuileries, where powdered-wigged nobles once strolled, near the Hotel des Invalides, where Napoleon is entombed, and at the Bois de Boulogne, the big, wooded park at whose southern end sits Roland Garros Stadium, where the French Open is held. As far as I could see, it is the only sport Parisians engage in publicly, unless you count driving motorcycles on the sidewalks.

Aside from the Pernod, my tutor had prepared me well. Not only does petanque rhyme with "clonk," but that's also the sound emitted—loudly—when the three-inch metal balls collide, so it was possible to follow my ears to games. Moreover, M. Budan's description permitted me to dope out the flow of play.

In one matter, however, I had been misled. M. Budan had said petanque was played on dirt. I discovered it also is played amid trees and tree stumps on pitted, rolling ground covered with stones and cigarette butts.

I did most of my petanque-watching at a grove across a highway bridge from Roland Garros, where six or eight games, ringed by kibitzers sitting on lawn chairs, were in progress most evenings. There, I met Monique Frenais, who endeavored to instruct me further in the game.

"Why don't they find a flat place to play, or, at least, clean up the stones and cigarette butts?" I asked Mme. Frenais, who said she'd honed her English during a stint in Detroit with her husband, an employee of a business-machine maker.

"The game is more amusing the way it is," she smiled.

I tried again. "When two balls look equally close, how do they determine which is closest?" I asked.

"They argue." (So that's what all the arm-waving was about.)

Mme. Frenais told me that the game's basic strategy involves the first player placing his shot close to, and in front of, the jack. That forces succeeding players to try to knock his or her ball out of the way. Because of the uneven ground, this usually requires a plomber rather than a rouler. A shot that removes another's ball is called a *tirer*, she said, and is a main test of petanque skill.

The men we were watching must have been pretty good, because they were making lots of tirers. The judgment was more than confirmed when one fellow ended a game by dropping his ball on a triangle of three that blocked the jack, leaving himself closest. The gallery sent up a cheer.

"What's that called?" I asked Mme. Frenais.

"A great shot," she answered.

• *June 23, 1989*

Issues and Circuses

HAMAR, NORWAY

A
•

man's gotta do what a man's gotta do, so yesterday I put on a red nose and floppy shoes and joined the circus. The media circus, that is.

The occasion was "The Meeting," the first confluence of Tonya and Nancy (no last names necessary) on Norwegian ice. The place was the small practice rink alongside the stadium where the women's singles figure-skating competition will be held, beginning Wednesday night. I got there 2½ hours before the practice's 1:25 p.m. starting time, and the place was already half full with about 250 bodies. By noon, it was SRO in the press section, or, rather, OSR, because everybody was standing to begin with.

What happened was this: Nancy arrived on time and Tonya was about five minutes late. They shared the ice with two other skaters. Nancy wore a bridal-white skating costume, the same one she wore the January day her knee was clubbed in Detroit. Tonya wore a flowered dress over black tights.

Both skated mostly in their own orbits, taking frequent breaks to confer with coaches stationed behind the boards about 20 yards (oops, meters) apart. Nancy smiled more than Tonya, who spent a lot of time coughing and drawing on an inhalator (she has asthma). They neither touched nor spoke, and didn't visibly recognize the other's presence. Nancy left first, Tonya about five minutes later. They practiced again in the main arena an hour and a half later, and it went about the same.

I'm glad to report that my colleagues behaved well, their only transgression being an occasional, rule-breaking camera flash while the skaters whirled. Some reporters shouted questions at Tonya as she left, but she responded only with a jaunty wave and thumbs-up sign. As circuses went, it was about as dull as they come. I could have left the nose and shoes at home.

I know that such an assurance will not calm the tut-tutting that has followed the full-court-press coverage of Skategate. Among the tut-tutters was one Patrick D. Gilroy, the Oregon judge who brokered the legal deal that cleared Tonya's path to Olympia. His order "urged" the news media to "remove their focus from these events [the Tonya-Nancy hubbub] in order that appropriate attention may be given the Games themselves."

Ha! If we news types should apologize for pursuing Tonya-Nancy, then our readers should apologize for gobbling up every morsel we feed them. This story has it all: violence, greed, betrayal and scantily clad young women. It's a tabloid's dream, ranking behind only "Dwarf Rapes Nun; Escapes in UFO," in headline Valhalla. There was a novel by that title.

Make no mistake, though—this is, at base, a serious matter, one that brought crime right into the sports arena, and we will have to deal with its outcome both inside and outside the world of fun and games. One question it raises is whether there's a difference between breaking the law and breaking the rules.

It can be argued that the attack on Nancy, by a man employed by Tonya's live-in ex-husband and bodyguard—and about which she has admitted knowing afterward but not telling—didn't qualify as much of a crime. All Nancy suffered was a bruise, and she was back on skates in a couple of weeks. Indeed, as the commercial offers flood in, there's no doubt the incident enhanced her career. But assault and battery isn't an exact science, and if the blow had landed an inch or two in another direction she might have been injured far more seriously. One wonders how much sympathy there'd be for Tonya if Nancy had been hurt too badly to compete here, while Tonya did.

It also can be argued that figure skating is, really, show biz, a strenuous entertainment like ballet or circus acrobatics that's a sport only because someone decided to keep score, and, thus, its participants shouldn't be held to sports' stricter standards. I think you can agree with the first part of that proposition without buying the second part.

The attack on Nancy both broke the law and altered the U.S. Figure Skating Championships, the Olympic-qualifying event, in a way that made it easier for Tonya to make the U.S. team. The law-breaking part will—or, should—be played out in criminal court with all legal protections due the defendants. The U.S. Olympic Committee was to have heard arguments on the rule-breaking part, but backed down in the face of a $25 million lawsuit by Tonya (how could she claim damages until she was injured, anyway?) and agreed to delay its hearing until after the Games, giving her what she wanted.

And that isn't right. Athletes can be suspended from competition for all sorts of offenses that don't involve criminal prosecution. These include drug-taking, hanging out with questionable characters, missing practice or curfew or, for student-athletes, even cutting class. The standards of proof for such offenses needn't match those of a court of law.

The closest recent parallel to l'affaire Tonya was Pete Rose's run-in with Major League Baseball. Rose was banned from the game not for tax evasion, the offense for which he went to prison, but for gambling on sports, which violated baseball's rules. It was his crime against his sport that has kept him out of the game's Hall of Fame, and, I think, rightly.

Tonya may or may not have to face criminal-charge music in the attack on Nancy, but the maiming of her chief rival by those near and dear to her, at the site of a major competition, breaks the rules of any sport I've ever heard of. It ought to cost Tonya at least a game, even a very big one. No circus, media or Olympic, should have distracted attention from that.

- *Feb. 18, 1994*

Brazil Not 'Bonito,' But Wins Anyway

PASADENA, CALIF.

T he World Cup ended with a whimper, not a bang. As his Italian teammates and Brazilian foes sprawled in exhaustion at midfield, their labors ended at 0-0 (that's nil-nil) after 120 minutes of soccer on a hot Sunday afternoon in a full Rose Bowl, Roberto Baggio sent too high a penalty shot that would have kept the deciding shootout alive. His head drooping, he turned to rejoin his motionless mates, while the boys from Brazil arose to rejoice around him.

It wasn't magnificent. It wasn't really soccer, either. It was as if the National Basketball Association championship had been decided by a free-throw contest, or the World Series by batsmen taking home-run whacks against a batting-practice pitcher. That's about the degree of difficulty of a soccer shootout try, in which the kicker blazes away from 12 yards against an 18-inch-wide goalie trying to guard a net that's 8 feet high and 24 feet across. You could park a truck in it.

But there were two good things about the conclusion of the quadrennial event that's the real World Series. One was that it ended a game that, given Italy's defensive single-mindedness, might be going on still. "It [the shootout] is not the most adequate way to decide a championship, but to play another 90 minutes would have been worse," Brazil's coach, Carlos Alberto Parreira, allowed later.

189

The other was that justice was served, and the best team won. Brazil dominated play from the outset and outshot its opponent, 22-8. It did about the same to all six teams it faced in its seven games (it played Sweden twice) during the month-long fest, winning six and tying one.

Never in the tournament did talented Brazil trail on the scoreboard, or alter a game plan that stressed attack. Its foes could make neither claim. "Every team that played us had to change its way of playing, and that included Italy," said the swift Bebeto, who with the fiery, pint-sized Romario gave the South Americans the cup's most dangerous one-two punch. "Everybody played us back, waiting for us. We were on top all the time. We were the best."

Arrigo Sacchi, the Italian coach, pretty much agreed, though not in so many words. "We did our utmost, and have to accept the results," said he, sunglasses atop his head. "We will not look for alibis."

This World Cup was staged in the U.S. partly to indoctrinate the American public in the joys of the sport that grips much of the rest of the world, and while a 0-0 championship game was hardly scintillating, no more instructional final matchup than Italy-Brazil could have been arranged. It was Brazil, in the years just after World War II, that loosed free-flowing "samba" soccer, or *jogo bonito*, for "beautiful game," upon the world. It was Italy, around the same time, that devised the defensive *catenaccio* style, meaning "big chain," to counter it.

Catenaccio is the game of the weak, designed, in the words of the soccer author Paul Gardner, "not to win games but to avoid losing them." It foils offenses by always outnumbering them around the goal, and if it produces a lot of 0-0, 1-0 or 1-1 outcomes, so be it, because it gives a lesser unit a chance. Europeans are fond of telling Americans that our desire for scoring is a character defect, and that, in sports, winning isn't everything, it's the only thing. Over time, theirs has become soccer's dominant philosophy. For worse rather than better, many think.

Neither the Italian nor Brazilian entry in this tournament offered a pure example of its historical model. The Brazilians were not as attack-oriented as their 1958, '62 and '70 cup winners, partly because of personnel differences, and they could play some "D," as shown by their five shutouts during the tournament. The Italians, led by the shifty Roberto Baggio, who scored five goals in his team's last four games, were classic counterpunchers, poised to strike when an opponent overcommitted. That's how they managed to qualify for Sunday's final despite having scored but eight goals in six previous games (Brazil's goal total was 11).

That Italy got what it wanted on Sunday—a chance to win— testified to the effectiveness of its strategy in expert hands. Indeed, the fact that it got as far as it did made the point more strongly. It lost its opener to Ireland, 0-1, qualified for single-elimination play as a divisional wild card, and needed late goals by Roberto Baggio to pull out round-of-16 and quarterfinal victories.

Moreover, it probably suffered more losses of key players than any previous World Cup finalist. Defenseman Franco Baresi missed four games with a knee injury, and goalie Gianluca Pagliuca, defend-ers Alessandro Costacurta and Mauro Tassotti and forward Gian-franco Zola all missed games for playing-field rules violations. Costacurta and Tassotti couldn't play Sunday. On top of that, forward Roberto Baggio and midfielder Dino Baggio, who aren't related, per-formed with leg ailments at various times.

Roberto Baggio pulled a hamstring in Wednesday's semifinal win over Bulgaria, and while he played a full game on Sunday he later complained of discomfort. He got off four shots in the game, but none had much snap. Baresi also played, for the first time since June 23, and experienced leg cramps in the late going.

Most of what controversy the final produced was over Coach Sacchi's decision to use his sore-legged stars among his five shootout kickers. Although neither pleaded inability, both missed their tries, which turned out to be crucial.

Taken as a whole, though, the results of the shootout merely confirmed what had taken place all afternoon. Brazil controlled the ball most of the time, and not only had more scoring opportunities but also better ones. Pagliuca smothered a free kick by Branco just in time to keep Mazinho from ramming home a rebound in the 25th minute. At 54 minutes, the goalie had to leap to snare Bebeto's header; at 76 minutes, a shot by Mauro Silva glanced off a goal post after Pagliuca bobbled it; and at 110 minutes, Romario was just wide from close in.

Italy's best chances came on a couple of shots by Roberto Baggio; one, at 114 minutes, was hard-hit but right at Brazil's goalie, Taffarel.

The shootout also was more a matter of misses than hits. Baresi, Italy's leadoff, put his shot over the crossbar, then Pagliuca guessed correctly and stopped Marcio Santos. The next four kickers—

Demetrio Albertini and Albergio Evani for Italy and Romario and Branco for Brazil—scored to make it 2-2. Taffarel stopped Daniele Massaro, Dunga scored to give Brazil the lead, and Roberto Baggio was high to make unnecessary a final kick, which Bebeto would have taken.

"Tell you about my saves [in the shootout]?" the blond Taffarel said later. "There was only one, you know. A shootout's like a lottery. You take a chance and hope you're right."

FIFA, the outfit that runs the World Cup, later said it probably will adopt sudden-death overtime instead of shootouts in future events, but that came too late to save this one from its lead-balloon ending. That's too bad, because otherwise the cup was a success, setting an official record for attendance (3,567,415 for 52 games) and an unofficial one for good cheer. At least we Americans did our part.

• *July 19, 1994*

A Day at Henley

T
•

he British have a hard time with summer, especially a warm one like they're having now. They never seem to expect it and, when it comes, don't quite know what to do about it.

The ordinary folk at least make an effort at comfort, exposing their limbs to the available breezes by wearing such summer-sensible clothing as shorts and T-shirts when they pursue outdoor activities. The monied class treats the season as an affront, and does its best to ignore it.

This again was clear at the Wimbledon tennis tournament, England's premier summer sporting event. Despite temperatures in the 90s some afternoons a week ago, male dress in the seats set aside for members of the sponsoring All-England Lawn Tennis & Croquet Club continued to be the pin-striped suits, long-sleeved shirts and neckties those fellas wear at their places of business. A few All-Englanders removed their jackets when the mercury rose, but the loosening of ties seemed beyond the bounds of propriety. The British flag may have been struck in many parts of the globe, but the British necktie, never!

England's ultimate summer dress-up party, though, is the Henley Royal Regatta. For five late-June-or-early-July days in this village on the Thames River west of London, the rowers row while the swells parade. "You have to see it—it's the Ascot races, only rowing," a U.S. rowing official told me before I came over. "It's the perfect British sporting event—six hours of chitchat with a drink in your hand," contributed a transplanted American I met.

Some homework revealed that the regatta possesses another element dear to the British heart—tradition. Save for the annual Oxford-Cambridge boat race, which dates from 1829, the Henley Royal Regatta's origin in 1839 makes it the longest-running annual sports show in the English-speaking world.

Henley-on-Thames was home to the early Oxford-Cambridge rowing contests, and their popularity spurred the town to launch the larger affair. Indeed, in creating the regatta, Henley may have been the first to set down the rationale for the community bankrolling of athletic endeavors that has reached monster proportions in the U.S.

"From the lively interest which has been manifested at the various boat races which have taken place [here] during the last few years, and the great influx of visitors to such occasions . . . the establishing of an annual regatta would not only be productive of the most beneficial results to the town of Henley, but would also be a source of amusement and gratification to the neighbourhood and to the public in general," reads a resolution of the Henley town council of March 26, 1839.

It was too tempting to pass up, so a week ago Sunday I was on hand for the regatta's final day, along with some 100,000 other people. With my press credential came the advice to dress properly. I interpreted this to mean a blue blazer and necktie, among other things. Lacking the club tie I thought would be most appropriate (my YMCA doesn't have 'em), I wore the one I got at the 1987 British Open golf tournament. I'd been waiting for the right occasion to wear it.

As it turned out, Henley seemed more like the Kentucky Derby than what I'd imagined Ascot to be from seeing "My Fair Lady." As at the Louisville, Ky., affair, the hoi polloi wore shorts, lugged coolers and had a fine time picnicking sloppily along the outer reaches of the course. Displays of sartorial finery were limited mainly to those who viewed the proceedings from the Stewards' Enclosure, named for the race's overseers.

There are about 50 actual Henley stewards, but for the equivalent of $35 one could enter their sanctum sanctorum, and about 6,000 people chose to do so. Each also had to meet a dress code that prescribed suit coats or blazers, flannel trousers and ties for men, and dresses or suits with below-the-knee skirts for women. The idea, the organizers say, is to recreate "the atmosphere of an English Edwardian garden party."

I don't know what Edward wore at Henley, but some of the men put on a blazer show that could only be called spectacular. There were blazers with piping and blazers with stripes. There were blazers with piping *and* stripes. There were blazers with two and three colors of stripes. Four, five and six colors, too, I think. By contrast, most of the women in the Enclosure wore single-color dresses and hats. For a change, the women looked nice and the men looked silly.

In matters of drink, local tastes prevailed, the most popular quaff being a Pimms Cup, a reddish, gin-tasting liquor mixed with lemonade. I tried it, and prefer regular gin and tonic. Champagne was big, too, and as the day wore on it was increasingly swigged from bottles.

My source's description of the length of the day proved accurate: The first race was at noon and, with breaks for lunch (12:50 p.m. to 2:30 p.m.) and tea (3:45 p.m. to 5 p.m.), the last of the 16 finished around 6 p.m. Each race took about six minutes, but since the course is about 1⅓-miles long, most spectators could see the boats for no more than a third of that. Given the opportunities such an action-light day presented, I thought the crowd handled its liquor well.

The rowing part of the program was serious, and good. The featured race, the eight-oar Grand Challenge Cup, was won by the U.S. national team. Steve Redgrave, whose numerous world-championship and Olympic medals have led some to call him Britain's greatest athlete ever, was part of the winning four-with-cox and pairs boats.

But other things were more memorable. I saw men walking with their hands clasped behind their backs, just like Prince Charles does. I saw a woman drink beer with a straw. In the event's bazaar section was a mechanical-bull-riding concession run by a couple of guys who said they'd never seen the movie "Urban Cowboy."

Best of all, a woman told me she liked my tie.

• *July 14, 1995*

I Went, I Saw, Iran

ATLANTA

T here was an Iranian demonstration here Wednesday, and it wasn't entirely peaceful. When the decision in the Olympic gold-medal freestyle-wrestling match at 220 pounds favored Kurt Angle of the U.S. over Abbas Jadidi of Iran after the two had tied on the scoreboard, 1-1, through the five-minute regulation round and a three-minute overtime, Angle knelt in prayerful pose while Jadidi knelt before the judges with anguished mien to protest their call.

The rhubarb continued into the medal ceremony that ended the session in the Georgia World Congress Center. Jadidi, still looking upset, had to be coaxed and pushed onto the medal platform by his coaches. He later was unrepentant about his display.

"I thought I'd scored points they didn't give me," he said. "I was hoping to the end they [the judges] would change their minds."

While that was going on, a group of about 60 Iranians and Iranian-Americans, together in the stands, were doing what fans everywhere do when they think one of their boys has been robbed. This is to say they moaned and gestured to one another and to the world at large. But they stood when "The Star-Spangled Banner" was played to honor Angle's victory, then quietly filed into the Atlanta twilight with the rest of the full-house throng of about 7,500.

196

"I thought our man won, but it was very close," Faramrz Fath-nezad, an Iranian who works in the Pakistani embassy in Washington, said on his way out. "But second place is not so bad, and we have the evening ahead of us."

So the score in the international-amity department came out about the same as the one for Angle-Jadidi did, and in this day and age that's not bad.

Much the same could be said about the session in general. The Olympics are supposed to bring the nations of the world together for friendly conflict, with the accent on the friendly, and if any session tested this notion, it was Wednesday's wrestling card.

Wrestling is a hard sport that attracts hard nations as well as individuals, and the usual USA-chanting majority was this day joined by groups supporting competitors from Iran, North Korea and Cuba, countries that have been known to take their international differences to the mat. Add in the Russians and the rest of the ex-Iron Curtain crowd, and the mix could have been, well, interesting.

Happy to relate, though, everybody pretty much cheered his own guys and either applauded politely or sat on his hands when the other guys were doing well. We couldn't ask more from Chicago Bears fans at a Bears-Packers game in Green Bay.

Man for man, the North Koreans in the crowd made the most noise, I thought. The 10 men sat unobtrusively in an end section, but unfurled their flags (blue on the top and bottom and red in the middle, with a red star centered in a white circle) and vocal chords when their man, Kim Il, the 1992 Olympic champion, came out for the final in the 106-pound class. When he won, 5-4 over an Armenian, several of the group sprinted from their seats to embrace him and give him a flag for his victory lap. They did the same for Sam Ri Yong, the only other North Korean in the competition, when he won his bronze-medal match at 125 pounds. Their business completed, they then departed, with more than half the card remaining.

The Iranians, also all males, were there to cheer on their own, but also to watch others perform; wrestling is their national sport, and they consider themselves connoisseurs. Iranians make the scene at all the big international meets, and were in Atlanta in greater force for last summer's world championships, for which tickets were easier to come by. On Wednesday, they sat front and center, and, waving their red, white and green flags and wearing T-shirts of those colors, were never unobtrusive.

The ones I talked to, including Iranian nationals and U.S. transplants (the two groups "get along fine . . . here," said one national), praised their Olympic reception by Americans. "The people like our spirit, the way we back our athletes," declared Amir Hajjari, another Washington resident. "Anybody says they don't like us, we give them a T-shirt," he added, smilingly displaying a stack of those.

The Iranians got their chanting and cheering in tune when their Amir Reza Khadem Azghadi won the bronze-medal match at 181 pounds, then waited expectantly for the burly, mustached Jadidi to appear. A 1993 world champion, he's a national hero of the first order, "sort of like your Ken Griffey Jr.," said Mr. Hajjari, helpfully.

Alas for the general peace of mind, Angle vs. Jadidi, the session's last and main event, was the sort of contest that pleases no one fully. Not only was it low scoring, which is typical when wrestling's big men meet, it also was full of instances where points might have been tallied but weren't, giving both men and their backers reasons for complaint.

The match was almost three minutes old before Jadidi scored by turning the thick-necked Pittsburgher, a reigning world's titlist, from an on-top position. Angle got even about 20 seconds later by reversing his foe's lunge for a takedown. A half-minute before the end of the eight-minute bout, Angle grasped Jadidi's legs and dumped him. The Iranian countered by locking his hands across Angle's neck and shoulders and holding on tight in a sitting position. A false move by either might have given the other a crucial advantage, so both stayed put until the buzzer and left things up to the judges.

Then came the decision, bringing joy to some and misery to others. That is until the next game, or bout, or round, when it all starts again.

• *Aug. 2, 1996*

SQUARED CIRCLES

Part 10

Tyson Vs. Spinks . . .

ATLANTIC CITY, N.J.

M ike Tyson had just finished enlightening the reporters and assorted tourists who attended the traditional post-fight press melee here very early yesterday morning when Michael Spinks arrived to do his turn. The two fighters grinned at each other and hugged. The hug knocked off Spinks's hat, a broad-brimmed, white number.

That was altogether appropriate, because some minutes before, Tyson had knocked Spinks's block off, figuratively speaking. This year's Fight of the Century, staged before 21,785 people who paid up to $1,500 for their folding-chair seats, lasted but 91 seconds. If the Iron One's gross purse reaches $20 million, as advertised, that works out to about $220,000 a second.

The fight ended quickly because Tyson hit Spinks very hard in the head three times in round one. The first blow, a right about 30 seconds into the heavyweight championship fight, did not knock Spinks down, but caused him to turn to his corner with a "what's going on here?" look in his eyes. The second was a left that dumped him on his trunks. He arose to take the last moments of the mandatory eight-count standing, but as soon as referee Frank Capuccino ceased to be his shield, Tyson was on him again. The finisher, another right, left Spinks on his back, his head beneath the ropes. If he had thoughts of continuing, he kept them to himself.

Spinks was supine when the bout ended, and took awhile to arise. That, perhaps, was because 100 or so handlers, officials, television-camera carriers and otherwise unidentified louts stormed and occupied the Atlantic City Convention Center ring as soon as hostilities ceased. A good five minutes elapsed before an elderly man with a medical bag—an M.D., I presumed—could make his way to the scene. That's typical of these affairs, another consequence of boxing's unregulated condition. If an injury had been involved, the delay might have been serious. Fortunately, Spinks exited on his feet, waving to signify that he could again function.

Tyson later said he knew the bout would be a short one before the first bell. "I saw fear in his face. I knew it'd be a first-round KO," he said.

Spinks disputed this. "I wasn't intimidated. If I was afraid I wouldn't have taken the fight," he asserted. And while he complimented Tyson's punching power, he stopped short of calling him the hardest hitter he has faced. "It doesn't take a hard shot to knock someone out if you hit him in the right spot," he noted.

He did, however, admit to a tactical blunder. "I came to fight like I said I would," he said. "Maybe I should have boxed him more."

But if he had, the fight might have lasted two minutes and 31 seconds. The action proved, probably to the dismay of those who make a living in this sport, that Tyson, who turns 22 years of age tomorrow, has no equal now or in the foreseeable future.

In the 31-year-old Spinks, he had a foe with no prior blemishes, a claimant to a slice of the formerly divided heavyweight crown who was unbeaten as a professional and, indeed, hadn't been bested since he stayed out too late the night before an amateur bout in 1976. Although he had previously campaigned as a light heavyweight, the 6-foot, 2-inch Spinks weighed in Saturday at a strapping 212 pounds, just six pounds less than the bullet-shaped Tyson.

But all that Spinks took out of the ring (in addition to his $13.5 million purse) was a boxing-history footnote he certainly could have done without. Monday night's go was the fourth-shortest heavyweight title bout ever, the record being Jim Jeffries's 55-second KO of Jack Finnegan way back in 1900.

It was the 17th time in 35 pro wins that the unbeaten Tyson had dispatched an opponent within one round, and the first time since 1986. The illustrious Spinks joined the likes of Marvis Frazier, Hector Mercedes and Sammy Scaff as Tyson's first-round victims. Even the aptly named Tony Tubbs, Iron Mike's previous foe, outlasted Spinks by a round.

Tyson's virtuosity did not, however, carry over to his post-fight interview session, which mirrored the confusion and siege mentality exhibited by his camp over pre-fight stories of discord in his relations with manager Bill Cayton and new wife Robin Givens. Tyson's trainer, Kevin Rooney, set the stage by inviting anyone who had picked Spinks to prevail (maybe 1% of those who had ventured predictions) to "eat your words," although he didn't specify how. Tyson then came on to say that maybe the fight would be his last . . . or maybe it wouldn't.

At one point, he said he was "a pro who could handle the pressures." Then he said he resented the attention paid to his private life by "people who tried to embarrass me and my family." Then he said prizefighting was in his blood, "something I have to keep working on." Then he said he might "go away for a while and think things over."

"Who knows?" he concluded. "I can't say now."

The betting, of course, is that this young man will, somehow, stay active. He has a fight booked for September in London against an English someone named Frank Bruno. Another possible foe is tall Carl "The Truth" Williams, who decisioned Trevor Berbick in a 12-round undercard match Monday night, but the truth about Williams is that he bounced punches off Berbick all night but didn't stop a fella Tyson flattened in two rounds in November 1986.

Evander Holyfield, the cruiserweight (190-pound) champ, is being touted, but he has yet to fight as a heavyweight. Angelo Dundee, Muhammad Ali's old trainer, is said to be grooming a 260-pound Brazilian ex-nightclub bouncer for a shot.

It seems hard to believe, but already folks are conjuring up non-boxer opponents for Mike. One who had thrown his own helmet into the ring—sort of—was Herschel Walker, the muscular Dallas Cowboys running back. Walker witnessed Monday's fray, though, and had second thoughts.

"The guy who can beat Tyson probably is a 10-year-old kid now," said Walker. "If he trains hard every day for 10 years, and does all the right things, he'll meet Tyson in 1998. Mike'll be 31 then, and maybe ready to get beat."

• *June 29, 1988*

... And Reflections on the Fight

O ccasionally, I go away from a sporting event wishing I had asked another question of one of the participants. I left Mike Tyson's one-round knockout of Michael Spinks in Atlantic City on Monday night with that feeling.

The question that occurred to me too late to raise would have been directed to Tyson. "Iron Mike," I should have said, "were you disappointed that the fight was so easy?"

I am sure that the query would have elicited hoots from some of my colleagues, and, I'd guess, a puzzled shrug from its target. If Tyson was in a mood to elucidate, which he isn't always, he might have explained to me that dispatching the party of the second part as expeditiously as possible was what boxing was all about, and, moreover, his duty as a professional.

He had, in fact, expressed his general philosophy on the matter at a press conference the Wednesday before the battle. "The Trumps, the Kennedys, the Rockefellers all come to the fights to see somebody get hurt," he said in answer to another question with a brutal logic that's useful for someone in a brutal business. "I intend to inflict pain as quickly as possible to get the fight over with fast."

The young man, however, is said to be a student of boxing history, and, given a chance for quiet reflection, conceivably could have responded in the affirmative. For the pity of his career so far—if you can call his three-year dash through the heavyweight division a career—is that he never has faced anyone who has even begun to test his skills and resources. An athlete needs a formidable opponent the way a violin virtuoso needs a Stradivarius. Without one, we—and he—will never know how good he really is.

That point has been addressed glancingly since the fray, mostly from the "we" perspective. Specifically, tears have been requested on behalf of those who paid anywhere from $1,500 for a seat at ringside to $30 for a seat at setside, but got to watch only 91 seconds of action. To have seen the ringsiders, however, was to wonder how many of them actually peeled off 1,500 of their own bucks for their tickets (would the glad-handing Donald Trump have accepted payment from the 500 or so dear friends he invited, including Jesse Jackson, George Steinbrenner—boo!!!—and Carl Icahn?). The rest can write off the expense to consumer education.

The "we" part that deserves greater note is the way we evaluate our sports heroes, both contemporarily and in retrospect. Rarely is an athlete's performance considered in isolation; rather, he is rated in comparison with the more memorable of his peers.

Thus, when we think of Muhammad Ali, we think mostly of his epic struggles with Joe Frazier, and when we recall Joe Louis it is in connection with his two goes with Max Schmeling. Same with Dempsey-Tunney, Marciano-Charles, and Leonard-Hagler.

Conversely, triumphs over inferior opposition ruin the pleasure of spectator and participant alike. U.S. Olympians will tell you that the Soviet-bloc boycott of the 1984 Games at Los Angeles devalued their medal haul. Soviet and East German medalists at the U.S.-boycotted Moscow Games four years earlier regard their own prizes similarly.

I thought the most interesting comment during the recent National Basketball Association playoffs came from a member of the Los Angeles Lakers (Magic Johnson, I think), who bemoaned the semifinal elimination of the Boston Celtics, his team's ertswhile nemesis and longtime sparring partner. He said the Celtics at playoff time always bring out things in the Lakers that the Lakers didn't know they had in themselves.

Tyson is unbeaten in his 35 professional fights, but that isn't what makes him unique; Rocky Marciano and Larry Holmes were undefeated heavyweight champions before him. Tyson stands out because he also is unscored upon, which is to say that his superiority never has been in doubt in any of his matches. Four of his fights have gone to decisions, the most recent coming last year against James "Bonecrusher" Smith and Tony Tucker. Both those worthies are large, strong men who survived by abandoning any hope of victory early on and clutching Tyson's arms at every opportunity.

It is, moreover, questionable whether Smith, Tucker or anyone else could today force Tyson to hear a last-round bell. "Mike's improved 50-60% since the Tucker fight. People forget he's only 21 years old," trainer Kevin Rooney asserted before the Spinks go. "No way anybody could hold him off like that anymore." And, indeed, Tyson's last four outings have ended in swift KOs.

Tyson's domination of his division could stem from the paucity of his opposition or his own, overwhelming gifts. I suspect it is the latter. The *Rocky* movies to the contrary notwithstanding, boxing at its highest level can be a subtle contest of styles and tactics, with two skilled professionals able to go many rounds before a solid blow is landed. That's why A. J. Liebling could write about the "sweet science," and the "cunning pressures" of arms and body with which the master Archie Moore manipulated foes. I confess I'd thought Spinks had much of the "Moore" about him.

But there is little subtlety to a Tyson fight. The opening bell sounds and he is there, in his opponent's face, pummeling him with punches of great force and unprecedented speed. "They all come in with plans, but they forget 'em quick," Tyson notes. Pretty soon, they forget everything else.

If there is anyone around who might test Tyson, he has yet to show himself. Boxing is not a sport that many engage in joyfully, so challenging challengers may remain scarce for quite some time.

There will be no lack of opponents because people will do a lot of things if the price is right, including accepting a beating. It's altogether possible that one day Tyson will become careless and lose to a lesser man, or, simply, get bored and quit. That would be sad for us, and doubly so for him.

• *July 1, 1988*

Chavez Beats the Bell, and Taylor

LAS VEGAS

T
•

he bout between the two 140-pounders was for the unofficial but real title of best-fighter-around, pound-for-
pound, and in most eyes Meldrick Taylor was beating
Julio Cesar Chavez for it with 25 seconds left in the 12th
and final round of a memorable brawl Saturday night in
Betsville. Then, amazingly, Taylor got pounded.

Chavez, the indomitable Mexican, staggered his foe
with a straight right-hand punch. A dozen or so seconds
later another right planted the muscular Philadelphian
on his trunks in a neutral corner as the red light signaling
the round's final 10 seconds began flashing atop the ring
post just behind him.

Taylor was up at the count of five, and the corner
light kept blinking. Referee Richard Steele extended the
count to nine, then waved his arms overhead, declaring
Taylor unable to continue and Chavez the victor.

The light blinked on. The time was 2:58 of the
12th. A couple more blinks and Taylor would have had
it. Maybe he should have.

It was an extraordinary end to an extraordinary
fight in what already has been an extraordinary year in
the sport of the fist. Like that other notable tussle of
1990, Tyson-Douglas, this one will be argued about over
and over, and with more reason.

The man in the middle was the veteran Steele, the
fight's third man. He was unequivocal about his decision.

"I asked Meldrick if he was OK. I heard no response. He could not continue," he said later.

Did he see the 10-second light flashing less than an arm's length from Taylor's head? "I don't keep time. I didn't see the red light. I saw a beaten fighter, a fighter that had had enough."

Lou Duva, Taylor's gnome-like co-manager, charged the ring as Steele waved his fighter out, and Steele asserted that Duva's action confirmed his call. Duva said he had moved only in the belief that the round had ended with his tiger a winner, and charged injustice. "It was a helluva way to lose; the ref took the fight away from us," he fumed. He added: "We had it." And again. "We had it."

That was demonstrably true, although as is common in boxing, one of the three judges seemed to have been watching a different fight from the one seen by his fellows, or by the objective-minded among the 9,000-plus people in attendance at the Las Vegas Hilton's Convention Center, including me.

Judge Jerry Roth had Taylor ahead 108 points to 101 after 11 rounds, or nine rounds to two, and judge Dave Moretti had it 107-102, or eight rounds to three, so the customary two-point (10-8) scoring edge for Chavez's knockdown in the 12th would not have changed their verdicts. Judge Chuck Giampa had Chavez ahead, 105-104, or six rounds to five, but would have been outvoted.

That was not the outcome anticipated by bettors who made Chavez a 2-to-1 favorite at the Hilton's sports book. The 27-year-old from Culiacan arrived unbeaten and untied in 68 fights with 55 KOs, boxing's proudest record. More-impressive testimony to his prowess is a smooth-skinned face all but unscarred by 11 years in the professional ring wars, despite a style that can only be described as warlike.

If Chavez were a heavyweight, his fame in this land would have percolated up from fight fans to sports fans to the tabloid-reading public that lionizes Sugar Ray and Iron Mike. As it is, he's champion of the World Boxing Council's super-lightweight division and a household name only in households south of Laredo.

Taylor, too, had labored in relative obscurity, despite his Americanness, a 1984 Olympic gold medal, and the ownership, now past, of a title belt in a division the International Boxing Federation calls junior-welterweight. That's the same class as the WBC's super-lights, which says volumes about the swamp that is boxing regulation.

Taylor is 23 years old. He has a twin brother named Eldrick. His fistic idol is the original Sugar Ray, the late Robinson, whom he has seen only on film. He came here undefeated, but once tied, in 25 goes as a pro, with 14 KOs.

More to the point of Saturday's contest, Taylor was a bigger 140 pounder than Chavez, brawnier in the neck, arms and shoulders, and straining towards the next-higher weight division, the true welters. As a puncher, Taylor is a volume dealer while Chavez is a stalker, seeking telling blows. The book on the fight was that Taylor had best keep outside Chavez's range, sticking and moving, staying off the ropes and out of the corners where Chavez could measure him.

Taylor, however, confounded both the form and his foe. He got the better of Chavez inside and out, beating him to the punch with his jab and pummeling him to the body at close range. In the early rounds, Chavez stalked and Taylor backpedaled, but Taylor usually got the best of it when the two men closed. In the middle rounds, he outfought the Mexican in the center of the ring, winging hard lefts to head and body and outlanding him roughly two-to-one.

The battle told more on Taylor, bringing blood from his mouth and nose and swelling around his eyes, but that probably owed as much to his own propensities as to Chavez. After round 10, his best, he raised both arms in symbol of a triumph that seemed inevitable.

But in round 11 Chavez rallied, and he did the same in 12 although his edge wasn't decisive until his winning punches. Manager Duva later agreed that Taylor would have been better advised to run in the final round, but said his code of the ring prevented it. "My kid is a fighter. You don't send him out there to dog it," he pleaded.

Taylor was not present to offer postmortem; dehydrated, he was sent to a hospital for observation, and was found to have suffered a broken facial bone. Chavez showed up and, through an interpreter, was eloquent in summation. "He was faster than I was, and stronger. But I had more heart," said he.

Was Steele right in stopping the fight even though Chavez probably wouldn't have reached Taylor again before the final bell? I say yes. Taylor can, and no doubt will, meet Chavez again. Better that than the risk of a far, far sadder conclusion.

• *March 19, 1990*

Taking After Big George

ATLANTIC CITY, N.J.

Inspired by the example of George Foreman, I stopped at a stand along the boardwalk on my way to the Foreman-Evander Holyfield fight here Friday night and ordered a cheeseburger. "Extra cheese!" I told the kid behind the counter. To myself I thought: "Let my arteries take care of themselves for a change."

"You goin' to the fight?" the kid asked. I told him I was.

"Holyfield's gonna win easy," he said. "He's too young, too fast. He'll hit 'im—bing, bing, bing. It'll be over in three."

I nodded noncommittally. "That seems to be the consensus," I said.

To myself I thought: "Maybe. We'll see."

A few hours later, I saw. The kid was right, in a way: Holyfield, the 28-year-old heavyweight champ, was too young and too fast for the 42-year-old Foreman. But he was wrong, too, because it was no "bing, bing, bing" bout. It was 12 rounds of heavy leather and hard breathing, and, in the end, they counted up the points instead of counting over a body. There have been better fights over the years, but few that deviated farther from form.

Here were two men who had fought their recent bouts as though they were double parked. And here was Big George, a redwood-like 257 pounds at the weigh-in. Who figured him to last 12?

Foreman himself had interrupted his pre-fight volley of age and food jokes long enough to predict a battle that would be short, if not necessarily sweet. "It'll be two of the best rounds you'll ever see," said he.

But that's how it sometimes is in boxing. The sport that looks the simplest—two guys bludgeoning one another inside a rope-framed square—also can be the most complex.

As George Benton, Holyfield's canny trainer, is fond of saying, "Style is everything."

As everyone in boxing is fond of saying, "You never can tell."

It was easy to denigrate Foreman going into this one. Not only was he overage and overweight by any sensible standards, but his 10-year layoff—between 1977 and 1987—was unprecedented for a top-flight pugilist. Ten years is longer than an era in boxing, it's practically an eon. Two of his contemporaries and former foes, Muhammad Ali and Joe Frazier, were introduced from the ring Friday night, and both are decidedly middle-aged gents. Ali is ill, too; he moves and speaks in an eerie slow motion. But I guess you know about that.

Moreover, while we chuckled at Foreman's patter—he was like the Ali of old, only without the cruelty—we'd laughed at the opposition he'd chosen for his comeback. He'd fought, and won, 25 times over the past four years, all against men who could be relied upon to stand still and be hit. Yet maybe we shouldn't have been so quick to sneer: It can hurt plenty if a 200-pound elevator operator hits you.

The 208-pound Holyfield shaped up as Foreman's opposite, which was what gave the bout some of the charge that caused it to rake in a pay-per-view television haul pegged at more than $80 million. Like any heavyweight who'd fought professionally in a lower weight class, the champ's "true" size (whatever that is) had been questioned. And while Foreman trained the old-fashioned way—by chopping wood, among other things—Holyfield seemed always to go about his business trailing electrodes, like that Russian fella who fought Stallone in Rocky IV (or was it V?).

In fact, though, the two fighters proved to be more similar than different. Both lasted the 12 rounds, showing that there is more than one road to fitness. Both displayed the quality of chin that enabled them to take punches that would have floored lesser men. And both showed themselves to be masters of their demanding craft.

Indeed, Holyfield owed his victory largely to his technical skills. He's no swifty, but he moved enough to make the ponderous challenger move to reach him, distracting him from more effective exertions. And Holyfield's tactic of hitting and then clinching foiled potential Foreman counterattacks. The champion was booed for this tactic in the late rounds, but shrugged it off. "I had to get close to George," he explained. "That was one place where I couldn't get hit."

Mostly, though, Holyfield fired and fired again, reasoning that "when I was hitting him, he wasn't hitting me." The computer setup that charts punches had Holyfield landing 355 times to Foreman's 188, but at times the ratio looked more like three or four to one in his favor. He staggered Foreman twice, in rounds three and nine, only to have the bell intervene both times.

Foreman did as well as he could with what he had. He landed some hard and unexpectedly fast left jabs, and some of his signature clubbing rights, and had Holyfield in trouble briefly in rounds five and seven. He won five rounds on one judge's card, and four on another's. But Holyfield's skillful clinching kept him from following up his advantages.

The judges' decision was unanimous and supported by the visual evidence of the fight's toll: Holyfield appeared weary but little-marked afterwards, while Foreman wore sunglasses and a badly puffed face. "I had the fight won, but Lou Duva [Holyfield's manager] sneaked a mule into the ring," George joked.

He added: "He [Holyfield] had the points, but I made my point, which is that if you can live, you can dream."

Foreman also made the point that he's a credible foe for any heavyweight, but one can only hope he'll take the money he earned Friday (his guarantee was $12.5 million; Holyfield's was $20 mil) and go back to being a preacher. Symbols are most effective when not struck too often. Dan Duva, Holyfield's promoter and Lou's son, declared that his tiger is bound and determined to meet Mike Tyson, whom many consider to be the real heavyweight champ. But in boxing, that sort of thing is rarely simple.

As for me, I went searching for a post-fight snack, and decided upon pizza. George's courage was contagious.

• *April 22, 1991*

Note: George Foreman was still boxing in 1996, at age 47.

'Lil Roy' Fights Big

GREAT GORGE, N.J.

B
•

oxing training is grueling and, often, painful, so fighters try to turn it into play when they can. The other day, at the spick-and-span gym here where he's preparing for his bout next Friday night with James Toney, Roy Jones Jr. and a sparring partner, Derrick Gainer, stood on opposite sides of a double-ended bag for a game of "Can You Top This?"

The idea was to see who could put the most combination punches on the device, a light bag attached to floor and ceiling that, depending on how it's struck, oscillates rapidly in every horizontal direction. Every time it's hit, the difficulty of hitting it again increases.

Jones began with a bam-bam-bam left-right-left tattoo and stepped back. Gainer answered. The latter, young and sleek, stayed even until Jones put together a flurry that numbered seven punches in about the time it takes you to scratch your nose. Then the two, and everyone else in the room, dissolved in amazed laughter. It was like watching Michael Jordan improvise a new slam-dunk.

Obviously, the 25-year-old Jones has talent. The question of how much talent—and, possibly, how he rates in terms of harder-to-discern qualities as well— should be answered next Friday. Toney-Jones, at the MGM Grand in Las Vegas, shapes up as that boxing rarity, a match between two excellent fighters in their primes. This promises a sharp contrast to last Saturday night's heavyweight-title go between George Foreman and Michael Moorer. Despite its dramatic outcome, that one pitted a man who, by any objective standard, is too old and slow for the sport (Foreman) against one who's too dumb (Moorer, who persistently placed himself in the only position where Big George could hit him).

Thanks to Foreman's high-cholesterol charisma, Foreman-Moorer was a "people's fight." Toney-Jones, for Toney's super-middleweight (168-pound) crown, is for aficionados. The hope in Ringland, though, is that the winner will vault into the esteem of the broader populace by laying strong claim to being the best boxer around, pound-for-pound. Aside from the heavyweight championship, that mythical title is about the only one that's saleable these days.

An additional twist on Toney-Jones is that the more intriguing fighter is not the one who's better known—or favored. Both those distinctions belong to the 26-year-old Toney, an unbeaten veteran of 46 professional bouts whose victims have included such marquee names as Michael Nunn, Mike McCallum, Iran Barkley and Prince Charles Williams. Toney, from the college town of Ann Arbor, Mich., is a rugged counterpuncher with a penchant for scoring late-round knockouts. He does not, however, possess Jones's speed of hand or foot. Perhaps no one does.

The trouble with Jones has been finding out about him. He first entered public consciousness with a loss, albeit a strange one. That came in the light-middleweight (156-pound) final of the 1988 Olympics in Seoul, South Korea, in which he thoroughly out-classed Park Si-hun, only to see Park get the nod. The decision outraged everyone to the point where qualitative judging in amateur boxing was junked in favor of a computerized punch-counting system.

Jones was so put off by his Seoul experience that he went home to Pensacola, Fla., and didn't fight again until eight months later, after the blush of his Olympic celebrity had faded. When he finally turned pro, it was under the wing of his father, Roy Sr., a one-time boxer who was, at various times, abusive toward and overly protective of his son.

The abuse came in the form of beatings: Jones has said that, among other things, his father would strike him across the thighs with an iron pipe to reinforce training lessons, and that he took to carrying a knife with which to retaliate if he was pushed too far. The protectiveness came because the elder Jones was leery of the entangling alliances in the sport's Byzantine promotional side; he kept his son close to home and largely inactive during his early pro years. From 1989 through 1992, Jones fought 20 times, a small number for a young fighter, against undistinguished opposition. Fifteen of those bouts were in out-of-the-way Pensacola.

Father and son split two years ago, but their ties, seemingly uneasy, remain. "We talk," says Roy Jr., but to the question of whether his father plans to attend the Toney match he answers, "You'll have to ask him." In training, Jones wears trunks bearing the nickname "Lil Roy." Big Roy is Roy Sr.

Since making the break, though, Jones has been anything but "lil." He has stepped up in class without breaking stride, running his victory streak to 26 and his knockout total to 23. He won a middleweight belt in May of 1993 with a decision over Bernard Hopkins and defended it last May by dispatching the mouthy veteran Thomas Tate with a single lightning left hook in round two. That earned him the Toney date, to be broadcast via pay-per-view television, and his name is now mentioned with Pernell Whitaker, Julio Cesar Chavez and his Friday foe as among the pound-for-pound best.

The main rap on Jones is that he's still untested. That's also the most interesting thing about him. "He's not a totally rounded fighter," says his tall, bearded trainer, Alton Merkerson. "His instincts are marvelous and he knows the basics, but he's still learning the tricks, the kinds of things you pick up only in the ring."

The fighter himself analyzes this differently. "Nobody's seen me fight yet," he declared after the Tate bout. After a lengthy sparring session here in the hills of northern New Jersey, which he spiced by holding a ring rope with one hand while fending off an adversary with the other, he elucidated further: "People have seen me box in the sense of hitting without getting hit, but I've never had to dig down and do whatever it takes to win."

Asked whether he hoped Toney would elicit such an effort, Jones paused before replying. "Part of me says yes and part says no," he said. "I guess you never know until it happens."

Maybe, on Friday, we will.

• *Nov. 11, 1994*

Note: We didn't: Jones's unanimous-decision victory over Toney was one-sided.

The Five-Ring Ring

ATLANTA

One of the troubles with the Olympics is the same as that of sports generally. It's that, stripped of their five-ring hullabaloo, they're just sports, which is to say they can range from very good to very bad, but usually are somewhere in between.

Sure, the Olympics are important, but just because a game or group of games are important doesn't mean they'll be well or closely played, as professional football's Super Bowl attests almost annually. Sports' unpredictability is its strength, because memorable things can happen in the least-promising contests. But if you want to be sure of a socko show, go see a good play.

There is, however, one athletic activity that consistently delivers things that aren't in the program. That would be boxing, sports' perennial one-ring circus. If you go to enough boxing matches, you'll see everything under the sun, plus a few things that rarely see the light of day.

Although I always feel obliged to apologize when I say it, I like boxing. It's not the mindless brawl its detractors make it out to be, and while A. J. Liebling's description of it as the "sweet science" strains credulity, it doesn't exceed it. Withal, the sport is elemental, and, thus, unbannable. Some men (and lately, it seems, a few women, too) want to do it, and if you legislate against it it'll pop up elsewhere—in back rooms, on river barges or across borders. As long as people are going to fight, it might as well be with boxing gloves on, and a referee present.

It's thus ironic that much of what's bizarre about Olympic boxing has to do with the officials who are supposed to civilize it. But that's an observation, not a complaint, because the prospect of such is part of what draws me to the squared circle when the Games roll around.

My initiation into Olympic boxing came in 1984 in Los Angeles. I was at the light-heavyweight semifinal fight in which the American Evander Holyfield knocked out a foe from New Zealand only to be disqualified because the Yugoslav ref said he'd hit the guy on a break. Because he'd been kayoed, the New Zealander was put out of the tournament, too, so the gold medal went, without contest, to the winner of the other semi. A Yugoslav.

The 1988 Games in Seoul went that one several better. Anthony Hembrick, the U.S. 165-pounder, was disqualified because his team misread the schedule and put him on the wrong bus to his first bout. A South Korean fighter was so distraught over a lost decision that he sat down in the ring and refused to move, for hours. Roy Jones Jr., the American 156-pounder, easily beat a South Korean in a final, but lost the decision. Three of the bout's five judges later said they thought Jones had won but decided individually to vote for his foe so the host country shouldn't be embarrassed by having one of its boys shut out.

The Jones decision was so bad the sport's powers-that-be junked qualitative judging in favor of a computerized scoring system that counts only punches registered within a second by three of a bout's five judges. The system made its Olympic debut in 1992 at Barcelona. Predictably, it worked badly, with fights being decided by scores like 4-2. More than a few fighters swapped blows with their foes for three rounds only to discover they weren't credited with landing any.

As these Games approached, the promise of extracurricular doings seemed high. Two members of the crack Cuban team had defected in the weeks before, a Ugandan fighter was arrested in Gainesville, Ga., for passing counterfeit U.S. bills, and David Diaz of the U.S. team claimed to have been run over by a bicyclist while running near the team's training base in Augusta, Ga. And if individual fighters didn't come through, the scoring system certainly would.

I arrived at Sunday afternoon's boxing session in Alexander Memorial Coliseum on the Georgia Tech campus and checked in with a colleague who specializes in covering the sport. He reported that all had gone smoothly on Saturday. That meant we were overdue for some weirdness, he said.

Alas, the 20 first-round bouts on Sunday's card produced nothing outrageous, but that was only by boxing's standards. A Colombian 105-pounder, irked that his Canadian opponent had thrown him to the canvas, took a couple of whacks at the guy while he was down. A Czech 132-pounder made up for about a six-inch height deficit to a Burundian by periodically grabbing him around the waist with both arms and taking a kangaroo jump. Lightweight Irvin Buhlalu, from South Africa, leaped from his stool as the bell rang beginning round three of his match with a Thai and pummeled him while his back was turned and his handlers were still in the ring. Buhlalu lost the fight anyway.

The first weekend's action showed that the judges' scoring fingers had limbered up since Barcelona: Punch-count scores were more likely to be around 15-8 than the above-mentioned 4-2. Still, that only reduced the system's absurdity. I couldn't keep punches-landed tallies manually, but by my count Jose Perez of the Dominican Republic threw 241 full-fledged blows in his three-round light-flyweight bout with Sabin Bornei of Romania, but got credit for landing only 10 in a losing effort. He could have done that well blindfolded.

Two American fighters were in action Sunday and both won, giving the U.S. victories in its first four bouts here. One of the winners was 132-pounder Terrance Cauthen, a stick-and-move lefty. He whipped an Uzbekistani, and said afterward he'd saved his best moves for later in the tourney, so we hadn't seen anything yet. He's probably right about that on other grounds, too.

• *July 23, 1996*

Note: He was.

TRUE-LIFE ADVENTURES

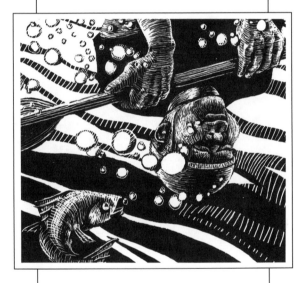

•

Part 11

Lawn Order

G otham is a long way from Wimbledon, where the world's championship of tennis is being contested, but one piece of it looked fairly close this week. That was the swatch of lawn in Forest Hills, Queens, snuggled amid the apartment towers, that contains the grass courts of the West Side Tennis Club.

They used to play the U.S. Open at West Side, and for a long time—until 1975—they played it on grass, just like they do at the Big W in London. Now, though, the club has pretty much joined the 20th Century, and all but seven of its 49 courts are made of Har-Tru, a form of clay, or DecoTurf II, a hard-court material.

The seven remaining grass courts were green and inviting on Tuesday, even though nobody much was using them. "The big majority of our members prefer to play on the clay," noted Michael Hoskam, the club's manager. "Clay suits most peoples' games better."

But I was there, at Mr. Hoskam's kind invitation, to play on the grass. I've played tennis for these past 25 years, and not only never have played on a grass court, but also never set foot on one.

This is despite the fact that I've covered three Wimbledon tournaments. At my first, in 1985, I asked the man who ran the press office if I might, quickly and between matches, tread upon Centre Court. He reacted as though I'd proposed staging a tractor pull at the place. I later would learn that he reacted similarly to requests of any sort.

I'd guess that 99% of all tennis players never have played on grass. That's because, even though the outdoor game was originally played on the stuff, in England, there are precious few grass courts around today. The U.S. Tennis Association (formerly the U.S. Lawn Tennis Association) reports that its last survey, in 1986, counted exactly 337 of them in this country, out of nearly 235,000 courts. England, Australia and New Zealand have some, too, but that's about it.

(In light of this, it seems odd that Wimbledon, tennis's most-prestigious event, still is played on grass; a parallel would be to play the National Basketball Association finals in a barn with peach baskets as goals. But what else can you expect from a sport in which 15-30-40 means one, two, three, and love means nothing?)

The main reason that grass courts are scarce is that they are expensive to build and troublesome to maintain. To construct one properly requires at least one-third more space than one of clay or asphalt, because a grass court's boundaries should be shifted from time to time so that its most-used parts don't wear out entirely.

Carl Peterson, president of C. R. Peterson Inc., a tennis-court builder in Elk Grove Village, Ill., says that a grass court requires a six-inch-deep base of crushed stone for drainage, topped by four inches of soil mixed with sand. The type of grass used varies from region to region.

In the rare instances he's been called upon to build a grass court —three times in 28 years—"we just put down the bottom," he says. "We call in a landscaper or golfcourse superintendent to do the seeding." Total cost usually runs to about $20,000.

Once planted, it takes about a year before the grass is full and tough enough to play on, and then it must be fertilized, aerated, rolled, watered, mowed and relined, forever. "Don't get one unless you have a gardener or a lot of time on your hands," Mr. Peterson advises.

Not surprisingly, most U.S. grass courts are old, and about 75% of them are in the Northeast, where tennis originated on these shores. Resorts in Florida, California, South Carolina and Texas also have them, as do so a few newish condo developments in search of cachet. As far as the USTA knows, vast areas of the South, West and Midwest have none at all save for an occasional backyard job.

As a resident of Evanston, Ill., I thus was forced to travel to find my place on the grass, and where else would I turn but to the West Side Tennis Club? The U.S. Open may have fled to the concrete acres of Flushing Meadows, but the memory of "Forest Hills," where I once witnessed a day of Open play, remains vivid. And, indeed, the place didn't disappoint, even though the old stadium is a bit the worse for wear and now houses the mundane hard court proscribed by the men pros for an exhibition tourney they once played there.

Wearing whites as requested (that kid Agassi isn't the only guy who's got 'em), I appeared at the facility's ancient Tudor clubhouse. After ogling the wonderful old photos of past Open champs, I was greeted by Rita Gladstone, a sunny assistant pro. She bore white tennis balls, which I hadn't seen in some time; she said they show up better against the surface than the yellows now in wider use. She reiterated a couple of things I'd read about grass-court tennis: Beware of the low bounces, and volley as many shots as you can because the best bounce is no bounce at all.

She finished her mini-lesson on an upbeat note. "Grass forces you to keep down and get your racquet back early," she smiled. "It should help your game no matter what you usually play on."

"I can use the help," thought I, but a few rallies showed me I didn't know the half of it. The ball hardly bounced at all, for heaven's sake, and when it did it sometimes skidded sideways. Add that I'm about as happy at the net as a flounder, and you had the makings of a long hour.

The grass felt good under my sneakers, though, and after several more minutes of application I got to where I was returning most (well, many) of her shots. She suggested we play a few games, and —lo and behold!—I won the first, thanks partly to a nifty forehand passing shot.

Giving away a game must be part of the assistant-pros' union rules, though, because I won only one more in the two-plus sets that followed. She came to the net to hit drop volleys that, literally, dropped dead, and her slice backhands didn't come up much higher. I tried to serve and volley a few times, but the results only reminded me why I don't do it more often.

But—hey!—it was a great experience, which will improve with the retelling, and it gave me a better appreciation of what Boris, Stefan, Steffi and that gang will be up to this weekend. I'm sure they'll be gratified to hear that.

● *July 5, 1991*

Cold Comfort

MADISON, WIS.

T. here comes a time every year, usually in February, when people in the northern tier of these United States wonder if winter will ever quit. The skies come only in shades of gray, the temperatures rarely rise above freezing. People know that darkness is supposed to recede each day, but the reverse seems true.

The sensible course is to turn up the thermostat, put on a sweater and watch it all through a window, and when the urge to exercise hits, there's always the YMCA. Racquetball is my idea of a winter sport.

As the perpetrator of an eclectic sports column, though, I feel obliged to range widely no matter what the season, and not just watch but, occasionally, do. Alas, the main winter alternatives in the latter regard are ice skating, which can involve jarring contact with a surface that's slick, cold and hard, and skiing, where ambulances wait at the end of runs. Cold weather is unpleasant enough without crutches.

But there's another winter sport that contains no such risks. In fact, it contains almost no risk at all save that of boredom. It's ice fishing, and millions of people do it. Well, maybe thousands.

They do it in seriously cold states like Wisconsin, Minnesota, North Dakota and Vermont. They do it for big fish and small. They do it indoors as well as out, in whole communities of fish houses that spring up on some lakes after the cold weather sets in, with the residents thereof fishing through holes in their floors. Some of those abodes boast wood paneling, carpets and generator-operated TVs and stereos.

Although I found it hard to believe, I'd heard that some people prefer ice fishing to the summer variety. When I'd located my ice-fishing guru, Sterling Bartlett of this state capital and university city 150 miles north of my home near Chicago, my first question was whether he is in that number. "I'd rather fish in shorts than leggings. Anybody sane would," he answered, reassuringly.

Bartlett is a square-built man of 43 years who's a carpet installer by trade but a sportsman by preference. A lifelong resident of the Madison area, he believes that one should make friends with the local climate, and in that spirit hunts whatever's in season with rifle or bow and fishes year-around. He used to ski before a neck vertebra broken in a diving accident convinced him that dangerous sports could be dangerous.

Testimony to his prowess in forest and stream are the trophies on walls of the home he shares with his wife, Ann, and children Eric, 15, and Heather, 13. Such decor also testifies to Ann's forbearance. "She's Norwegian," he smiled, as though that explained everything.

Bartlett ice-fished far and wide in his younger days, but now sticks pretty much to the lakes around his home. This meant we would be fishing mainly for perch. "They're here, and they're good eating," he said of the species. "Why go farther?"

As it turned out, our party on a recent Thursday morning numbered four. I brought my friend Seymour Shlaes, a former copy editor for this newspaper who's retired when he isn't operating his wood shop. Bartlett brought along his friend Maurice "Mo" Schlimgen, who is retired when he isn't helping his son install office partitions.

Shlaes is like me in that he's not so much a fisherman as someone who enjoys catching fish. Schlimgen is the real McCoy, a man who spent much of his working life as a tavern owner so he could work nights and fish days. Driving to the north shore of Lake Mendota in 20-degree temperatures, he waxed enthusiastic about the big lake's fishing heyday.

"I remember one day—in 1952, I think—pulling 174 perch through the ice inside of four hours. Two days later I caught 176. Summers, you could walk across the lake on the boats," he said.

In some ways, ice fishing beats fishing from a boat in summer— you can get up anytime and walk around, for instance. On the other hand, there's no boat in which to haul equipment, and because ordinances prohibit most vehicles (and fish houses) on Lake Mendota, we had to carry ours about a mile across snow-covered ice, and, later, back. That was the day's exercise.

In ice fishing, like real estate, three things are important: location, location and location. Bartlett picked our spot on the basis of where and when he'd caught fish previously, and on reports from fellow anglers. But he warned us not to expect too much. "Ice fishing's funny," he said. "You can catch fish and the guy a few feet away can get blanked."

Others had come to the same site conclusion he did, because about a dozen fishermen had planted themselves in the area before we arrived. Using the augers we'd brought, we drilled our fishing holes over a space of about 20 square yards. Based on a rule of thumb of a ½-inch per turn of the auger, we were on ice about 13 inches deep.

Bartlett handed Shlaes and me sawed-off fishing rods with large, open reels. For bait we used tiny white maggots he said he'd ordered by mail and kept in his home refrigerator (wonderful women, those Norwegians!). He said to let our hooks fall to the bottom and then raise them a couple of feet.

And then?

"And then you sit," said he, pointing to the buckets we'd used to hold our equipment that now would be our seats.

Action was brisk at first, but, true to form, uneven. Schlimgen reeled in 10 or so nice perch or white bass in the first half-hour, Bartlett got four and Shlaes got two. Sitting but a few feet from each, I got blanked.

There were compensations. The towers of Madison may be modest by megalopolis standards, but they shimmered handsomely at the far end of the lake's vast, white, silent expanse. The homemade venison sausages Bartlett cooked up for lunch on a small portable stove were tasty. The term "cold beer" gained new meaning.

When three more hours produced red noses but no more fish, we called it a day. But even our modest catch was better than that of others on the lake.

"Any luck?" we asked a soul sitting huddled along our path to shore.

"I'm hoping a fish will pull my pole into the hole and I won't have to do this anymore," said the fellow.

Great sport, ice fishing.

• *Feb. 19, 1993*

A Bumpy but Boffo Ride on the Colorado

MOAB, UTAH

ick and I steered our inflatable kayak straight into the rapids, just like we'd been told to do. The ride was bumpy but exhilarating. Everything was going fine until Nick, sitting in front, plunged his paddle's left blade deep into the river and held it there.

The boat turned sideways into the current, just like we were told not to do. Waves crashed over us. Dunk City beckoned. But we thrashed around a bit, righted ourselves and emerged unscathed, albeit dripping.

"Why'd you do that?" I inquired of his unorthodox maneuver.

"Do what?" he replied.

We river rats call that kind of response "White Water Madness."

Nick and I attained river rathood (well, at least mousehood) last month during a kayaking-rafting weekend above and through Westwater Canyon on the Colorado River, between Grand Junction, Colo., and Moab, Utah. Part of a company of 30, we communed with nature and our fellow humans, soaked up some rays and, for brief periods, placed in doubt our safety and sanity. It's the sort of thing guys do when middle age threatens to become a memory.

It is, actually, the sort of thing many people do; about 15,000 people run the Westwater rapids annually, either on their own or, more usually, as passengers of professional guides. Navigable white water can be found elsewhere in this land: the Ocoee River in Tennessee, the Gauley in West Virginia, the Kennebec in Maine and the Rogue in Oregon, for example. If you haven't gotten your seat wet, you should.

My companion was friend Nick Farina, whom you may recall if you have a good memory. Eight years ago, he and I formed an entry in the annual 19-mile Des Plaines River Canoe Marathon near our native Chicago, which I later described in these pages. Unaccustomed to such exertions, we didn't finish first, but we didn't finish last either, and we still count that among our achievements.

Nick, a large, bearded fellow who looks like he knows what he's doing whether he does or not, is an enthusiastic outdoorsman. At a recent meeting, I noted that our combined ages had advanced from 89 at the time of the canoe marathon to a current 105, and opined that if we desired further joint adventures, soon might be a good time. He concurred, and suggested white-water kayaking.

He said he'd done it once before, and immediately launched into a description of the Eskimo Roll, the maneuver used to right an overturned kayak. "You twist your butt one way and your paddle the other. You have to do it fast because you're upside down in the water," said he. "Really," he added, "it's not hard."

"Do Eskimos wear eyeglasses?" I wondered.

In search of an outfitter we tracked down Sheri Griffith Expeditions, based here in Moab. Its 41-year-old proprietor, a river vet, said she'd be glad for us to paddle along with one of her regular rafting runs. When she inquired about our experience with the vessel, and learned it was slim (Nick's) and none (mine), she said it'd be best if we rowed the kayak through some mild rapids and hopped a guided raft through the really treacherous ones.

On the appointed Saturday, hot and clear, we gathered at the river's edge near Grand Junction. Besides the tanned, fit-looking Sheri and four other guides, our group included vacationers from Germany, Belgium and Canada, and six robust teenage boys from Brazil accompanied by the infinitely forbearing parents of three of them. The Brazilians and a guide would paddle their raft; the others would ride fixed-oar models rowed by the guides.

We were introduced to our kayak. It had pointed ends, all right, but was made of rubber and had no deck like the Eskimo variety does. If this baby rolled, we'd be swimming. The guides called the thing a "rubber ducky," hardly a heroic appellation. Sheri pointed out its advantage. "If you hit a rock, you'll bounce," said she.

A few strokes and I was handling the two-bladed paddle niftily, but the mighty Colorado River is a good deal swifter than the sluggish Des Plaines, and holding a course took a bit of doing. We quickly got the hang of that, though, and learned to go with the flow. There was choppy water here and there, and while the stretches little altered the Colorado's predominant tan color—"The key word in white water is 'white,'" noted guide Grant Amaral—some patches definitely were foamy. Emboldened by success, we soon were seeking them out.

The second day we were to run the canyon, which cuts through 200-foot-high black-granite cliffs and contains 11 countable rapids. Sheri thought we could handle the first two, but judged the others to be beyond our ken. If we'd intended to protest, the names of some of those—Big Hummer, Skull, Sock-It-to-Me—would have convinced us otherwise.

We hit the first serious rapid, Wild Horse, just past midday. Unlike the modest chop of previous stretches, this one had two- and three-foot waves that were quite white and coming from several directions. But except for Nick's gaffe, we did well.

The second one, Little Dolores Rapid, was longer and tougher. We didn't so much bounce through it as buck—this must be what bronco riding is like, I thought—and large rocks, strewn irregularly, added to the challenge. Our guides assured us the run rated a solid four on a 1-to-10 scale, well worthy of respect. We felt we'd not only survived, but conquered.

We then boarded a raft and went through the remaining rapids as passengers, our participation limited to bailing. I thought that part of the trip rated, maybe, a six for thrills, but a 10 for spectacle. The scenery, in fact, was gorgeous throughout. All it lacked was John Wayne standing atop a bluff, scanning the horizon for Apaches.

There were other things to recommend the journey. The star show Saturday night, seen from our sand-beach camp, was unrivaled. I learned that cottage cheese, horseradish and chives make a great dip. One of the guides showed me how to score a beer can diagonally with my thumb so I could crush it without gashing my hands.

I came out smiling, as did Nick. "One thing," he said. "When you write this, will you tell about your goofs as well as mine?"

"In my story," I replied, "I'm the hero."

• *Aug. 27, 1993*

Scratching Up
Katahdin . . .

A. ndrew, my English-major stepson, had spotted a volume by Henry David Thoreau open on my desk in my home office in Evanston, Ill.

"What a hypocrite that guy was!" Andrew guffawed. "He wrote about how he loved living in the woods and getting by on beans, but when he got too cold or hungry he'd run over to Emerson's for a hot meal."

So maybe the Sage of Walden wasn't a perfect human being, but I can report that he must have been some kinda man. In 1846, before Nike, Gore-Tex or Cutter—before there was a *trail*—he climbed Mount Katahdin, Maine's tallest summit and, by some lights, the foremost mountain of New England.

Now I, too, have climbed Katahdin, in the company of Raymond Sokolov, the estimable editor of this page. We've been climbing a mountain every few years to prove to one another and, I guess, ourselves, that we can still get, uh, up something. It's a middle-aged-male thing, I think.

Regular readers might recall previous Klein-Sokolov (the billing is alphabetical) expeditions. In 1985 we scaled Mount Massive in Colorado, in 1989 Guadalupe Peak in Texas and, back to Colorado, in 1990 Mount Harvard. While none of those required technical skills, all were considerable hikes, and the two Colorado peaks *each* exceeded 14,000 feet in height. When Ray, my mentor in these matters, suggested that we next try Katahdin, whose Baxter Peak is but 5,267 feet above sea level, my reaction was, "Piece of cake."

Hoo-boy, was I wrong. About two-thirds of the way up, halfway through a seemingly endless boulder field, I seriously considered turning back, and would have if I'd thought I could have. Two weeks have passed since the journey, but my scratches and blisters have yet to fully heal. It was a week before I could walk down stairs without clinging to the railing.

Even Ray, an experienced mountaineer much younger than I (well, three years younger) and in better shape because of his devotion to a ridiculous-looking race-walking regimen, confessed that, at Colorado heights, he couldn't have done the strenuous climbing that Katahdin required.

Days after the climb I spoke with Jean Hoekwater, the naturalist at Baxter State Park, of which Katahdin is a part. She allowed, with evident amusement, that my reaction was fairly typical. "People who've climbed in the West come here thinking that Katahdin will be easy," she said. "They come off it shaking their heads and asking if we've ever heard of switchbacks."

Switchbacks are the gradually rising, serpentine trails that make a lot of the big Western mountains more hike than climb. Katahdin doesn't have 'em. You hit the trails at about 1,400 feet, and don't stop climbing until you run out of mountain. "We tell people they need to be in good shape to try it, but a lot of them choose not to listen," Hoekwater said resignedly.

Withal, Katahdin is a people's mountain, climbed by thousands annually. This is both a favorable commentary on the national state of physical fitness and a tribute to Katahdin's allure. In central Maine, about 80 miles north of Bangor, it's a beautiful part of a beautiful state, ringed by lakes and forest. It's the northern terminus of the Appalachian Trail, which stretches almost 2,000 miles down to Springer Mountain, Ga.

Katahdin's best PR came from Thoreau, whose account of his trip there is a chapter in his book *The Maine Woods*. He waxed eloquent about then-empty land while foreseeing, and bemoaning, its civilizing. His assault on the peak of the mountain he spelled "Ktaadn" came when he was aged 29. He was stopped short by a mist that all but enveloped the craggy heights, but glimpsed enough of them to come away awed.

"The mountain seemed an aggregation of loose rocks, as if some time it had rained rocks, and they lay as they fell on the mountain sides," he wrote. "It was vast, Titanic, such as man never inhabits. Some part of the beholder, even some vital part, seems to escape through the loose grating of his ribs as he ascends. Nature has got him at a disadvantage. . . . She does not smile on him as in the plains. She seems to say sternly, why came ye here before your time?"

I was to ask myself that same question.

Thoreau reached the mountain from Bangor by carriage and canoe; Ray and I drove up on I-95 from the Bangor airport. Undoubtedly, Thoreau's route was more scenic, but we also got some of the flavor of the state. "Eat lobster. It's good for you and good for Maine," said one radio commercial we heard. "Moose Crossing," read a road sign when we reached the woods.

We spent the night at an old inn near the park, and were up at dawn for the climb. Starting at about 6:30 a.m. from Roaring Brook Campground in warm, sunny weather, we covered the 3.3 miles to Chimney Pond in about 2½ hours, not too badly the worse for wear.

We intended to proceed from there to Baxter Peak via the relatively friendly Helon Taylor Trail, but missed a turn and found ourselves on Cathedral Trail instead. Bad mistake. So named because it passes three immense "cathedral" rocks, it's one of the steepest and toughest of the 13 routes to the top. It's 1.7 miles, all rock and all up, and marked only by dabs of blue paint at irregular intervals.

I had to stop for breath many times, and might be there still if Ray hadn't pointed out that, there being nowhere to plug in my laptop, I couldn't set up housekeeping. Ultimately finding it easier to go up than down, we reached Baxter Peak at about noon. The descent, by a more gradual route, was easier on the lungs but harder on the calves. That's why I went down stairs one at a time for a week.

We saw lots of other climbers along the way, most of them far younger and more agile than us. Mountain climbing is easier at age 20 and 130 pounds than at 50-something and 190 (OK, 195). But hats off to the kids anyway.

In retrospect, I found the experience comparable to my Army service: something nice to have done. The scenery was lovely. Driving out of the park at day's end, we saw a bear. And, afterward, there was Nuprin.

Thoreau didn't have that either, did he?

• *Aug. 19, 1994*

. . . And Conquering Wheeler

QUESTA, N.M.

A ll of us can point to pivotal experiences in our lives, and I am no exception. My latest came at about this time last year.

I was two-thirds of the way up Maine's Mount Katahdin, in the midst of a considerable boulder field. I was scratched, blistered and thoroughly tired, and a lot of mountain still loomed above me.

I would have turned back if I thought I could have easily, but continuing to the summit and finding a smoother return route appeared less daunting than scrambling down the big, jagged rocks I'd already traversed.

That's what I did, but the pain of the climb eclipsed the elation of its successful completion. I realized I had overestimated my state of physical fitness, and, as a consequence, almost bit off more than I could chew. In other words, I discovered I was out of shape.

What's the big deal? you might ask. Well, none of us likes to have our illusions punctured, and one of the reasons I was climbing the formidable but not overwhelming Katahdin was to write about it as part of the informal series of "average guy" adventures I have described in this column. I do this to remind people that, your typical daily-newspaper sports section to the contrary notwithstanding, sports needn't be the sole province of young and agile mesomorphs who spend all day in the gym. A

233

confession of failure in that context would have had philosophical as well as physical implications.

The idea of climbing mountains to make that point was that of Ray Sokolov, the editor of this newspaper's Leisure & Arts page, and a veteran mountaineer. Ray had to persuade me to try our first joint expedition, up Colorado's 14,421-foot Mount Massive, in 1985, but once I did it I was hooked by the splendor of the experience. The Klein-Sokolov team (the listing is alphabetical) later climbed Guadalupe Peak in Texas (8,751 feet) and Mount Harvard in Colorado (14,420). All were rugged hikes but required no technical skills and so qualified as average-guy-accessible. We topped them in fine form.

Thus, at 5,267 feet high, Mount Katahdin promised to be easy. Trouble was, five years had passed between it and our Mount Harvard climb, and I'd slipped from middle-middle-age to a later phase (OK, I'm 57). Also, I'd gained weight. The upshot was that my usual fitness regimen of tennis in the warm months, racquetball at other times, and fitful stints on a home exercise bike didn't fully prepare me for Katahdin's rigors.

When I recounted that observation, friends sneered. That's what friends are for. "Guess you won't do that any more," several said. If I was sensible, I would have agreed, but something else (vanity, probably) was stronger. I resolved to climb again, only better.

In retrospect, that was a fortunate choice, because a goal is a great thing for someone seeking to be fitter, and what goal could be more tangible than a mountain? I ate less—cutting way down on the french fries, snacks and, uh, aperitifs—and my exercise-bike sessions became regular instead of occasional. By this summer, my weight had dropped to the low 180s from the high 190s. Even my daughter noticed the difference.

The mountain Ray and I picked for my comeback was Wheeler Peak in north-central New Mexico, north of Taos. Ray had to be in the area to review the Santa Fe Opera, and, at 13,161 feet, the peak is the highest in the mountainous state, making it suitably notable. *The Hiker's Guide to New Mexico* called it a "very strenuous" day hike, but one that required no bodyshredding rock scrambles. Good and good.

The hike's first mile or so, up a steep, rocky trail starting from the Taos Sky Basin at about 9,400 feet, was its toughest stretch, the guidebook opined. It added a caveat: Get an early start because summer-afternoon lightning storms are frequent on high.

That we did, and were climbing by 7:15 a.m. on a recent Monday. The first mile was, indeed, difficult, but we were still smiling at its end, a favorable sign. Then came a more-gradual climb through a wooded area, another steep stretch, and a slight descent into a gloriously beflowered valley that was welcome for the reprieve it offered but resented because we knew that, coming back, we would have to reclimb it.

From there the trail rose through the treeline to a four-mile-long series of switchbacks along exposed mountainsides. In two slanty stretches the trail was covered by the snow that stays on the mountain year-round. A peak loomed just behind the second snowfield, but it was Mount Walter, 13,133 feet high. We had to descend it and climb for another half-mile before reaching Wheeler.

We arrived at the summit at 11:45 a.m., planning to catch our breath (it comes in short pants up there) and eat lunch. The view was marvelous, but it also revealed dark clouds coming our way. Not wanting to have our sandwiches toasted from above, we postponed lunch and hotfooted it down, hoping to get off the ridges ahead of any atmospheric unpleasantness.

Within an hour of starting down, we met three separate pairs of climbers on their way up. We told them a storm was coming, but none turned back within our view.

No sooner did we reach the trees than the storm hit, bringing pea-size hail mixed with lightning. We donned the Hefty bags Ray had brought for the purpose, and they almost kept us dry. The lightning was scary, and the hail stung, but they just made for a better story. After lying low for 40 minutes, we were able to slosh the rest of the way down, arriving at our car at 4:15 p.m. feeling fine, and heroic. If anything bad befell the dopes we had passed, it didn't make the next day's news.

It was, in summary, a wonderful experience, as has been that of pulling my belt a couple of notches tighter. I recommend both to you other average guys, and gals. If I did it, so can you.

• *Aug. 18, 1995*

ODD BALLS

Part 12

The Slow Road
to Seoul

INDIANAPOLIS

L et it be recorded that the first member of the 1988 U.S. Olympic track and field team qualified at a few minutes before noon here Sunday. He won his event in a walk, but that doesn't diminish his achievement. His event *was* a walk.

It stretched (or, rather, looped) for 50 kilometers up and down New York Street in the Hoosier metropolis, or 31 miles in real distance. The winner, Carl Schueler, traversed it in three hours, 57 minutes and 48 seconds. That works out to a pace of almost 7½ miles an hour, a pretty swift hike.

About 200 spectators were on hand in gray, chilly weather to applaud when Schueler, a land-use planner from Colorado Springs, Colo., entered the Indiana University Track Stadium alone for the final laps. The throng wasn't large by Olympic standards, but the winner thought it made up in quality what it lacked in size. "I bet I knew half the crowd here today," the trim, bespectacled redhead said later. "Not a lot of people follow race walking, but those that do are a kind of fraternity."

Schueler won the title of earliest track Olympian by a couple of hours over Mark Conover, who won the men's running marathon held later Sunday afternoon in Jersey City, N.J. Those two events were conducted early, partly, I guess, because that'll give contestants time to catch their breath before the September Summer Games in Seoul, South Korea.

239

Sal Corrallo, race-walking chairman for The Athletics Congress, the U.S. governing body for the sport, said that another reason for the early 50K walking trial was that many of the men who competed also will be in the 20K trial here in July. That's a mere sprint of 12.4 miles, and requires "speed work—a whole different kind of training," Corrallo said. No kidding, he really did.

That there have been two walking races in recent Olympics represents something of a triumph for the usually overlooked activity, whose supporters claim Rodney Dangerfield as their spiritual father. In 1976 at Montreal, when the Olympics were in a temporary streamlining mode, each sport was asked to jettison an event, and track and field volunteered the 50K walk.

The 20K event has a similarly spotty history. Beginning with the 1956 Games in Melbourne, Australia, it replaced 10,000 meters as the sport's "short" event because of continuing disputes over walkers being disqualified for running, i.e., proceeding without one foot in contact with the ground.

Lengthening the race and slowing the pace did not end such hassles, however. After Daniel Bautista Rocha of Mexico won the 20K at Montreal in '76, photos clearly showed him airborne during some strides. Officials at the 1980 go-around in Moscow got nasty and disqualified seven members of the field, including the two leaders at the 9,500-meter mark, for this offense. The winner, Maurizio Damilano of Italy, moved up from third because of the misdeeds of his opponents.

One fella got the hook here Sunday, not for running but for "creeping." That's what they call not fully extending the leg at each step. If you've seen race walkers in action, you know that they do not stroll as do you and I. They pump their arms and wiggle their hips vigorously, producing a motion that Red Smith once likened to that of earthworms out after a thunderstorm. This can evoke hilarity among unhip spectators, but it also permits the racers to move as fast as they do.

"The hip and arm movements allow full leg extension and a very quick step turnover," explains the lean Mr. Corrallo, a researcher at the U.S. Department of Education in Washington when he's not supervising walking races or competing in master's events. "The most speed you can get walking in the normal way is maybe four miles per hour, while experienced racers can go twice that fast. I get a kick out of changing gears when I'm walking on the street with someone who doesn't know my background. I love to see his eyes bug."

Walking has gained ground as an exercise in recent years, and the sport's competitive ranks have grown apace. Still, it is pursued seriously by only a few hundred soles in the U.S., hardly a large enough figure for world domination. East Germans placed 1-2-5 in the 50K at the World Championship in Rome last summer, and an Italian won the 20K.

The U.S.'s best finish at 50K in the worlds was a 16th by the 32-year-old Schueler. Right behind him was Marco Evoniuk, 30, of San Francisco, who placed second here and is the American record-holder at the distance. Evoniuk, a financial consultant, also qualified for the Olympics, along with third-placer Andy Kaestner, a part-time bartender from Racine, Wis., who at 24 is the youngster of the group.

Schueler and Evoniuk are old sparring partners, and 1988 will be their third Olympics. The difference between them on Sunday, about four minutes, might have been attributable to the weather: Schueler likes it cool, Evoniuk warm. "Another 15 degrees and I might have had him," joked Evoniuk between deep breaths.

After the event, the race-walking people held a public clinic, and about half the audience stuck around to attend. Before long, the IU track was filled with people of various ages and shapes, swinging their arms and wiggling their hips.

Winner Schueler stayed, too, and while he was too sore to take part, he chatted with the folks, patted children on the head and signed autographs. He was still there when I left, two hours after the post-race interviews.

"Waiting for my lift," he shrugged.

Carl Lewis always has a car waiting.

• *April 26, 1988*

Bowling 'The Petersen'

CHICAGO

The sign on the battered building at the intersection of 35th Street and Archer Avenue on this city's industrial South Side reads "BOWLING—20 LANES, 10 TABLES." That is not exactly true. There are 22 lanes and no tables, pool having been dispensed with long ago because it was attracting the "wrong" kind of traffic.

The sign in the tired blue tile over the door reads "Home of the Petersen Classic." That is true. They've been bowling the Petersen here since 1921, when the game, and the neighborhood, were a good bit younger.

To get to the Petersen, you must climb 22 shabbily carpeted stairs to the building's second floor, no mean feat when you're lugging a couple of bowling balls. Then you must avoid the temptations of a 70-foot-long bar dispensing every beverage one is permitted to imbibe without a prescription. The tournament alleys (no fancy business about "lanes" here) are in back, illuminated by bare bulbs hanging from a ceiling that has allowed water to pass on many a rainy day. The place was described in print as a "dump" as far back as 1942.

The proprietor, erect, gray-haired Mark Collor, says that, yes, he has pondered renovating or even replacing the building, but has always decided against it. "We'd lose our mystique if we went modern," he declares. "The Petersen wouldn't be the Petersen any more."

If you're not a bowler, you might not know what the Petersen Classic is, so a description is in order. It's the most-enjoyed, most-griped-about annual event in the 10-pin sport. It also is one of the oldest, largest and richest. By the time its 10-month run concludes on July 17, more than 14,000 bowlers from around the country will have vied for upward of $875,000 in prize money, some $50,000 of which will go to the singles champ. More likely than not, that fellow's name will have been a household word only in his own household; no full-time professional has won it since 1950.

"The pros used to come here, but they don't much anymore. Their schedules are too tight, I guess," says Mr. Collor.

"You mean their egos are too tender," scoffs Jim Lawshe, his less-diplomatic aide. "They can't stand having to put up our entry fee and then get beat by some guy from Peoria."

That wasn't what husky Louis P. "Pete" Petersen had in mind when he launched the tournament 67 years ago. Petersen was a carpenter who turned entrepreneur in 1908 when he bought the building at 35th and Archer and installed eight used and eight new alleys. His first "Classic," designed to call attention to his establishment, was a 64-player invitational with a then-princely first prize of $1,000. He hyped it by having a "banker" present to fondle the winner's check while the bowlers rolled.

"Pete was a heckuva promoter, ahead of his time in a lot of ways," says the 73-year-old Collor, Petersen's son-in-law, who has been associated with the tourney for 50 years and has run it since Petersen's death in 1958. "He was a pretty good hustler, too. He never bowled very well 'til there was money on a game. Then he'd beat you in his street shoes."

Tourney fields stayed smallish—and were dominated by pros—until the end of World War II, when Petersen came to see it as a more direct revenue producer. Entries passed the 10,000 mark in 1959 and hit a high of 18,720 in 1972. They've slid since, mostly because of the inroads televised sports and other entertainments have made in bowling's ranks, Mr. Collor thinks. But the current basic entry fee of $63 a bowler, plus bar tabs and additional fees for a dozen or so other prize categories besides the featured singles pot, still furnishes a hefty prize purse and a nice profit for the house.

Commercialization in the form of corporate sponsorship has been stoutly resisted. Even the organizers of the 32-man squads that make up the bulk of the field can't dub them with their business names. "Pete wouldn't let 'em, and I won't, either," Mr. Collor shrugs.

The Classic's format also remains untouched from Pete's days. Each bowler rolls eight games across the main bank of 16 alleys. That's a big factor in the event's legendary toughness; keeping the bowlers moving doesn't give them a chance to "zero in" their shots.

The tourney uses the heaviest available pins (three pounds, eight ounces) and prohibits pre-event practice. Thirty years of wear have made lane fronts as bumpy as roads under repair. Some alleys are oily, others have Saharalike dry patches. Ancient pin-setting machines don't always work uniformly. "It's equally fair for everyone," Mr. Collor sniffs. Then he pauses and adds, "Make that equally unfair."

It is thus no wonder that Petersen scores are among the lowest in bowlingdom. Winners usually average no higher than 210 a game for their eight-game sets, and a 1,600 score—a 200 average—always nets one of the 93 $1,000 prizes awarded. Indeed, with the present tourney two-thirds over, a 1,600 would put a bowler in 17th place in the standings.

"You gotta go in there with the idea that nothing that might happen can bother you. You try for a good time first, and a good score second," says Guy "Buddy" Deluca, a 40-year-old government employee from Pittsburgh whose winning of two Classics, in 1969 and last year, must rank among the most astounding feats in all of sports.

To say that a good time was being had by all at the Classic on an afternoon this week would have been incorrect, though. The 32 men on the lanes from in and around Lansing, Mich., were emitting a cacophony of hoots, cheers, curses and groans.

Beefy Jim Edmonds, a Petersen first-timer from Belding with a 171 average, bowls a score of 93. "I didn't believe what I was told about this place. Now I do!" he exclaims. "One set of lanes hooks like crazy. The next set doesn't hook at all," wails Dale Fox, a machinist from Eaton Rapids, about his first four game scores of 128, 212, 145 and 235.

"I've been coming here for 18 years, and every time I see something different," says Dale Dunham, a school administrator from Lansing. "Even if you bowl lousy, you always have a couple of stories to tell."

• *April 29, 1988*

Death in the Brickyard

U sually, I have little trouble ignoring the Indianapolis 500-mile automobile race, but this year I've read a couple of things I thought were worthy of comment as the Sunday-before-Memorial Day event approaches.

The first was one of those "special advertising sections" that seem to be stapled into every issue of *Sports Illustrated* magazine these days. This one ran on May 9 and was titled "Indy." It covered 14 pages, eight of which were full-page ads for some of the products that like to hitch themselves to auto racing's ample star.

The text was by Patrick Bedard, who has driven in a couple of 500s. It was about the evolution of the engines that contest the 77-year-old go-around, and its tone was both upbeat and lyrical. "An Indy car at full song is a vivid symbol of the thoroughly optimistic and exquisitely cock-eyed spirit of man," Bedard wrote. Nowhere in the piece do the words "crash," "injury," "death" or, even, "safety" appear.

The other work was the 1988 edition of the *500-Mile Race Record Book*, published annually by the *Indianapolis News*. It's a pocket-sized book that the newspaper sells for $2.61 at its offices, or $3.80 by mail. It lists the order of finish and highlights of each of the 71 500s that have been run on the Indianapolis Speedway to date, as well as of those of the other U.S. 500-mile events for

Indy-style cars. It also lists the individual annual finishes of the nearly 600 present and former drivers who have piloted vehicles around the one-time "Brickyard," and, where appropriate, the dates and manner of their deaths.

The book has no literary content, much less style, but it speaks more eloquently of the reality of the Indy 500 than do the well-crafted words of the *SI* supplement. In the sparest language, cars are depicted spinning and hitting walls, burning and coming apart. People get hurt. People die. If the race was a movie, it would be rated "X," for violence.

Of the 1981 running, for instance, we learn:

"Lap 33—[Don] Whittington hit wall in backstretch.

"Lap 58—[Rick] Mears pitted while leading, caught fire. Mears and six crewmen suffered burns.

"Lap 64—[Danny] Ongais hit wall at Turn 3, suffered fractured leg, internal injuries as car disintegrated."

Oh, yes. Bobby Unser won in 3 hours, 35 minutes and 41.78 seconds, averaging 139.029 miles per hour in a "Norton Spirit" car.

Information of a different sort comes from leafing between the race results in the front of the book and the driver histories in the back, and toting up a few scores. This process reveals race-car driving to be a pursuit of unsurpassed danger. Of the 492 former Indy drivers listed—some of whom appeared at the Speedway only once—130, or better than one in four, came to their deaths in races or through race-related injuries.

Furthermore, superior driving skill seems to involve either greater danger or recklessness. Of the 35 deceased winners of U.S. auto racing's premier event, 14, or 40%, died on the tracks. These include five of the last six decedents: Mark Donohue (the 1972 winner), Jimmy Clark (1965), Jimmy Bryan (1958), Bob Sweikert (1955) and Bill Vukovich (1953 and '54). The sixth, 1966-winner Graham Hill, was killed in the 1975 crash of a plane he was piloting.

Of the 71 fields that have started the Indy 500, the 1955 one was the most ill-starred: 16 of its 33 members, including seven of the top eight finishers, wound up being carried off on their shields.

Four of those deaths came on the Speedway. Two-time winner Vukovich died in a smash-up on Lap 56 in the race itself. Second-placer Tony Bettenhausen was killed in a 1961 practice run. Pat O'Connor, who finished eighth, was a casualty of the 1958 race, and 20th-place Keith Andrews died in practice in 1957. The Class of '55, incidentally, fared even worse than those figures indicate, because Manuel Ayuho was killed during practice for that run.

The *Indianapolis News* book indicates that race-driver safety has improved in recent years; since 1973, only one has been killed on the Speedway, compared with 36 in the years before. He was Gordon Smiley, who died during qualifying runs in 1982. Race officials say that better materials get most of the credit, along with the fairly recent practice of building cars so that they come apart on impact, dispersing the energy of the crash and lessening the injury risk to drivers.

But the injury beat goes on, so maybe luck also has been involved. In practice runs for last year's 500, for example, crashes resulted in a broken neck and foot for Dennis Firestone, a broken heel and ankle for Johnny Parsons, and two broken ankles and a broken leg for Jim Crawford. Roberto Guerrero spent 17 days in a coma with head injuries suffered last September in a tire-testing run on the Speedway.

It is possible to disagree on what conclusions are to be drawn from the above. Racing's supporters point out, properly, that the drivers are consenting adults who know the risks of their activity. Some of these aficionados are fond of contrasting their sport, favorably, with boxing, where the contestants *intend* to harm one another.

I regard the difference between auto racing and boxing as one of degree, not kind, with auto racing getting the worst of the comparison. In addition, I fail to see in auto racing the man-against-man drama that sports should generate. Too much metal and too many corporate stickers get in the way.

Most distressing to me is auto racing's tendency to involve innocents, i.e., spectators, in its mayhem. The total Indy 500 death toll of 62 includes not only drivers, but also mechanics, track personnel and spectators. The latest of 10 spectator deaths occurred last year. As the "500-Mile Race Record Book" describes it:

"Lap 131—Bettenhausen lost wheel in Turn 3; wheel hit by Guerrero bounced into stands with fatal injury to Lyle Kurtenbach, 41, Rothschild, Wis."

Mr. Kurtenbach, a salesman, was survived by his wife, Karen, and daughter, Dawn.

• *May 27, 1988*

Candide On Mike

HOUSTON

T
•

ank McNamara may lack Brent Musberger's motor mouth, Frank Gifford's classic profile or Bob Costas's cute smile, but he has something those more-celebrated sportscasters lack.

"Tank always will be 35 years old," says his creator, Jeff Millar. "Brent, Frank and Bob will grow old, as will you and I, but not him. He's frozen in time, like Little Orphan Annie."

Tank also gets frozen in mouth from time to time, but less often than previously. He may not be getting older, but he is getting better—learning his trade as the sports anchor for the television "On the Spot News" team. Additionally, he is overcoming a tendency to scream "Fumble!" and leap on any object that happens to drop in his presence.

"Poor Tank suffers from Delayed Stress Syndrome. His 20 years as a football player conditioned him to react to anything that falls as if it were a fumble," Millar explains. "But he's pretty much over that now, partly because the joke wore thin."

The continuing joke of the "Tank McNamara" comic strip, which the bearded, 46-year-old Millar co-authors with Houston artist Bill Hinds, a bright-eyed 38, is made of sturdier stuff, however. It's that big-time sports have become such an overblown part of life in these United States that it's laughable. "There is," Millar says, "never any need for Bill and I to resort to fiction to make a living. The stuff on the sports pages every day is funnier than anything we could ever make up. The wonder is that nobody thought of doing a strip about it before we did."

"Tank McNamara," which is carried in about 375 newspapers, has been around since 1974. It was the brainchild of Millar, then, as now, a movie critic and humor columnist for the *Houston Chronicle*. Millar was put in touch with Hinds through a mutual friend. The pair sold the idea for a satirical sports strip to Universal Press Syndicate before they had a main character. At one point before its birth, it was to be called "Jocks" and feature a lunatic fan named Sweatsox, who now appears as a sometime character. Tank wasn't cast for the lead until about a week before the strip was to make its debut.

"It was a fortunate choice," Millar says. "Tank's being a TV reporter gets him into everything. And who has a better seat than the TV cameras?"

The Tank McNamara of 1974 didn't look much like today's Tank. The current version is less craggy than the original and, in keeping with the styles of the times, has shorter hair and wears jackets with narrower lapels. Most noticeably, his jaw is larger—much larger.

"The jaw just keeps growing, like it has a will of its own," exclaims Hinds in mock horror. He adds: "We get letters that we've made him look grotesque, but I pitch 'em. That's because he looks a little like *me*."

One thing about Tank that hasn't changed, though, is his outlook. He wanders oafishly through the wonderful world of sports biz like a mike-toting Candide, innocently seeking enlightenment.

"Tank is an ex-jock—he played defensive tackle for the Houston Oilers—but he's not really an insider, and he's neither cynical nor even particularly hip," Millar says. "He wants sports to be like what they seemed to be when he was 12 years old. He suspects there's a gap between the image and reality, but he resists fully recognizing it.

"I think most people are that way. They want sports to be uplifting and ennobling, and want to reject the evidence of their senses that they're often anything but. Bill and I see ourselves doing a sort of public service there. Our being cynical saves Joe Fan the trouble."

Even the dimmest Joe Fan, of course, has little trouble recognizing the cast of characters who parade across the Millar-Hinds panels. There are paranoiac coaches, egomaniacal owners, conniving agents, airheaded groupies and greedy, insouciant jocks. "All the folks you know and love," Hinds opines.

And the characters are saying pretty much the same things their real-life counterparts said the week before. That's because Millar and Hinds turn out their Monday-through-Saturday strips only 10 days in advance, one of the shortest lead times in cartoondom.

"Thursday's our day," says Millar. "I think about material all the time, of course, but I do the actual scripts Thursday mornings and Bill does the drawings the same afternoon. I guess you'd call it quasi-journalism. It keeps things fresh."

This week's strips, for instance, burlesque Wheaties' signing of basketball star Michael Jordan to a megabucks endorsement contract by having a breakfast cereal called "Empties" announce it is reducing by 75 cents a bushel the price it pays for wheat so it can hire an un-named athlete to grace its boxes with his picture. "The farmers of America are happy to subsidize this great example to America's youth," an Empties spokesman assures Tank.

"Tank" marked football's Heisman award week by having a college run a series of "negative" TV ads attacking other schools' player-of-the-year candidates. "Does America want a Heisman winner who hears footsteps?" one asks.

The Mike Tyson-Robin Givens marital bout also got recent treatment.

"Eight whole months I invested in that marriage. I'll never get those eight months back," laments Mrs. Champ. "All I'm asking is that you give money a chance," her lawyer tells her, consolingly.

As the above indicates, things financial are a stock humor subject in "Tank." "It's easy to make the money side of sports sound absurd, because the real figures are absurd," Millar observes. Also good for laughs, he believes, are football, basketball and baseball, in that order. "Football gets the edge because people react crazier to it than to other sports, although maybe we think that just because we live in Texas," he says.

"If we want to get letters, though, we deal with hunting," he goes on. "Hint that it's violent and people write threatening to shoot you. With material like that all around, how can we miss?"

• *Dec. 16, 1988*

Pool Goes Straight

CHICAGO

"Machine Gun" Lou Butera, short and gray haired, eyed the schedule for the U.S. Open Pocket Billiards Championships here last week. "They got us playing at 11:30 a.m.," groused the man who lived up to his nickname by once sinking 150 consecutive balls in a world-record 21 minutes during tournament play. "The only time I ever used to play at 11:30 a.m. was if I started at midnight."

But that was then and this is now, and pocket billiards, a/k/a pool, has targeted Yuppiedom as a market. Thus, contestants were required to arise early, and, presumably, eat an oat-bran cereal for breakfast as well.

Relatedly, talk about betting on the outcome of contests involving the game with the 15 balls, a/k/a hustling, was discouraged. No sooner had Loree Jon Jones, a slim brunette from Hillsboro, N.J., captured the women's title Friday night than Sam Jones, her bearded husband, coach and manager, approached me with a request.

"Promise that when you write about this, you won't mention hustling or that movie, *The Hustler*," pleaded Sam, in reference to the wonderful 1961 film starring Paul Newman and Jackie Gleason that set in slate the sport's seedy image. "We're trying to line up corporate sponsors for a tournament tour, but they say pool still brings up pictures of gambling and smoky bar rooms."

I told him I couldn't make any promises, especially since the men's final later that evening would match a kid from nowhere (West Germany, actually) and a fat man, just like in the movie. Amazing how life keeps imitating art, isn't it?

I can honestly report, however, that the air in the ballroom of the Congress Hotel, where the tourney was staged, was pleasantly clear thanks to a ban on spectator smoking, that the players looked spiffy in their tuxedos (gentlemen) or evening clothes (ladies), and that while money changed hands, it was in the form of checks for top finishes rather than in crumbled bills across tables.

And in the main event, the Paul Newman type, 22-year-old Oliver Ortmann of Munich, defeated the Jackie Gleason type, old pro and beer-commercial star Steve Mizerak, 200-186, in a three-hour match, ending after midnight. Aficionados ranked it among the most closely contested in memory. "If this match would have been on live TV, it would have made millions of new fans for us," said Charles Corley, the event's organizer. "As it is, we were lucky to get five minutes on the late news."

Indeed, the fact that the national 14.1, or "straight-pool," championship was held at all was something of a victory for the sport. It was inaugurated in 1966, and continued annually through 1977, but lack of sponsorship and squabbles within the players' ranks prevented its resumption until 1983, and another six-year gap preceded last week's fest.

Part of the trouble stemmed from the switch to nine-ball from straight pool as the predominant U.S. tournament game. In nine-ball, players' shots must touch, but not necessarily sink, each ball in numerical order, and the game ends once the nine-ball is pocketed. It's possible for that to happen quickly, even on the first shot.

In straight pool, competitors can play balls in any order, and must call each shot. When 14 balls have been pocketed, they are reracked, with the remaining ball and the cue ball staying where they were. The shooter usually seeks to continue his run by pocketing the 15th ball while also breaking the new rack to set up future shots.

Each ball pocketed counts for a point in straight pool. Matches run to 100 or 125 points for women and 150 or 200 points for men. That can take awhile, as Friday night's final illustrated.

"TV likes nine-ball better because it's faster and more unpredictable, but straight pool is the classic game. It's what really determines who's best," asserted Mike Sigel, a many-time national and world champ, who placed fourth here.

With recreational pool making a comeback, and I. W. Harper whiskey putting up $52,000 in prize money, a "who's who" field of 40 men and eight women gathered for four days of double-elimination play to decide just that. The women's draw went predictably, with the top-ranked Mrs. Jones, 23, prevailing. Elegant in a blue satin blouse and long, black velvet skirt, she defeated Robin Bell, a mother of five from Costa Mesa, Calif., 125-29, in the final.

The winner was a child prodigy, winning a world's championship at age 15. She's a full-time pro now, and operates a pool room back home with her husband when she's not out playing. "Encouragement keeps me going," she smiled. "First my Dad, then the nuns at high school, now Sam." Holding up her winner's check of $4,000, she added: "This helps, too."

The boys, on the other hand, were anything but formful. Young Ortmann is a six-time European champ with a reputation as a skilled shotmaker, but in need of seasoning. "I am maybe not so good in the head," he cheerfully admitted during tourney week, referring to his shot-selection skills.

Mizerak, 45, has four U.S. and two world titles under his substantial belt, but the last came in 1983. He has played few tourneys since gaining fame in ads for Miller Lite beer, preferring to make exhibition rounds for a number of corporate sponsors. He also has gained considerable poundage in his travels. "Everywhere I go, somebody knows a great restaurant," he lamented. "I'm really not in shape for this."

But once play started, "Miz" glided through the field undefeated, while Ortmann dispatched such stars as Nick Varner and '83 champ Dallas West. He had runs of 34, 33 and 23 balls in the final, to Miz's 43, 39 and 26.

Ortmann led, 193-166, before Mizerak ran 14 balls and left his foe frozen on a rail. From there, the two maneuvered through a dozen, intricate "safety" shots and two intentional fouls each before a sweating Mizerak played boldly and missed, opening the table, and the $10,000 winner's prize, to his foe.

Ortmann later said that while he was surprised at his triumph in total, he wasn't overawed by his individual foes, including Mizerak. "In Munich," he noted, "we drink normal beer, not light."

• *Dec. 4, 1989*

Tanking It

A •
perusal of the sports calendar for Memorial Day weekend revealed lots of baseball, the middle games of the pen-ultimate NBA playoff round, a bunch of routine-looking golf "classics" and the Indianapolis 500, an event in which cars and drivers vie to see which can carry the most advertising stickers.

I rejected that last thing out of hand (I went once and found it ghastly), and reasoned that I could catch up with the others at other, more critical times. I chose instead to attend the National Underwater Hockey Championships at the Chicago College of Osteopathic Medicine in this western suburb of the Windy City.

I did so for several reasons. One is that I'm a sucker for anything with "national" in its title. Another is that I'd never seen anyone skate underwater. Finally, I hadn't seen Brent Musberger in awhile, and was hoping he'd be covering it for ABC.

I was disappointed in two of those quests. They didn't skate here, they swam—in a pool—and Brent and ABC were elsewhere. The event, however, was quite na-tional, with 12 teams representing 10 cities. The winner was Club Puck, from San Francisco, which defeated a Se-attle team in the Sunday afternoon final of the single-elimination tournament.

En route to the crown, the team from the bottom of the Bay also beat Club Psychopuck, from St. Louis, and the gang I was rooting for, Club Fred, from Chicago, the 1987 champs. The Freds recouped somewhat by winning the unofficial congeniality award for providing a covered truck in the parking lot equipped with two battered sofas, a boom box, a large keg of beer and chairs for tanning.

"Our guys got older, and a bit out of shape, but our pre- and post-game parties have held up well," noted Club Fred stalwart Heinz Werning, who sported a Mohawk-style hairpiece taped to his bald pate.

Inside, though, the sport was spirited and altogether serious. Underwater hockey is played by six-person teams (the tourney was co-ed) equipped with fins, masks and snorkels. They use 14-inch, unbladed sticks to try to shoot or push a leaded puck about the size of a can of tuna fish into a three-meters-wide (10-foot) goal at the pool's bottom. Besides general athleticism and the usual aquatic skills, it requires strong lungs, the better to stay submerged long enough to do some good.

The idea, however, isn't to see who can stay down the longest. "The best work is done in 5-to-12-second bursts," explained mustached Joe Grandov, a Club Puck member and coach of the U.S. men's all-star team that will compete in the sport's world championships next month in Montreal. "You dive under, pass the puck to a teammate, and get back to the surface to catch your breath and track play until you can be useful again."

He added: "Positioning and teamwork count most. We can't be Wayne Gretskys and take the puck the length of the pool alone to score. We have to come up for air; Wayne never does."

The tourney was conducted by the Underwater Society of America, which oversees a number of sports. There's also fin swimming, which includes above- and below-surface events; free and scuba diving; underwater rugby (!); spearfishing; and underwater photography. In that last activity, each contestant gets a roll of film and four hours to paddle around a defined area and shoot underwater scenes, with a panel of judges determining the winner.

The society is an affiliated member of the U.S. Olympic Committee, and, as such, would like to see underwater events in future O Games. Interestingly, underwater swimming does have an Olympic past. The 1900 Games, in Paris, gave medals for an event in which two points were awarded for every meter a competitor covered underwater, and one point for every second he stayed down. The winner, France's Charles de Vendeville, got 188.4 points for traversing 60 meters in 68.4 seconds. By contrast, the third-place finisher, a Dane, stayed under for 90 seconds, but managed to swim only 28.5 meters.

The 1904 Olympics, in St. Louis, included a plunge for distance that measured how far swimmers could get on a single dive without surfacing or further movement. The U.S.'s William Dickey won at 62 feet, 6 inches, but his triumph was ascribed largely to the absence of a couple of Englishmen who'd previously bettered 75 feet. Alas, that was to be that for underwater events, and they joined things like the 100-meter freestyle for sailors (Athens, 1896) on the Olympic-swimming reject pile.

If any underwater sport makes the Games, it probably will be fin swimming, which features both speed and athlete visibility. Underwater hockey is notably short on the latter; neither the puck, nor much significant underwater activity, can be glimpsed from poolside. Sans underwater video or windows below water level, the sport resembles nothing so much as feeding time in the shark tank.

That's kind of what it's like where the action is, too, players say. "There are rules against rough stuff, but there's still plenty. We all have bruises," averred Mary Jo Ferris of Club Fred. "It's like NBA basketball—a non-contact sport with contact."

Club Puck, featuring several U.S. world-team members, cruised through the tourney with relative ease, beating St. Louis in the semis, 9-1, and Seattle in the final, 7-3. The pool in which the contests took place measured the proper 25 meters long, but, unlike the even-bottomed venues for international competitions, varied in depth from six to 12 feet, with a down-slope at the deep end that strongly favored teams attacking in that direction.

That edge was balanced because teams changed ends for each 15-minute half, but it was a mark of Club Puck's dominance that, defending the deep end, it held the Seattleans to a 2-2 tie in the first half of the championship go.

"We did some nice work, or at least I think we did," smiled Grandov, an engineer at Stanford University's linear accelerator lab. "In underwater hockey, you're never really sure what's going on unless you're down there yourself."

• *May 30, 1990*

It Must Be the Genes

ews item: Scientists have announced they have discovered the gene that determines whether or not people will be sports fans. They have dubbed it the "F Factor," and speculate it is linked to such other behavioral characteristics as the tendencies to paint one's face and waggle an index finger aloft while shouting "We're No. 1!" The finding is expected to stimulate new controversy over the ethics of altering a baby's genetic makeup before birth, with pressures from fan and nonfan parents alike.

OK, I'm joking. As far as I know, scientists haven't found any F Factor, or, probably, even looked for one. I strongly suspect, however, that one exists and will someday be uncovered.

The subject of who's a fan and who isn't came to mind last weekend when I read that some 125 million Americans watched the telecast of the Super Bowl contest between the Dallas Cowboys and Buffalo Bills. That meant just about half the population of this country had at least a passing interest (no pun intended) in professional football's annual big game. It also meant that just about half did not. The split seemed too neat to be coincidental.

It's tempting to ascribe the division to nurture rather than nature, but my own experience indicates otherwise. I grew up the only sports fan in a family of four, with both parents and a sister in the opposing camp.

My father was particularly adamant about his nonfanhood—for instance, he was fond of calling football "foolball." He had less against baseball, but not much. Whereas in many families fathers take sons to their first baseball games, I took my father to his.

A similar condition exists in the family I've helped raise; among the children, the four boys are fans to one degree or another, but Jessica, the lone girl, is not.

Her lack of interest doesn't stem from lack of exposure. When younger (she's 20 now), she was taken to athletic events of all sorts, and plied with goodies to sugar-coat the experience. But the effort at indoctrination failed, and, retrospectively, she bemoans the MTV time it cost her.

To see whether my observations were common, I did what newspaper reporters do: I called an expert. He's Allen Guttmann, professor of American Studies at Amherst College. He is the author of a book titled *Sports Spectators*, which seems right on the mark.

Alas, Guttmann quickly confessed he'd given little thought to the factors that separate fans from nonfans, pointing out that his book is concerned mostly with the history of fandom (sample chapter titles include "Greek Spectators" and "The Roman Arena") and its pathology ("Spectator Hooligans").

He said that, off the top of his head, he supposed that nonfans either have other obsessions—music or Civil War history, for example—or verge on the apathetic. He also thought fanhood is associated with competitiveness in other spheres, and that this might well be a predisposition.

He remarked that having written about sports has given him an appreciation of the unpredictable nature of fanhood. "Often, when I'm with colleagues, I'll want to chat about the news or the weather or their research, but *they'll* keep switching the subject to sports," said he.

Guttmann surely has a point about the obsessive nature of some fans; it's not by accident that the signs carried by ticket seekers outside stadiums on big-game days always read "Need 1 (or 2 or 3)," not "Want 1."

The same goes for competitiveness; besides whatever rooting for their teams they might do, fans compete among themselves in such categories as boisterousness, bizarre dress and knowledge of sports trivia. Nonfans think it's redundant to link those last two words.

There are, of course, grades of fandom, and listing them might be useful. Starting with the most fanatical we have:

—"Get a Life." These people would rather watch or talk about sports than do anything else. They don't just look at ESPN, they mainline it, and keep the phones lit at the all-sports radio stations that recently have spread, plaguelike, across the land. Whatever their chronological age, their mental age averages about 12.

—"Has a Life." Most fans think they belong in this class, although not all do. They like sports, but also go to an occasional movie, read an occasional book and can talk about things like the news, the weather or their colleagues' research. They're more likely to root for specific teams than to care about sports in general. It's my observation that most female fans fit here.

—"Cares That Mike Ditka Was Fired." These people pay attention only to sporting events of transcendent importance, like the Olympics, Super Bowl, World Series or the Chicago Bears' firing of Ditka, and then only because they're afraid of being left out of the next-day conversations. They may root, but don't really care if their teams win or lose, and when they do go to games often leave before they're over. Many Californians fit this description.

—"Who's Mike Ditka?" These would be the other-obsessed/apathetics that Guttmann mentioned and, are, I'd guess, about as numerous as the get-a-lifers. They think that Kirby Puckett is a country-western singer, and the NBA is a lawyer's group. They should not be scorned, because it takes a real knack to avoid sports in this day and age.

Looked at in this way, it becomes apparent that, once scientists locate the F Factor, they'll find it strong in some, weaker in others and nonexistent in a few, and readily manipulable when "designer genes" come into vogue.

But what's that you say? You don't think it's the genes? Well, then, maybe it's the shoes.

● *Feb. 5, 1993*

New York's All Smiles for 26.2 Miles

NEW YORK

L
•

ike Calvin Coolidge, I do not choose to run, and I heretofore also had chosen not to watch others do so to excess.
This reflects a longstanding aversion to experiencing or
witnessing acute discomfort, a trait I think I have in common with the bulk of the race. The human race, that is.

I realize, however, that others do not share my preference. This was brought home forcefully here on Sunday, the day of the 24th annual New York Marathon.
Some 26,000 men and women of various ages and nationalities came to run the 26.2-mile event, and the
crowd-estimate experts said some two million others
came to watch. One big difference between the runners
and the watchers was that the watchers looked happy,
while, except at the start, the runners did not.

By and large, the runners also were skinnier than
the watchers. This is a characteristic of a sport whose
motto should be that one never can be too thin or too
wretched. It was significant, I thought, that the second-
place finisher among the men was Bob Kempainen of
Minnetonka, Minn. Pain isn't his middle name, but it is
in the middle of his last one.

Of saving graces, though, there were several. With
the sun shining and temperatures mostly in the 60s, Sunday ranked among the best November days in history. It
was so pretty that even the graffiti along New York's streets
looked good. And for five or so hours, the components of

Gotham's oft-fractious mosaic united to urge on the competitors. People were so good-natured, they even cheered the press bus.

"You gotta understand that the marathon's become our biggest sports event," explained a New Yorker of my acquaintance. "We never have a World Series anymore, the Super Bowl's always somewhere else even if a New York team's in it, and ordinary people can't get tickets to the U.S. Open [tennis tournament]. It's pretty much this or nothing."

The man most responsible for the New York Marathon's ascension is Fred Lebow. Like many gung-ho New Yorkers, he was born and lived elsewhere (Romania, Czechoslovakia, England, Ireland, Kansas City and Cleveland) before settling here. He came to running 30-odd years ago as a way to gain stamina for tennis, and says that since his first run he hasn't lost a set. That's because he hasn't played one.

"Running opened new worlds for me . . . it was like this great secret no one had let me in on," he rhapsodizes. He soon was running marathons, then organizing them, eventually quitting his job as a garment-industry consultant to spread the secret. Wearing running clothes and his signature bicycle cap everywhere, he became a walking advertisement for his sport. He ran daily until struck by brain and thyroid cancer in 1990. After that, he walked.

Last year, his disease in remission, he marked his 60th birthday by again competing in—and finishing—the race he built. "It was my gift to myself. It was better than a cake—and I love cake," says the bearded vegetarian.

The first New York Marathon was run in 1970, four times around Central Park, with 126 contestants. The race was expanded to all the boroughs in 1976. It made headlines in 1980 when it was discovered that Rosie Ruiz, the first woman across the finish line, had taken the subway for part of her trip. National television coverage began in 1981.

The race long has been among the world's largest in terms of participation, with 28,000 starters in 1992. More than 90% of those finished, but the number was unwieldy, so the entry list was trimmed by almost 10% this year. About one-third of the runners are foreigners, a third are from the New York area and a third come from the rest of the U.S. Last year, lawyers were the largest single occupational group, with 1,139 entered. Bet you didn't know there were that many skinny lawyers.

Pretty much the same top runners run in marathons everywhere, so what really sets the New York Marathon apart is New York. The people of the city fill the race's route, taxing a police contingent big enough to stage a St. Patrick's Day parade. Some spectators are there to cheer specific runners ("Yo, Vinnie, All the Way," read one representative sign on Sunday). Others come to press their own agendas, however obscurely (a group along Bedford Avenue in Brooklyn wore white coveralls and hoisted large photos of human skulls; maybe they were promoting dental hygiene). But even the ideologues seem to join in the festive air.

"The crowd is so . . . so proud of the runners. They make you go faster than maybe you would otherwise," said Uta Pippig, the blond, 28-year-old German who won the women's side of Sunday's race in the time of 2:26:24.

The men's winner was the wiry veteran Andres Espinosa, a 30-year-old Mexican who was second here last year. His time was 2:10:04, 59 seconds faster than that of Kempainen. They, like Pippig, looked relatively comfortable throughout.

Not so fortunate were the 55 runners who were taken to hospitals for heat exhaustion, and more who were treated by on-site medics. One elite runner, Kim Jones of Spokane, Wash., was hospitalized with an asthma attack, and released. Temperatures in the 60s, pleasant by most standards, are considered high by a marathon's. It's not for nothing that the route was lined with first-aid stations.

The winners gave the kind of postrace interviews marathon runners give: Espinosa mentioned the "hard work" of his preparation three times, and Pippig twice.

Pippig finished about a half-mile in front of the second-place woman, and said she was surprised she did so well. "I ran through Central Park alone. It would have been better to have had two or three men running with me," she said.

She meant for pace. On this day, among happy spectators in the thousands, protection wasn't required.

● *Nov. 16, 1993*

Go! Fight! Tie!

CHICAGO

T
•
here's a new college football "Game of the Century" every year or so, and some years there are two or three, but for me there will ever be just one, and tomorrow will mark its 50th anniversary.

That was the Army-Notre Dame game played in Yankee Stadium in New York on Nov. 9, 1946, and its objective qualifications for G-of-the-C honors are substantial. Army, at the crest of its wartime glory, came in carrying a 25-game winning streak and ranked No. 1 nationally, the place where it had ended the 1944 and '45 seasons. The names of its stars, running backs Glenn Davis and Felix "Doc" Blanchard, are remembered by people who recall little else of that era.

The Fighting Irish, unbeaten in '46, were ranked No. 2, but, then as now, many thought the top spot was theirs by right. With the likes of quarterback Johnny Lujack and tackle George Connor back from military service, they looked like a dynasty in the making, which is what they turned out to be.

My own reason for enshrining the game is less, uh, catholic. I was eight years old at the time, living around the corner from Our Lady of Lourdes Church on the North Side of Chicago, the only Jewish kid in a mostly Catholic neighborhood, and not nearly the biggest. Some of my pals, and most of my nonpals, were vocal Notre Dame fans, and in the weeks preceding the game their bleatings became too much for me. I'd never seen adults play football except in newsreels, and wouldn't have known "Doc" Blanchard if he'd stuck a tongue depresser in my mouth, but, in an attempt to silence them, I made a number of bets that Army would win. A rather large number.

If the gesture made me feel good, the sensation was fleeting. It quickly became apparent to me that one of two things would happen: I'd lose the bets and suffer the consequences of being unable to pay because my net worth amounted to, maybe, 35 cents, or I'd win and be forced to try to collect, a process that would yield more in bruises than in cash. Nov. 9 loomed as doomsday, for sure.

Those were radio days, and I tuned into the contest on our home Emerson. I groaned whenever Notre Dame threatened to score, and reacted similarly to each Army thrust. Back and forth the two sides heaved through the long afternoon, and my stomach heaved with them.

The last heave went Army's way, when Davis, a triple-threater, threw a long, last-minute pass to Blanchard around the Notre Dame 20-yard line. He was ruled out of bounds when he caught it, though, and the remaining seconds ticked off uneventfully. The game ended in a 0-0 tie, which everybody said suited nobody. But everybody was wrong, because it suited me fine, providentially so.

It doesn't take much for me to harken back to that game, but I hadn't thought about its signal anniversary until reader David Varner, who lives in Palm Coast, Fla., phoned this week to point it out. As a 10-year-old with his father, he was among the 74,000 people who attended the game, and remembers it in an altogether sunny way. That's because he wasn't an unwise, underaged gambler.

Varner's call caused me to look up a few things about Army-Notre Dame, '46, and some of the results seem worth mentioning. Most startling was the size of the players: tackle-to-tackle, mighty Army's starters averaged 194 pounds a man, while Notre Dame's averaged 214. That's about 100-pounds-a-man less than big-time college interior linemen now weigh, and it makes one wonder where the extra weight is coming from.

The length of the teams' schedules also stand out; both played just nine games, against the 12 their current counterparts will play, including a bowl (Army's good again, for a change). Still, theirs was a long-enough campaign to create impressions that have lasted quite a while.

Those were the days of so-called one-platoon football, and some of the game's more-important plays were defensive ones turned in by players better known for their offensive talents. Arnold Tucker, the Army quarterback, and Terry Brennan, Notre Dame's leading ball carrier in the game, made pass interceptions, and Lujack made a saving tackle on a run by Blanchard.

On the other hand, the tactics of Frank Leahy, the Notre Dame coach, presaged the game's present era. While eschewing two platoons, per se, Leahy substituted so freely it amounted to about the same thing, and his year-round approach to football ("spring" practice in South Bend before the 1946 season began in February and ended in June) mirrors the current situation, albeit in a primitive way.

The tie permitted Army to retain its No. 1 ranking for the next week, but while the Cadets ended the season without a loss they beat a weak Navy team only 21-18 in their finale. Meantime, Notre Dame finished strong, thrashing Northwestern, Tulane and Southern Cal by a combined score of 94-6, and, as they do today, such displays enabled them to top the year-end writers' poll.

Notre Dame would win 21 straight games after the tie with Army, taking the 1947 national title and leading the chase the next season until it was derailed by a last-game tie with USC. The Irish won all 10 of their 1949 outings to reclaim the crown, so their four-year players who entered in '46 would win 36 games and tie two in their careers.

I have my own epilogue on the game. While I didn't exactly root against Notre Dame in that long-ago battle, my childhood experiences have never left me unhappy when they've lost. Still, I rooted for Lujack and Connor when they played pro ball with the Chicago Bears. Brennan later became Notre Dame's coach, and while his 32-18 record would have been good enough at most places, it got him fired after five seasons. I did a story about him some years ago, and liked him very much.

And when the NCAA this season instituted overtime to play off ties, I sighed on behalf of foolish little boys everywhere.

• *Nov. 8, 1996*

Index